THE PRESTIGE OF VI

SALLY BACHNER

the prestige of violence

AMERICAN FICTION, 1962–2007

The University of Georgia Press   Athens and London

Published by the University of Georgia Press
Athens, Georgia 30602
www.ugapress.org
© 2011 by Sally Bachner
All rights reserved
Set in Minion Pro by Graphic Composition, Inc., Bogart, Georgia

Printed digitally in the United States of America

Library of Congress Cataloging-in-Publication Data

Bachner, Sally, 1970–
    The prestige of violence : American fiction, 1962–2007 /
Sally Bachner.
        p. cm.
    Includes bibliographical references and index.
    ISBN-13: 978-0-8203-3889-7 (alk. paper)
    ISBN-10: 0-8203-3889-3 (alk. paper)
    ISBN-13: 978-0-8203-3910-8 (pbk. : alk. paper)
    ISBN-10: 0-8203-3910-5 (pbk. : alk. paper)
    1. American fiction—20th century—History and criticism.
    2. Violence in literature. I. Title.
    PS374.V58B33 2011
    813'.5209—dc22

                                                2010044006

British Library Cataloging-in-Publication Data available

contents

acknowledgments

Although this book bears few traces of the dissertation from which it originated, it bears the indelible stamp of Michael Wood. Michael was the reader and interlocutor I needed to begin working out these ideas; his generosity, curiosity, and inventiveness were (and still are) a reason to keep thinking and writing about literature. I was also fortunate to have Maria DiBattista, Diana Fuss, and Starry Schor in my corner as advisors, readers, and mentors. Their collective brilliance and kindness were very important to me. Karen Beckman, Gage McWeeny, Amada Sandoval, and Stuart Burrows made the slog of graduate school far merrier. A fellowship I received from Princeton University's Center for Human Values was also invaluable.

This book really came into its present shape at Wesleyan University. My colleagues in the English Department have, to a person, been models of professional support and generosity. I owe a special debt to Sean McCann. He not only read and commented on countless drafts with unmatched analytical precision but also helped me envision the bigger picture. The boundaries, stakes, and potential value of my project all came into focus through my discussions with him. Other colleagues in and out of the English Department demand a shout-out of their own for the help they provided both intellectually and personally: Henry Abelove, Joshua Chambers-Leitson, Lisa Cohen, Christina Crosby, Ann DuCille, Joe Fitzpatrick, Mary Alice Haddad, Indira Karamcheti, Natasha Korda, Jill Morawksi, Kirsten Ostherr, Joel Pfister, Richie Slotkin, Elise Springer, Bill Stowe, Khachig Tololyan, Stephanie Weiner, Elizabeth Willis, Krishna Winston, and Yves Winter all made this process richer. Claire Potter merits a special spot in my acknowledgments. Not only did she pore over draft after draft with enthusiasm and insight, she even came up with the idea of a chapter that was not part of the original plan for the book. I can't imagine making it through this process without her expertise, curiosity, practical advice, and friendship. A sabbatical and two fellowships at Wesleyan's Center for the Humanities gave me time to immerse myself more fully in research and writing.

Away from Wesleyan, I was fortunate to participate in the Post45 conference. Reading the work of, and being read by, such an incredible group of scholars gave me an enviably concrete sense of my audience. I am very grateful to the steering committee for inviting me and to all the participants for providing such an intensely stimulating intellectual community. Erica Stevens brought my manuscript to the University of Georgia Press. Nancy Grayson and the rest of the staff shepherded it through the editorial process with great care. The anonymous readers who reviewed the manuscript gave generously of their time and expertise.

This book wouldn't exist without the help provided by all those friends and family members who looked after and nurtured my child while I was researching, reading, and writing. My friends in Middletown—Gloster Aaron, Kate Alloco, Rani Arbo, Monica Belyea, Mary Alice and Rami Haddad, Ken and Heather Hoffman, Scott Kessel, Ed McKeon, Lucy McMillan, Marcella Oteiza, Jenny Royer, Steve Smith, Trish Thompson, and Sogwol and Paul Zakarian are all part of the village that has helped me raise my child and stay, for the most part, sane. All my family—my mother, Miriam Simpson; my mother-in-law, Barbara Shire Magro; my sister, Annie Bachner; my father, Paul Bachner; and my stepmother, Susan Bachner—have given me love, cheered me on, played with my son, and lent considerable financial assistance along the way.

Most important, my husband, Stephen Magro, and our son, Elias Bachner, made all this worth doing, even when it kept me away from both of them or left me crankier than any of us would have liked. They are the constant source of love, joy, and fun in my life, and I never want to stop thanking them for it. This book is for them.

THE PRESTIGE OF VIOLENCE

the prestige of violence

AMERICAN FICTION, 1962–2007

"Unspeakable thoughts, unspoken." This is the prefatory phrase with which a character in Toni Morrison's singularly influential novel *Beloved* characterizes the lyrical climax to come. What follows are four remarkable chapters in which we become privy, through Morrison's words, to the unspeakable thoughts of three women: Sethe, a woman who escaped from slavery and murdered her daughter to prevent her being returned to a life as property; her surviving daughter, Denver; and the murdered girl, who has returned in the form of the titular character. Although the first three of these chapters are specific to a single character, their three voices meld in a fourth chapter, not only with each other but with the voice of an unnamed African woman who speaks in the present tense of her suffering as she survives the Middle Passage. These chapters offer a miniaturized version of *Beloved* as a whole, which is committed to showing that slavery continues to harm long after its prohibition. Yet the logic whereby the legacy of slavery is both preserved *and* transformed as it affects subsequent generations is exchanged for a model whereby the suffering of all the characters can be represented by the horrific violence of the Middle Passage. What is offered as unspeakable in these chapters is the horror of slavery, rendered through fragmented images of the mass death, manacles, starvation, and sexual abuse that defined life on the slave ship.

These chapters are small miracles of verbal virtuosity that render slavery's horror with more vividness and emotional force than could be reasonably expected. And yet the novel insists that we *not* read this account as the bringing into language of a horror long since dulled by time and sanitized by collective bad faith. Nor are these "thoughts" unspeakable merely because they are too painful or socially taboo for the characters to speak about. Instead, *Beloved* insists that the horrors of slavery are fundamentally and intrinsically resistant to articulation in either spoken or written form. The insistence, against all evidence to the contrary, on the unspeakability of the story reemerges at the very end of the novel in the form of a challenge to the reader. The narrator vacillates between insisting to the now explicit "you" that Beloved's story is alternately "a story to pass on" and "not a story to pass on." The play on the phrase "to pass on," which signifies both transmission and death, invites us into a seemingly unresolvable paradox. Should Beloved be exorcised as a demon for the health of the community? If so, might her exorcism entail a rejection of the past that she embodies, and thus prevent the collective healing that can only occur when the past is recognized and preserved? Can the collective recover from slavery only if her story is transmitted?[1] And yet such a transmission is impossible if the story is fundamentally, essentially, unspeakable. The resolution lies in the novel's counterfactual image of transmission as a bodily rather than textual act. Instead of passing on her story by telling it, we are invited by the narrator to place our feet in the empty footsteps that Beloved has left by the side of the Stygian river into which she disappeared.

Like the unspeakable thoughts that the novel claims against all evidence to have left unspoken, we are invited to understand that the transmission of her story involves not so much telling or writing but the nonlinguistic embodied act of walking beside a river. This repudiation of the text's own status as a linguistic act exists in a strange tension with the overt lyricism of the final paragraph. How can any of this be meaningfully unspeakable when it has been communicated with such striking literary language? And why would Morrison *want* to insist upon its unspeakability?

ᑌᑗ

Beloved is a singular text but it is also typical: genocide, terrorism, war, torture, slavery, rape, and murder are the favored subjects of the most celebrated postwar American novels. A list published by the *New York Times* of the "Best Works of American Fiction of the Last 25 years," based on the votes of over a hundred "prominent writers, critics, editors and other literary sages," testifies to the hold novels about violence have had over the imagination of elite taste-makers.[2] *Beloved* took the number one slot. Dominating the rest of the list are novels by three authors—Don DeLillo (three titles), Philip Roth (five titles), and Cormac McCarthy (two titles: a single novel and a trilogy)—whose works have been centrally concerned with the bloody massacres and catastrophes of American life.[3] Many of the same texts honored in the list, along with other seminal novels from the years between 1962 and 2007, are the subject of my book. The degree of overlap is neither intentional nor accidental; I take it as a confirmation that violence does indeed carry a peculiar prestige in American fiction of this period. This book explores that prestige, showing how it is forged by novelists and reinforced by the acclaim that they win.

These novels do not merely insist that violence lies at the center of American life and of the project of fiction. They locate in violence the ultimate source and site of authentically unmediated reality, even as they claim that such a reality cannot be accessed directly by the novel. Again and again, these works insist that violence is beyond their ken, that it is unspeakable and thus only to be gestured at but never represented. Their enduring literary value—the fact that critics rate them so highly—is not unrelated to their ability to persuade readers of this central tenet: that violence is at the center of American life but remains unknowable and unspeakable in ordinary terms. Yet, that these texts *have* persuaded so many readers is remarkable given that the unspeakability of violence is a promise perpetually broken by the texts themselves. We readers only know violence is unspeakable because the texts keep *saying* that it is, and we are meant to discount the evidence at hand.

This book aims to uncover and elucidate a complex set of unstated propositions about language, violence, and the real that underwrite the claim that violence is unspeakable. These propositions can be reduced to two: that violence brings us into contact with an otherwise hidden and inaccessible reality, and that ordinary speech habitually occludes and falsifies the real. Such propositions are all too often passed off as eternal verities, incontestable facts, or mere common sense. In fact, these propositions have a literary history that has played an important role in rendering them persuasive and compelling. By analyzing some of the most influential and celebrated fiction from the early 1960s through the first years of the twenty-first century, I track the emergence of the peculiar prestige of violence in literary fiction.

The central premise of such works is a dramatic opposition between conventional language and the suspect sociability with which it's equated, on the one hand, and a violence that appears to be prelinguistic and thus indubitable, on the other. Alongside the conviction that violence is unspeakable—that violence remains outside, above, or below the reach of language—is the conviction that violence is the ultimate source and location of reality. Or rather, while such a formulation presents these two ideas about violence as merely contiguous, their relationship is more intimate: the ontological prestige of violence entails, at least among those who have come to see language as the mediating and distorting matrix of sociality, the claim that it is unspeakable. It is precisely because violence is understood to be unspeakable that it can function as a locus of the real, and precisely because violence is understood as a source of the real, we must continue to insist upon its inviolability from the encroachment of language. Violence, in other words, has become the last redoubt of the real, which is the reason its unspeakability occasions more pride than it does handwringing. However much we may abhor violence, our claim that it is unspeakable is a tribute paid to its perceived authenticity and desired inviolability.

Given the continued reach of Foucauldian thought, in which it is a commonplace that violence is generated by and circulated through the power-saturated discourses that we wield, the prestige of violence conceived in supralinguistic terms may seem unlikely. However, the opposition between ordinary speech and violence these texts activate tends to presuppose the operation of various poststructuralist paradigms that see language as the primary matrix through which violence originates or is perpetrated. The contradiction is, however, only apparent. Language in most of these texts is represented as fundamental to the production of a violence to which it proves subsequently inadequate. A similar logic is at work in Lacan, whose theory of the real my own use of the term surely calls to mind. But while my use of the term "the real" has unavoidable associations with Lacan, the fiction I analyze is animated by an idea of the real that is not strictly Lacanian. For Lacan the Real is the state of full communion with the world that we lose upon our entrance into a linguistic order he calls the Symbolic. While Lacan often claimed that the Real "is impossible" once we leave infancy, whatever residual contact persists occurs through the experience of trauma and through awareness of our own embodiment and materiality.

As his accounts of the Symbolic order make clear, for Lacan language is in-extricable from socially constructed meaning, from ideology and law, and all of these function as a screen—however inevitable or structural—that prevents us from truly encountering, or reencountering, some prior presocial reality. As Malcolm Bowie explained it, "[I]n all its modes [the Real] successfully resists the intercessions of language."[4] Thus, Lacan is important to this study insofar as his theory of infantile development offers a thoroughgoing theorization of a set of assumptions that underwrite much post-1960s literature and theory. Readers will encounter a much more eclectic and flexible concept at play in this book. So while the "real" invoked by some of the writers I discuss looks loosely Lacanian, I use the term to designate a range of purportedly authentic, non-social truths to which these authors seek access through violence. For this reason, I use the terms "the real," "reality," and "the authentic" as rough synonyms: although they inflect and emphasize the concept somewhat differently depend-ing on context, they all refer to the extralinguistic ontological order to which these texts gesture but insist they cannot reach.

Another central term in this book, prestige, draws attention to the special value and power that is accorded to violence in many of the most enduring novels of the period. My conception of prestige draws on a Bourdieuian theory of cultural capital in which "taste"—in this case, taste in particular subjects by authors and critics—participates in the legitimation and replication of class values, positions, and interests.[5] As in Bourdieu's work, my argument here is not that these ideas about violence are deployed intentionally by a particular class to shore up and reproduce their privilege. Instead, I aim to show how the ideas about language, violence, and ultimately, about the exercise of American power described here register anxieties about and offer solutions to affluent Americans as they make sense of the world in which they live. In place of a strictly Marxist or even neo-Marxian analysis of class, I provide a literary and historical context in which to understand why the idea of the unspeakability of violence has resonated so powerfully with a cultural elite defined not just by its influence and affluence but by its discomfort with the economic conditions and political practices that sustain its power.

In this book, I argue that the fascination with violence that underwrites fiction and theory of the period is an index of the discomfort that privileged Americans feel by virtue of the fact that they are at once citizens of a relatively peaceful and prosperous society and the inhabitants of a larger, much less peaceful and prosperous world. At the heart of this anxiety is the suspicion that the violence and suffering that takes place elsewhere is the product of the very economic and political practices that guarantee U.S. prosperity and security. The structural opposition between violence and conventional language, and the foregrounding of a violence guaranteed by its material absence at the center of American life, enables a deeply therapeutic and illusory reckoning with that violence. It converts the typical perception of violence held by members of the nation's dominant class—that it cannot be directly experienced, that it is most present in its absence, that it evades conventional discourse—into a truth about violence itself.

A commitment to the prestige of violence is by no means universal in American letters or among the most celebrated writers of the period. Cormac McCarthy, although among those writers singled out for praise along with Morrison, DeLillo, and Roth, is not a part of this study. He is absent in part because his accounts of the centrality of violence are rooted in, and organized around, the brutal facts of American history. But just as important as the concrete historical basis for much of the violence in McCarthy's work is my sense that the relentless silence of his landscapes and characters doesn't reflect the sublime sanctity of the violence being committed or the inadequacy of language to the task of representation. McCarthy's works contrast the fullness of the English language with the bleakness and emptiness of the world that has been deadened, not regenerated, by violence. McCarthy's work, in my reading, endlessly demonstrates the way that violence can indeed be represented; he does so in a language as thorough, unflinching, and elaborate as the deliberate acts of cruelty inflicted by one human upon another. By the same token, I have not written about Bret Easton Ellis's *American Psycho*. I read that novel as a brilliant if necessarily repulsive account of how the language of consumer fetishism participates in the violence of capitalism without that violence ever being reducible to language. *American Psycho* is a novel that is about, rather than an example of, the kind of displacements of violence that are my subject.

Another instructive counterexample to the ideas about violence pursued in this book can be found in the works of Joan Didion. On the surface, her novels and essays would seem to fit the pattern I describe. After the publication of her first two novels, Didion became an increasingly political writer, focusing, like Don DeLillo, on places either anticipating or reeling from revolutionary violence. Yet she repeatedly critiques the privileging of violence over language in which so many of her contemporaries engage. The title essay of *The White Album* (1979), which looks backward to the sixties she covered in *Slouching Towards Bethlehem* and investigates the feel of the 1970s that she is currently living through, begins with the assertion that "we tell ourselves stories in order to live." She explains that she suffered a nervous breakdown, which she attributes to the fact that she "began to doubt the premises of all the stories [she] had ever told [her]self, a common condition but one [she] found troubling" (11).

While DeLillo, Pynchon, and Roth have all anatomized the psychological difficulties characters confront in the wake of the collapse of specific cultural narratives, they are also all united in their sense that such stories necessarily hide and falsify the real. Although Didion also understands these narratives to be the product and substance of our social world, she does not appear to be convinced that there is a sublime beyond a language worth seeking. This becomes clearer as the historical dimension of her argument emerges: the failure of the stories we tell ourselves in order to live "began around 1966 and continued until 1971" (11), the same historical moment that she described in her previous collection of essays. The apocalyptic note sounded in that earlier book by her allusion to Yeats's "Second Coming" prepares us for something a good deal bloodier than the louche scene of the Haight in 1967 that she describes with laconic and melancholy revulsion. In "Slouching Towards Bethlehem" she tells of the Doors and the Diggers and of runaways and ends with a chilling anecdote about a jumpy acid-head's two children: the five-year-old has been dropping acid and taking peyote for the last year, while the three-year-old has been setting fires and chewing on electrical cords. But at the heart of the essay is her evaluation of "what was then called the movement," which she argues has been profoundly misunderstood and underestimated by the press.

Her analysis rests on a distinction she makes between those activists "whose approach to revolution was imaginatively anarchic" (122) and the idealistic and romantic children who have shown up for the drugs and the freedom and who stand ready to be unwittingly mobilized by the former. While the former have a political program, albeit one about which she has grave misgivings, the latter are "immaculate of political possibilities." Arguing against the common view that they are engaged in protest "against the culture which had produced Saran-Wrap and the Vietnam War," she offers this counterexplanation:

> We were seeing the desperate attempts of a handful of pathetically unequipped children to create a community in a social vacuum. Once we had seen these children, we could no longer overlook the vacuum, no longer pretend that the society's atomization could be reversed. This was not a traditional generational

rebellion. At some point between 1945 and 1967 we had somehow neglected to tell these children the rules of the game we happened to be playing. Maybe we had stopped believing in the rules themselves, maybe we were having a failure of nerve about the game. Maybe there were just too few people around to do the telling. (122–23)

Although this view is among those that has earned Didion her reputation as a conservative, that label does not tell the whole story. She bemoans the breakdown of community, knowledge, and traditions that she describes, but by calling it a game it seems clear enough that she would mind far less if there were an alternative story put in its place. It is here that she is not merely a conservative but something of a radical relativist: whether we like it or not, we are, Didion suggests, caught up in a game. We might as well become knowledgeable about the rules. Her understanding of the traditions that are waning is not that they are natural or even, in their specifics, necessary. To transpose this into the terms of *The Prestige of Violence*, the real cannot be isolated from either social life or ordinary language because it is produced out of the dynamic interaction of the two.

Didion is less interested in encountering the real than she is in uncovering the material bases of our social practices. The essays collected in *The White Album* in particular evince a robust curiosity about the mechanisms and institutions that sustain our speculations, fantasies, and ruminations. Didion recounts her visit to the Operations Control Center for the California Water Project to understand how water is moved, in massive quantities, around the state and in the process provides a view of the state's economy in which agriculture takes precedence over Hollywood. She visits the Los Angeles Operations Center of the California Department of Energy to learn how traffic is manipulated on the "42-Mile Loop"—"the rough triangle formed by the intersections of the Santa Monica, the San Diego, and the Harbor freeways" (79). She offers a participant's ethnography of Hollywood, explaining the pay structure and hierarchies among all those involved in writing, producing, and financing a movie.

The distance between Didion's view of language and that articulated in the novels I explore in this volume is nowhere better expressed than in her essay about the new residence built for California's governor during Ronald Reagan's tenure. In "Many Mansions" Didion aims to speak about that which she insists is *actually* unspeakable in the political culture of the moment: social class. Didion played in the older mansion, a "large white Victorian Gothic house," as a girl; one of Governor Earl Warren's daughters was her schoolmate. She describes the nooks and crannies, the numerous staircases, and the private bedrooms as embodiments of the values of a no-longer-dominant class. The new mansion, by contrast, built under Nancy and Ronald Reagan's direction, although never lived in by anyone, is of an open design that optimizes "flow";

Didion is nonplussed by the way it combines the banal, the luxurious, and the ersatz. The chapter closes with her characterization of the new mansion as "a house in which one does not live, but there is no way to say this without getting into touchy and evanescent and finally inadmissible questions of taste, and ultimately of class. I have seldom seen a house so evocative of the unspeakable" (72). The unspeakable, in other words, is not really unspeakable. It is merely that about which we prefer not to speak.

Didion cannily articulates the way that the unspeakable is actually a social code passing itself off as an organic fact, one that regulates speech about the intractable embarrassments, contradictions, and conundrums of contemporary life. In this book I explore the way that the unspeakable generates a fictional space in which solutions of a speculative, fantasized, and rhetorical nature can be explored without our ever having to talk about that which remains prohibited. As in Didion's work, this book is animated by a curiosity about those things we say are unspeakable and about those things that are habitually left unspoken.

DEFINING AND DELIMITING VIOLENCE

As will become clear in the following chapters, I identify a wide range of phenomena under the umbrella of "violence," sometimes in ways that will strain my readers' sense of the flexibility and capaciousness of the term. So, what counts as violence in these texts and in my readings of them? Political theory, and to a lesser extent philosophy, has been the main field in which violence has been subject to systematic attempts at definition. Violence has typically been understood in relation to force, and thus violence is read in terms of its instrumentality in the field of politics.[6] Most of these theories distinguish between legitimate and illegitimate uses of force: for Max Weber, for example, only the state has the legitimate right to wield violence, and then only under particular conditions. Just war theory, such as in the writings of Michael Walzer, defines what conditions need to be met for the state violence of war to be practiced legitimately.[7] In other theories, violence is always necessarily illegitimate. In *On Violence*, for instance, Hannah Arendt distinguishes between the legitimate power that derives from the implied consent of a group and violence that requires implements to compensate for the lack of popular support. Another way violence has been defined is in positivist terms: violence is known by the empirically verifiable damage it inflicts on bodies and property. In this model, violence is instantiated in a bank robbery, in a massacre, and in a suicide bombing, or in any other place where its direct harm to bodies and property can be detected. At odds with this positivist account is the theory of structural violence, a term first used in the sense we know it by Johan Galtung in 1969.[8] It "is defined as a reduction of human potential that is not immediately attributable to an acting subject . . . and manifests itself as inequality of power, resources, and life opportunities."[9] Related to this is Pierre Bourdieu's theory of symbolic violence, in which social capital, the value of which has been naturalized, perpetuates inequality.[10]

Although the previous terms are useful in sorting through what does and does not count as violence in the books I discuss, my use of the term violence throughout this book is not supported by any single consistent theory. It is in conversation with the texts in question that I have derived and delimited the category. On the most basic level these texts demonstrate a fascination with what we might call obvious, commonsense examples of violence, those that entail empirically verifiable injury and that have obvious political origins: war, genocide, terrorism, and assassination. Yet many of these same texts conflate paradigmatic acts of violence with structural and symbolic violence. For example, in Margaret Atwood's *Surfacing* the structural violence that underwrites patriarchy is made visible in the potentially verifiable "crime" of rape but also in the continuities the text establishes between the woman traumatized by misogyny, the soldier traumatized on the battlefield, and the animal hunted and eaten by ravenous humans. Perhaps most striking in these novels—and where they depart most vividly from any theoretically coherent account of violence—is the fact that they metaphorically extend violence to phenomena that don't seem to have much to do with it. It is the relentlessly labile quality of violence in these texts that marks their distinctive engagement with it. In Vladimir Nabakov's *Pale Fire* and Thomas Pynchon's *The Crying of Lot 49*, for example, ordinary deaths, or even trivial moments of loss and obsolescence, are associated with conventional instances of violence and assimilated into the category. And while in both of those texts the metaphoric extension of violence can be read as part of their activation and anatomization of paranoia, acknowledging the paranoia doesn't fully defuse the special reality charge that such metaphoric instances of violence hold. So while it can be legitimately noted that violence in my argument is a portable concept, I hope to demonstrate that this portability derives from and is responsive to the novels in question.

THE STRUCTURE AND GEOGRAPHY OF VIOLENCE

The starting date for the period I cover in this book is 1962; the closing date is 2007. These numbers correspond to the publication dates of the earliest novel examined in this book (*Pale Fire*) and the most recent (*Falling Man*), respectively. Although different years and different novels could be substituted to shift the period a few years forward or back, I am arguing for the conceptual continuities that extend from this second phase of the cold war all the way to the initial aftermath of September 11, to which the two most recent novels discussed in this book respond. My argument hinges on a distinction between the earlier "duck and cover" phases of the cold war and the period after the Cuban Missile Crisis, when despite ongoing concerns about nuclear warfare and fall-out, the safety of the United States from direct attack seemed increasingly clear.[11] Whatever the reality of the threat to Americans at home throughout the cold war, Americans expected and prepared for physical attack within the United States throughout the 1950s in ways that were no longer as plausible in the decades after. There were exceptions of course, including a brief renewal of nuclear panic in the 1980s. But as a whole, cultural discourse about violence throughout this period conceives of cold war violence as something that happens elsewhere but that has its mysterious origins at home.

Understood in these terms, it makes more sense that representations of violence after the official end of the cold war were so little disrupted by the collapse of the nation's presumed foe.[12] Successive administrations managed to transfer the models of conflict that were dominant in the cold war to other threats. Countless critics have noted the way the declaration of rhetorical war on various entities—on drugs, terrorism, AIDS—attempted to apply cold war logic to very different problems. But despite these ideologically charged metaphoric extensions, direct political violence was continually conceived of in the literature of the period as something that happened both outside the physical boundaries of the nation and to other people. The deadly events of September 11 may have broken down that confidence, but in many ways it served to illuminate (if also delegitimate) the rules we believed the world would follow.

My point is certainly not that the material realities of American military power were *actually* invisible or materially absent. But many affluent Americans—including those who write and read literary fiction—live at a remove from the domestic impact of U.S. war-making. Their children are less likely to serve in the military (especially since the end of the draft); the machinery and infrastructure of the U.S. military was and continues to be—as such disparate scholars as Trevor Paglen and Catherine Lutz have argued—hidden from civilians, albeit often in plain sight.[13] This suggests that the claim that state violence cannot be directly experienced was, like the claim that violence is unspeakable in fiction, an aspiration rather than a neutral description of the facts on the ground. But the claim does register some important features of the way American power was wielded throughout this period.

Particularly since the early 1960s, the looming threat of atomic warfare transformed the way the United States used violence to pursue its objectives. Uncertain whether nuclear threats could be used without courting total world destruction and unable to pursue explicitly imperialist practices in a period of massive decolonization, successive administrations increasingly sought to exert their power in ways that obscured and mystified the use of violence.[14] The obsession with the inherently abstract and unmeasurable "credibility" of the United States, the increasing prosecution of covert and limited wars under an expanding executive claim to the right of secrecy, the concurrent refusal to declare war openly and with public approval, the centrality of client states to the pursuit of policy objectives—all of these interrelated features of the postwar exercise of power transformed the way violence was deployed by the state and how Americans thought about what violence is, who suffers from it, and why. These characteristics of state violence lent support to the perception of a radically unbridgeable gap between appearance and reality, one in which language itself seemed to be the underlying matrix of dissimulation and distortion.

In addition to being marked by the obfuscation of state violence, the period I cover is set off from earlier years by the collapse by the late sixties of public confidence in the major institutions and authorities that had stood for and guaranteed the ideals of the United States.[15] To name just a few of the biggest crises to public confidence of the period: the inner-city riots that erupted in Newark and Detroit in the summer of 1967 exposed the anger and desperation of the black urban underclass and gave the lie to the myth of American classlessness; the organized police brutality of the 1968 Democratic convention in Chicago made representative democracy look like a sham; the appearance of the Pentagon Papers in 1971 contradicted a range of claims about how and why the war in Vietnam was prosecuted; the Watergate hearings and eventual resignation of President Nixon in 1974 revealed the meanness and dishonesty at the heart of the executive branch; and the Church Committee of 1975 exposed the extralegal violence practiced abroad by U.S. intelligence services. Read alongside these events, the conceptual privileging of violence over language becomes visible as a philosophical analogue to the discovery by Americans that they were lied to about the benevolence of the social order and that the lies covered up the reality of extensive and sometimes illegitimate violence being committed abroad in America's name.

In one sense then, the unspeakability of violence can be read as a symptom of the covert violence of proxy wars, of the unspoken but looming nuclear threat in world affairs, and of the unreliability, if not outright mendacity, that characterized so much political discourse. Yet the same novels that promote this model of violence are clearly capable of more-nuanced accounts of how and why violence is distributed—or rather, perpetrated—so unevenly across the globe. Although nearly all of the authors in question express, in interviews, letters, and essays, or through their political activism, their sincere moral qualms about the practice of American power, this is not the primary problem to which the texts are addressed. These novels instead emphasize their presumed lack of access to violence and to the authority thought to flow from it. While the unequal distribution is represented in these texts as a genuine and worrisome political problem, this inequality also becomes the ground upon which a new and authoritative relationship to violence is forged. These novels suggest that violence is fundamentally unavailable for language or experience, but not because you are not there or because you are not the victim; this is just what violence is really like. To know that it is unspeakable and to rehearse its unverifiability is to gain a new kind of authority in relationship to it.

⟶

While I read these novels as being singularly fascinated and troubled by the practice of violence abroad, this fascination also entails the mystification, if not the outright denial, of the violence occurring at home. There was plenty of *actual* violence in America, whether it was located in the riots that devastated American cities abandoned by whites, industry, and anyone else with the economic means to escape; in the more mundane street crime fed by unemployment, poverty and lax gun control laws; in the state violence of law enforcement; in racial violence that pervaded (and still pervades) society; or in the form of violence against women. The race and class dimensions implicit in this list are particularly important here. For any account of violence in this period must address the violence generated by the massive gap between rich and poor that widened during the postwar economic boom. This gap only added to the discrepancies between the way that Americans of differently racialized classes experienced and understood violence. The threat of violence was banished, at least in the most obvious and explicit ways, from the daily lives of the affluent even as the increasingly numerous urban poor endured an epidemic of violence, criminal and structural, in their neighborhoods.[16]

As Michael Harrington argued in his bestselling *The Other America* (1962), the poor became increasingly invisible to the affluent. Although affluent Americans had long ignored poverty in their midst, Harrington argued that the process had become far more extreme: "[T]he very development of American society is creating a new kind of blindness about poverty. The poor are increasingly slipping out of the very consciousness and existence of the nation" (5).[17] Poverty was now masked by sharper economic segregation, by the expansion of suburbia, by the growing political alienation of the poor, and by cheap consumer goods that allowed impoverished people to appear prosperous.

Yet *this* material is surprisingly underutilized in the fiction of the period. Many of the most esteemed American novels of the thirties, forties, and fifties—John Dos Passos's U.S.A. trilogy (1930–36), John Steinbeck's *The Grapes of Wrath* (1939), Richard Wright's *Native Son* (1940), and Ralph Ellison's *Invisible Man* (1952), to name a few obvious examples—anatomized the suffering of America's underclass. By contrast, the most celebrated postwar texts of the 1960s and later focused only rarely and indirectly on urban poverty and violence. Instead of domestic crises, the most honored writers in this period focused on the specter of bloody conflicts abroad. It is not that novels were not being written about the violence wrought at home by economic inequality, racism, and misogyny. Yet these were not the novels that resonated most powerfully with the elites, who play a disproportionate role in determining which works are reviewed in periodicals, honored with prizes, reissued in special editions, chosen as fit subjects of scholarship, and taught to high school and college students.

Some of the absence of actual, local, and contemporary violence in mainstream American literary fiction reflects a literary historical process in which crime came to be the domain of more-popular genres of fiction. But it is worth noting that even the fiction written by and about groups that are disproportionately victims of the contemporary violence of American culture tended to turn away from the most obvious material. Much of the most prestigious African American fiction of this period focused far less on the city street than on the temporally distant violence of slavery; much of the feminist fiction of the period, despite being staked on the centrality of violence to women's everyday lives, transposed that violence into the register of war or revolutionary conflict. Instead of representing the pervasive violence that is regularly understood in public discourse as a social crisis, violence is increasingly characterized in the acclaimed fiction of the period as absent, immaterial, and unreachable.

Sustained literary inquiry into the institutions, practices, policies, and norms that sustain economic inequality, racism, and patriarchy, for instance, appears to be doomed from the outset in both novels and theoretical accounts that share this view of language—such inquiries depend on language to apprehend and communicate social relations. Within the logic of unspeakably real violence, the ordinary capacities of language *must* fail if the text wants to succeed in other, more important, terms. According to a rigorous application of its own models, such violence cannot really be violence at all: we know *real* violence only by its unverifiability, by its appearance not as concrete, lived reality but in its rigorous absence or ghostly trace.

NOVELISTIC AUTHORITY AND THE "LINGUISTIC TURN"

Throughout this study, I privilege fiction in my anatomization of contemporary ideas about violence and language, ideas that I nonetheless want to suggest have broader cultural currency. I see novels as the preeminent cultural texts in which the limits of language and the ontological preeminence of violence have been asserted, and through which they have been disseminated. Supporting this claim and explaining why this is the case requires a foray into the history of the genre and into the role of fiction, and literary language more generally, in the postwar university. Since its emergence in the eighteenth century the novel has been the primary textual form for locating individuals within a complex social totality. Critics as diverse in their methods and political commitments as Georg Lukács, Ian Watt, Mikhail Bakhtin, and Michael McKeon have understood the novel as singularly engaged in the representation of the individual within social collectives and, more particularly, in generating accounts—whether illuminating or mystifying—of the world wrought by capitalism.[18]

Examined in this light, the preoccupation in much postwar fiction with apparently internal and self-reflective matters of representation, narrative, and discursivity would appear (except perhaps to Bakhtin) to signal novelists' collective indifference to or ignorance of such social totalities. Yet the long-standing expectation that novelists reconstruct the social matrices in which individuals move *is* being met in this turn to self-reflexivity. The unspeakability of violence in particular registers social transformations by which novelists have been impacted with particular force. In sociocultural terms, postmodernism is the literature of post-Fordism. The massive expansion of white-collar workers, the feminization of the labor force, the birth of the information economy, and the concomitant decline of manufacturing—these are the main features of the social and economic world that the authors of the period I cover must represent if they are to fulfill the historical task of the genre. It is a world dominated, at least symbolically, not by the making of concrete material objects but by the production, proliferation, and processing of information.

Andrew Hobarek has suggested that we can understand the obsession among postwar novelists with language and their development of increasingly hermetic styles as "responses—however displaced—to the expansion and ultimate proletarianization of mental labor."[19] These responses reveal that "our understanding of the era's novels as rejecting political and economic concerns in favor of individual and psychological ones" is untenable (25). While I attend to different sets of anxieties than Hobarek, I too argue that the turn to issues of language constitutes a substantive response to, rather than an evasion of, the larger political and economic world in which the novel has always placed its individuated human narratives. Mark McGurl takes the "proletarianization of mental labor" noted by Hobarek to a different place—that is, to the university, where so much mental labor is realized in the form of books or, as Bourdieu would have it, as objectified cultural capital.[20] His focus is on the rise of creative writing programs, and he offers an explanation of the self-reflexivity of postwar fiction that is consistent with Hobarek's. McGurl relates "the metafictional reflexivity of so much postwar fiction . . . to its production in and around a programmatically analytical and pedagogical environment."[21] He wants us to see that even writers who have not logged time in creative writing programs are part of a culture in which the category of literature is mediated institutionally by the university.

McGurl's emphasis is on creative writing programs, and he is right to direct long-overdue attention to this invention of a radically new form of literary training and patronage. But it is worth noting how profoundly the most celebrated texts of this period are marked not just by the intellectual imprint of the university in general, and not only by the focus on craft in creative writing programs, but also by the theoretical and philosophical currents that transformed the study and teaching of literature. I am referring to what has been variously called the linguistic turn, the rise of structuralism and poststructuralism, and the ascent of theory. Although surely this generalization will be misplaced in a few cases, the theoretical work gathered under this big umbrella is organized around two fundamental insights: (1) that knowledge is socially constructed, and (2) that language is the underlying medium and matrix of that knowledge. If accepted, these insights have profound implications for the kind of claims that can be made for the authority and value of the novel and novelist. If the social world is a realm of mystification and mediated knowledge constituted in and mediated by language, the novel is at once enormously consequential—because it can produce what we take to be reality—and utterly worthless—because that reality is, in some important sense, inauthentic. This concern persists even if the third tenet of poststructuralism attacks the so-called metaphysics of presence that would underwrite concepts like authenticity, reality, and truth.

I will turn in a moment to a fuller account of how these ideas are registered in the postwar novel, but the significance of theory's emphasis on the constructed nature of knowledge cannot be adequately appreciated without a look at the institutional context in which it intervened. American universities were transformed during the cold war by the influx of government money, the redirection of research toward governmental aims, and the wholesale penetration of academic life by the state.[22] English departments played an idiosyncratic role in this new dispensation.[23] Compared to science departments, the budgets of which were swollen by military and other government funding, literary studies was "an indirect beneficiary, at most, of scraps of 'overhead' redistributed by administrations to the shabbier precincts."[24] Especially in the earlier years of the cold war, English departments were places where the structural politicization of knowledge occurring in other fields was largely resisted; literature was celebrated as a cultural sphere presumed to be uncontaminated by both crass consumerism and jingoistic patriotism.

Looking at the role "theory" played in shifting the discipline's political center of gravity, Richard Ohmann draws attention to the symbiotic relationship between theory and the political activism associated with the civil rights movement, the antiwar movement, feminism, and gay liberation. He suggests that theory enabled a disciplinary self-critique of the rearguard contribution English departments made, as bastions of supposedly depoliticized freedom, to the cold war and to norms in support of the status quo more generally. John Guillory's analysis focuses instead on the way that theory functioned as a solution to the marginalization of English departments and literary study within the cold war university. The mastery of theory's difficult texts, the learning of its esoteric vocabulary, and the ability to perform its grueling interpretive maneuvers on new texts all look in his analysis like an effort to lay claim to the kinds of specialized knowledge valued in the information economy more generally and the cold war university in particular.[25]

While there is ample wisdom in both these perspectives, my interest lies in what happens to the novel and to novelists, less so in the departments in which they are studied. The core tenets of theory—that knowledge is socially constructed and that language is the medium of that construction—combine with the priorities of the cold war university to entail a radical deauthorization of what had long been the novel's raison d'être. In the period this book covers, the apolitical pastoral of academia is revealed to sponsor, under the cover of disinterested research, the brutal execution of American policy goals abroad. In this sense, the practical marginalization of the humanities occurs in tandem with a theoretical account of its centrality and complicity in the perpetuation of power. After all, according to much of this theory, language *is* power. The philosophical positions of theory recuperate for literature a place at the white-hot center of world affairs, even as the practical marginalization of literature and literary study continues apace.

This newly discovered power of literary language lies in its ability to generate a reality that is, according to an older but still active worldview, patently false. In this sense, the ongoing obligation of the novel to represent expansive and verisimilar social and cultural worlds through the use of a transparently meaningful vernacular comes into tension with the poststructuralist suspicion of the social as a site of real meaning and of the narratives the novel has produced. The novel, precisely because of its long-standing ties to social realities, registers the deauthorization of its own aesthetic capacities with greater force than any other genre. The novel seems destined to map a world that is not truly "real," and it is in this sense that fiction is uniquely positioned to articulate the vexed mythology of an unspeakably real violence: it is charged to represent the reality of a violence—that is, something that is understood to be essentially *outside* or *beyond* the social—through its deep complicity *in* the violent social world.

There is yet one more important aspect of these developments that make the fate of fiction such a singular one. If any mode of linguistic practice has been singled out for special scrutiny by poststructuralist and constructivist theories, it is narrative. And while poststructuralism may have taught students in a range of disciplines that narratives are everywhere, they are associated more closely with fiction than any other popular form. When Hayden White, in his influential *Metahistory*, identified "Romance, Comedy, Tragedy and Satire" as the four modes of "explanation by emplotment" used by historians, he initiated a frenzy of comparison between the prose narratives of history and those of literature.[26] Although White was interested in many genres, it was fiction that became the dominant point of comparison. This was an unsurprising outcome given that, at least since Sir Walter Scott, novelists had produced as many if not more narratives about the past as historians. Indeed, the comparison, which came not just from White but from many others, was powerful enough that American fiction has been dominated since by what Linda Hutcheon famously called, with a nod to White, "historiographic metafiction."[27]

By contrast, poets, however influenced by these same theories of language, were mostly practicing a form that had long since ceased to be importantly tied to narrative. And while various poetic schools—such as the language poets—insisted that its language was also necessarily that of the social world, poetry continued to be conceived by many practitioners and readers alike as a generic space in which language was capable of being reinvigorated with every poem. Art forms with strong visual components—like film, drama, and visual art—could, and often did, gesture at a mimesis untainted by linguistic mediation. So while many works in these media identified violence with the extralinguistic real, they did so from a very different aesthetic, formal, and historical relationship to language.[28]

SUBLIME VIOLENCE, MODERNIST PREDECESSORS

The conviction that violence is an important source of human contact with the real is surely not original to this period. Postwar American fiction, like the modernist fiction that preceded it, drew on much older theories of the sublime and on even older religious associations between apocalyptic violence and the cessation of a merely human, nonsacral order; important work has been done exploring those connections.[29] By the same token, the association of violence with the sublime has served a range of dubious political projects, from the explicit support that futurism lent fascism to the more ambivalent aesthetic recuperation of colonialism provided by primitivism. But while it is true that postwar American thinking about violence is connected and indebted to these earlier iterations, my focus is on the ways that the prestige of violence as limned in postwar fiction does its own particular work in its own specific historical moment.

The degree to which postwar novels are continuous with or depart from their modernist predecessors is instructive on this point. Although some useful terms of differentiation have been proposed in the now-cooled debates over postmodernism's relationship to modernism, only a few—Brian McHale's distinction between a modernist epistemology and postmodernist ontology comes to mind—have gained real critical traction.[30] But we need not erect a wall between the postmodern and the modern to acknowledge the different political and economic issues, and the different location of fiction within literary culture, that inflect, and are in turn reflected upon in, the fiction of the postwar years.[31] The antirealism of Anglo-American modernist literary practice was, like that in much postwar American fiction, strongly idealist. Virginia Woolf, Ernest Hemingway, T. S. Eliot, and James Joyce, to name just a few important authors, all aimed to penetrate to a shimmering core of reality that they often conceived of as obscured by the veil of convention and socially circumscribed perception. But these modernist works are staked on the hopes, if not always the confidence, that the artist wields tools appropriate to the task.

Lionel Trilling perfectly articulates the modernist conception of the role of the artist in this respect:

> [T]he art and thought of the modern period assume that it is possible for at least some persons to extricate themselves from the culture into which they were born. Any historian of the literature of the modern age will take virtually for granted . . . the actually subversive intention that characterizes modern writing—he will perceive its clear purpose of detaching the reader from the habits of thought and feeling that the larger culture imposes.[32]

This subversive capacity exists because while language habitually serves and expresses the falsities of social life, it is not constitutive of it. Language emerges as the primary instrument that can be taken up and repurposed for illumination by the sufficiently talented artist. To offer but one brief example of how this plays out textually, we might look at the moment of Virginia Woolf's *Mrs. Dalloway* when Clarissa intuits and experiences Septimus Smith's suicide. The real is located by Clarissa, and by the novel as a whole, in the moment of his agonizing death. This moment passes from Septimus to Clarissa with only the barest intercession of words. But looked at within the novel as a whole, the episode appears as emblematic of the power of Woolf's own literary language to capture and concretize the evanescent connections that exist between seemingly unknown and discrete persons. The novel condemns "chatter" and "lies" as that which defaces the spiritual purity each person possesses, but that purity is also produced by the communication that the narrator generates between Septimus, Clarissa, and the reader. Modernists like Woolf found a partial compensation for or alternative to the ruination of the world in literary form and language. But for postmodern writers, literary language, and the novel in particular, is a theater in which the failure of language, especially literary language, can and must be staged again and again. American novelists attempt in their work to write about the very violence whose value lies in its presumed resistance to representation.

CRITICAL PARADIGMS

The genre-specific sense that novelists have of being at once complicit in and cut off from the real world of power belongs not strictly to the university per se but to the unequal distribution of power and the geopolitics of violence during the cold war. The postwar expansion of the university is itself a product of the affluence and hegemonic power of the United States, which in turn relied on researchers in a range of disciplines to advance national aims. The complex role of the university as simultaneously a haven *from* and laboratory *for* American militarism is a particularly apt symbol of a much broader social contradiction. This account of how the geopolitics of violence is registered and serially reworked by novelists from this period owes a substantial debt to the groundbreaking work of Richard Slotkin, particularly to his account of the myth of the frontier in his landmark trilogy: *Regeneration Through Violence* (1973), *The Fatal Environment* (1985), and *Gunfighter Nation* (1992). While I can't claim to offer anything like the culturally and historically differentiated analysis that he provides, my work here is inspired by his insistence that the study of culture should occur in conversation with the conditions of its production. The goal is not to reduce literature to the status of the symptom, or the author to unconscious vector, but rather to recognize what Slotkin calls the "reciprocity that characterizes the functional relation between cultural constructions and 'material' experience" (24). Slotkin himself is adamant that, in such work, "myth and ideology are created and recreated in the midst of historical contingency, through deliberate acts of human memory, intention, and labor—that myth has a human/historical rather than a natural or transcendent source and is continually modified by human experience and agency."[33]

An account that recognizes artistic agency and insists upon its responsiveness to local historical and material conditions is all the more important given the dominant explanatory paradigms in the field. According to some of the most influential and enduring accounts of fiction of the period, the fascination with postwar violence can be taken for granted because it is taken to be a natural response to the fact of violence. Linda Hutcheon, for example, while usefully identifying the metafictional and metahistorical impulses of fiction in the period, takes the preoccupation with violence largely for granted.[34] The turn in these novels to a relentlessly *catastrophic* history is visible simply as a turn to history more generally. Frederic Jameson, although rightfully understood to be the most forceful antagonist of Hutcheon's view, nevertheless shares her belief that, in his words, "history is what hurts." The significant difference in this respect is that Jameson is in possession of a theory for why history is what hurts: it is because capitalism has yet to cave in under the weight of its own contradictions.[35] But what both critics respond to in fiction is not so much an obsession with history but with what the novels understand to be the violence that makes history interesting in the first place. Jameson's and Hutcheon's assumptions about history are replicated in much of the scholarly work on postwar American fiction. Many critics have noted the obsession with violence in the period, but the dominant scholarly paradigm interprets this trend as a symptom of history itself; the twentieth century (and now the twenty-first) is characteristically described, without justification or explanation, as the most violent in human history.[36] Fiction that addresses such events is characterized as a form of "traumatic realism" or as the product of a "traumatic" or "post-traumatic imaginary."[37]

The most influential, explicit, and extreme theoretical expression of this view is undoubtedly that found in trauma studies. The term has come to describe the academic but nonclinical body of writing on trauma that has emerged as an interdisciplinary subfield since the early 1990s.[38] Strongly indebted to post-structuralism in its working models of language and the subject, the seminal works of the field include Shoshana Felman and Dori Laub's *Testimony: Crises of Witnessing in Literature, Psychoanalysis, and History* (1992), a 1991 volume of *American Imago* edited by Cathy Caruth and published in book form as *Trauma: Exploration of Memory* (1995), and Caruth's own dense and lyrical monograph *Unclaimed Experience: Trauma, Narrative, and History* (1996).[39] Trauma studies has in turn had a powerful influence on a range of disciplines and scholarly areas, especially Holocaust studies, queer studies, ethnic studies, African American studies, art history, media studies, sociology, and anthropology.[40]

Despite drawing on the clinical and therapeutic regimes of psychiatry, practitioners of trauma studies have tended toward a commitment to preserving the silence and speechlessness that trauma is often said to engender. The first sentence of Caruth's introduction to her landmark *Trauma: Explorations of Memory* is a quotation from an anonymous veteran of the Vietnam War who defiantly proclaims, "I do not want to take drugs for my nightmares, because I must remain a memorial to my dead friends" (vii). Caruth goes on to endorse the view, held by some survivors, that "to cure oneself—whether by drugs or the telling of one's story or both—seems . . . to imply the giving up of an important reality, or the dilution of a special truth into the reassuring terms of therapy." Eschewing such false reassurance, Caruth aligns herself in solidarity with those who valiantly resist speaking about their trauma, which becomes tantamount to its narcotic erasure.[41] But if for Jameson and Hutcheon history bears upon trauma largely because its unprecedented violence tends to induce trauma, in trauma studies the trauma that must be preserved is suffered by history itself. History in turn acts upon individuals insofar as they make up the collectives who come in history's wake and are invested by and with its trauma. On the first page of the first chapter of *Testimony*, Shoshana Felman refers twice to what she calls "our post-traumatic century" (1), what she further describes as a "century that has survived unthinkable historical catastrophes." Caruth echoes this diagnosis in more circumspect language when she speaks repeatedly throughout *Unclaimed Experience* of "our own catastrophic age."

⁓

Although Cathy Caruth's *Unclaimed Experience* is written in the cryptically oracular style adopted by many poststructuralist thinkers when they address matters of moral gravity, it can be usefully analyzed to clarify both the underlying logic by which the prestige of unspeakability is attributed to violence and the moral hazards of doing so. One important chapter is built around a dream cited by Freud in *The Interpretation of Dreams*. Freud recounts the dream as follows:

> A father had been watching day and night beside the sick-bed of his child. After the child died, he retired to rest in an adjoining room, but left the door ajar so that he could look from his room into the next, where the child's body lay surrounded by tall candles. An old man, who had been installed as a watcher, sat beside the body, murmuring prayers. After sleeping for a few hours the father dreamed that the child was standing by his bed, clasping his arm and crying reproachfully: 'Father, don't you see that I am burning?' The father woke up and noticed a bright light coming from the adjoining room. Rushing in, he found that the old man had fallen asleep, and the sheets and one arm of the beloved body were burnt by a fallen candle. (93)

After rehearsing Freud's own analysis of the dream as a form of wish fulfillment, Caruth turns to Lacan, who she says would understand the father's awakening as exemplary of both trauma and our ethical obligation to the deaths of others. The father's awakening to the death of his son instantiates "the psyche's relation to the real." Here, the real emerges because the death of the child is incommensurable with the symbolic realm of language. The real is coterminous with experience of the traumatic event, in this case the father's awakening to the death and burning of his son.

It would, however, be more accurate to say that for Caruth the real emerges in the *nonexperience*. In Caruth's theory the traumatizing event can only be experienced belatedly. Shocked out of full awareness by the event, that event is only registered experientially later in the form of flashbacks, nightmares, and other traumatic repetitions. For Caruth it is precisely *because* the traumatic event *is not* experienced initially that it functions as an encounter with the real. For if the subject does not experience trauma, then she does not encode it into language, and it is the immunity of the traumatic experience from the symbolic realm of language that makes it real (or rather, *the* real).

Yet Caruth takes this to mean that the ultimate witness of an event, and thus the paradigmatic victim of trauma, is someone who is entirely absent from the scene of traumatogenic horror. This idea is given its extreme articulation in an earlier chapter on the film *Hiroshima Mon Amour*. Caruth declares that a Japanese soldier who is represented in the film as being away when the bomb is dropped is in fact the traumatized witness of the bombing par excellence.[42] Since, according to Caruth, our encounter with the real is always a nonencounter, the very materiality of violence is not just superfluous but an obstacle. Caruth's theory of trauma thus begins with an absolute equation of the real with violence, but by the end, that violence has become wholly dematerialized.

Such nonencounters become the substance of the imperative to ethical action Caruth discovers in the father's awakening. The father's awakening to the burning of his son takes on the metaphoric significance of our ethical recognition of the real violence that is happening both outside and inside of us as trauma. Caruth explains:

> The awakening embodies an appointment with the real. The awakening in other words, occurs not merely as a failure to respond but as an enactment of the inevitability of responding: the inevitability of awakening to the survival of a child that is now only a corpse. The pathos and significance of this awakening derive not simply from the repeated loss of the child . . . but rather from the fact that it is the child itself . . . who, from within the failure of the father's seeing, commands the father to awaken and to live, and to live precisely as the seeing of another, a different burning. . . . It is precisely the dead child, the child in its irreducible inaccessibility and otherness, who says to the father: *wake up, leave me, survive*; *survive to tell the story of my burning.* (*Unclaimed Experience*, 105)

Caruth's deliberately confusing syntax makes it hard to decipher the ethical imperative being outlined here, but the task is not impossible. Here, the fulfillment of our ethical obligation entails waking up too late, awakening, that is, to a corpse. Somehow, in this model, our failure to prevent a death becomes the truest realization of what it means to meet the ethical challenge of violence. And as I suggested a moment ago, our encounter with the real is not so much our *own* encounter with death as it is the encounter with the death of another. Violence and death may be the very stuff of the real, but the real, handily enough, always happens to someone else.

So while these dead others allow us to encounter the real, it is also an encounter that can hardly be said to happen at all. And from a purely theoretical perspective, this seems to be Caruth's claim. But in practice, this narrative bears the burden of establishing a relation to the death that would otherwise be absent. In Caruth's ethical theater, we are all the fathers of dead sons, and in that sense, our necessary traumatization by that death need not be established. Indeed, such a death cuts so close to our own death that we are recast by Caruth as survivors.

But once we recognize this incredibly moving story of a father's loss as a figure for our ethical obligation to the threat and fact of death, the terms of survivorship grow problematic. It is one thing to tell us that we should act to prevent the death of strangers as if they are our own children, but this is not what Caruth is after. Instead, we are invited to assume that these deaths can never be anticipated, never prevented—indeed, never acknowledged at the time of their occurrence. The establishment of a parent-child relationship does little more than justify our claim to having been traumatized by the deaths of strangers.

The fact that someone who was never present at an event can be said to be a witness is not just a sign of her rejection—as a student of de Man—of the metaphysics of presence but a sign that for her, history itself is that which is traumatized. People are always necessarily witnesses, not just because people do not possess the kind of presence that would make them masters of their experience, but because it is history itself that has been traumatized. We are *all* witnesses, for we are all subject to a history long passed but still suffering.

Caruth's concept of the real acts as a deus ex machina that produces, inevitably and inexorably, not just death and violence but our inevitably ethical response to it. We do not need to do anything; merely by being human subjects we both fail and succeed (by failing) in our encounter with the real, a real that is paradigmatically located in the death of our own child. Indeed, it seems that because the deaths of others are recast as the death of our child, we can then, by moving on, count as *survivors*. It becomes our duty to survive the deaths of others, the trauma of others, a duty to survive what then becomes the trauma of our own survival.

Like Morrison's *Beloved*, Caruth's *Unclaimed Experience* offers a singularly condensed and powerful account of the unspeakability of violence, but it does so with the tools of criticism and as a form of theoretical argument. Although Caruth's text is indeed extreme in the directness of the claims it makes about violence, unspeakability, and the ethical status of the absent "witness," those claims are more exemplary than exceptional. Her work lays bare the logic that operates in far more circumspect theoretical and critical work about violence. Nor has all of the work that shares her assumptions about the unspeakability of violence been explicitly poststructuralist. Only two years before the publication of *Beloved*, Harvard philosopher Elaine Scarry published *The Body in Pain*, an eclectic and enduringly influential reading of human rights data on torture, Clausewitzian theory, Marxist materialism, and the Old Testament. Scarry's argument is that the experience of physical pain is singularly and uniquely resistant to language. She says:

> Why pain should so centrally entail, require the shattering of language . . . may be partially apprehended by noticing the exceptional character of pain when compared to all our other interior states. . . . If one were to move through all the emotional, perceptual, and somatic states that take an object—hatred for, seeing of, being hungry for—the list would become a very long one . . . [Physical] pain—unlike any other state of consciousness—has no referential content. It is not of or for anything. It is precisely because it takes no object that it, more than any other phenomenon, resists objectification in language. (5)

Scarry suggests here that pain's supposed lack of referential content is itself a kind of, or source of, pain. But why should the failure of pain to "take an object" entail the "shattering of language"?[43] Must every affective state find some kind of analogy in the syntactical structure of a well-constructed sentence in English in order to be expressible? Surely the experience of pain can be articulated in grammatically complete formulations, even if those sentences do not—as in Scarry's less ambitious point—ever fully capture that experience? Even if we were to accept Scarry's doubtful claim that pain is the sole state of consciousness that does not take an object, this does not tell us why it should entail the "shattering" of language.

The violence inherent in the image of shattering is not accidental. Rather, it indicates the way pain becomes all but inseparable from violence. Scarry is far more interested in pain when it has a human agent; she writes about biblical vengeance, about war and about torture, but only occasionally about the pain caused by disease. Indeed, as Scarry sees it, a particularly vexing ethical problem arises in our habitual ways of thinking about the origins and agents of pain. She notes that when suffering from illness we might speak of "stabbing" or "shooting" pain, incorrectly assigning our pain to a violent agent. While she acknowledges that in the momentary representability of pain such metaphors are beneficial to the sufferer, the process is problematically linked to the very figurations that, in Scarry's analysis, allow torture to be used by regimes to shore up their power. In torture, Scarry argues, pain's reality is used to lend unearned legitimacy to those who inflict it: "[T]he physical pain is so incontestably real that it seems to confer its quality of incontestable reality on that power that has brought it into being" (27).

What I have just characterized as an ethical problem is also, as I have already insinuated, a theoretical one. For it acknowledges that language does indeed get produced in the face of pain and, by implication, by the violence inflicted by the torturer. To resolve this apparent contradiction, Scarry makes a move that should be familiar from *Beloved*: she declares the language produced by and in the experience of violence to be a nonlanguage. "To bring them together," she writes, "to bring pain into the world by objectifying it into language, is to destroy one of them" (51). Like Morrison's unspeakable and unspoken but undeniably *written* thoughts, the language that arises out of violence must be explained away, reclassified, so that the experience of violence can preserve its authority.

The political and theoretical ambitions that animate Caruth's and Scarry's texts are clearly divergent. But beyond the enduring influence that these two very different texts have enjoyed, what they have in common is a view of language and violence that places them in dynamic opposition. While both authors are explicitly and sincerely concerned with violence, they also both equate violence with the real. And in both texts the reality of violence is inseparable from its resistance to language.

This book proceeds chronologically from 1962 to 2007, and from individual close readings of novels to broader, but still textually based, discussion of individual authors. In doing so, there is an obvious temptation to allow specific texts to stand in for and exemplify whole periods. Such generalizations are only sustainable to a point. Although I argue, for instance, that Mailer articulates a worry about the march on the Pentagon that illuminates pervasive concerns about the distant violence of the Vietnam War, a large measure of the power of and interest in his text lies in the idiosyncratic and ingenious solutions it develops to resolve problems of historic scope.

Chapter 1 offers a close reading of Nabokov's *Pale Fire*. The novel's importance to this study has much to do not only with its seminal status as an artifact of the transition from modernism to postmodernism but also with the terms by which it has been celebrated, studied, and canonized. The book's reputation—general and scholarly—is built in part on the way it plays the historical tragedy of Nabokov's well-known personal history against a mischievous and deflating metafictional game. The novel draws much of its power from the very historical violence that it tells us is a joke. Getting the joke of the novel, getting that it *is* a joke, proves that we are like its author—marked by loss, violence, and revolution—even if, especially if, we appear superficially untouched by it.

Pale Fire is also important because Nabokov's privileging of violence is crucially different from the authors that follow him. In *Pale Fire*, literary language serves as the primary ambassador for the invisible ever-presence of violence. Real violence for Nabokov is located in a Russia that has been lost to cataclysmic revolution, and all we have left of that place is *art*: the miracles of literature maintain an authentic relationship to the pain, suffering, loss, and violence that inspires it. Thus by virtue of the distinction that the novel draws between high art and everyday speech, his text is able to preserve a conduit between language and the real. Language does this not by representing violence but by transforming, transfiguring, and transcending it.

Pale Fire's essentially modernist confidence in language is not present in any recognizable form in Pynchon's *The Crying of Lot 49* or in Mailer's *The Armies of the Night*. In chapter 2, I show how the reality that Pynchon, in his essay "A Journey Inside the Mind of Watts," identifies with the violence of life in the black ghetto is recuperated for the white Los Angeles of Oedipa Maas in *The Crying of Lot 49*. Although it alludes to the "Other America" made famous by Harrington, the novel authenticates its own seemingly unreal literary language not by engaging with the material reality of local violence but by yoking its art to the unspeakable and unreachable horrors of Vietnam.

Vietnam is equally important to my reading of Norman Mailer's *Armies of the Night* in chapter 3. I argue that Mailer solves the problem of his immersion in the symbolic world of writing and the deanimalized sphere of American liberalism by introjecting the violence of Vietnam into the march he represents. The figure of the self-immolating Buddhist monk, central to my reading of Pynchon's text, merges in Mailer's text with the burning women and children of Vietnam, and all of them are symbolically relocated by Mailer in the figure of the radical Quakers. The "real" trial by state violence of the Quakers, who remain in jail long after his own departure, rescues Mailer's own literary language by turning it into the conduit of the real.

The Crying of Lot 49 and *The Armies of the Night* are among the most frequently read of these two figures of American letters, not least because most of their other books are massive doorstoppers. Their significance lies in their enduring popularity and in the role both texts play in constituting readers' only contact with these two important authors. It also lies in the way their interest in harnessing the authority of violence is relatively explicit and at least partly reconcilable with their stated politics. For both writers, violence can be explicitly and directly venerated as a source of the real: the problem is trying to find a way for their literary language to access that reality without contaminating it.

Chapter 4 addresses the emergence of Posttraumatic Stress Disorder (PTSD) and the impact that it had on feminist representations of patriarchal violence. Focusing on two novels—Margaret Atwood's *Surfacing* (1972) and Marge Piercy's *Woman on the Edge of Time* (1976)—I argue that the emergent discourse of PTSD has had curious and politically paradoxical effects on these fictional accounts of sexual violence. Whereas nearly all feminist theory of this period insists that powerful ideological forces and group interests collude in the silencing of women's speech about patriarchal violence, in these fictions violence looks essentially and fundamentally unspeakable. These writers draw on the figure of the American soldier abroad, suggesting that we must leave both the nation and the bodies of women to truly encounter violence. Using the battle over, and eventual medical institutionalization of, PTSD as a nodal point, I explore the consequences of linking the plight of the Vietnam vet with that of the oppressed woman through trauma.

This chapter marks a more vexed relationship between explicit politics and the conceptions of violence at play. These writers dematerialize violence and thus remove it from the sphere of direct political intervention. The trauma induced by violence must be preserved for the feminist project to maintain its authority. Although these books are not broadly representative of feminist fiction of the time, they do anticipate in important ways the ways violence is invested with an authority and a value that undercuts political programs that might seek to reduce it. Trauma is no longer the affective correlate to the physical effects of violence, but a diffuse form of authority that resides in various classes, genders, sexualities, races, and, most broadly, "cultures."

In chapters 5 and 6, I explore the transformations that have marked the careers of two major writers of the postwar period. Both Philip Roth and Don DeLillo have taken up the theme of violence and have meditated extensively on the nature of representation throughout their long and prolific careers. In chapter 5, I trace the way Roth's early and controversial insistence that postwar American Jews, with their safety and affluence, live at an unbridgeable remove from their persecuted European counterparts evolves into the erasure of historical difference between the two in *The Plot Against America*. Whereas in his earlier work Roth's conception of the "real" was rooted in the material and the interpersonal world of sex, friendship, ambition, and betrayal, in Roth's later work he seeks to ground American history in the ultimate reality of a violence that cannot be directly experienced and that can be written about only indirectly.

DeLillo is the more consistent writer on this topic, and in chapter 6 I outline the continuities and refinements in his account of the relationship between violence and language. Throughout his career, DeLillo explores the total and inescapable complicity of language in violence *and* its inability to fully represent that violence. This contradiction is characteristically resolved by the distinction his novels draw between narrative, on the one hand, and nonsemantic language, on the other. DeLillo's career-long effort to develop a literary language that can do more than acknowledge its complicity in and failure to represent violence is realized in *Falling Man* (2007). *Falling Man* locates the violence of 9/11 not so much in maimed bodies or in destroyed buildings but in the collective acts of horrified spectatorship. No longer defined through its complicity—since violence has become a wordless spectacle—literature emerges as a therapeutic act of the performance artist, reintroducing words that will, eventually, allow people to heal.

Ↄℳ⌒

The book closes with an afterword in which I address literary fiction of the present moment and the immediate future. As I ask questions about the present and the future it will become even more clear that I read the valorization of violence in these texts with skepticism. But while I aim throughout this book to show how this valorization distorts and mystifies the political realities of violence, this book is not primarily a brief *against* the prestige of violence. There have been some excellent and impassioned works that, while they use a different vocabulary, describe and largely condemn similar currents in contemporary culture. Tali Kal's *Worlds of Hurt: Reading the Literatures of Trauma* (1996), one of the earliest and still one of the best treatments of the subject, shows how the literature of trauma written by actual survivors is co-opted and then redirected toward the consolidation of the status quo. Naomi Mandel's excellent *Against the Unspeakable: Complicity, the Holocaust and Slavery in America* (2006) is an impassioned writ against the theoretical and political work that unspeakability performs in recent literature and scholarship about the Holocaust and slavery. In this book, by contrast, my focus is on close readings that lay out the logic of the novels from within. Better models for what I aim to achieve are Gary Weissman's *Fantasies of Witnessing* and Amy Hungerford's *The Holocaust of Texts*, books in which the authors' ethical and political qualms about the textual operations they describe are apparent but not the main focus.

But in the spirit of full disclosure, and so as not to be coy about my own sense of the ethical and political stakes of the ideas about violence I describe, I will state categorically that I am unconvinced that violence is uniquely resistant to articulation or that ordinary speech fails the phenomena of violence in ways that are inherent to violence or to ourselves. To put it another way, I understand violence, our experience and responses to it, and the language we use to describe it, to be largely socially determined. No language, surely, is capable of expressing every feeling or phenomena; every American grade-schooler learns of the paucity of their vocabulary for snow compared to that of "Eskimos." But in the case of English, I can see no reason to single out the available vocabulary for the experience or the phenomena of violence as particularly impoverished. Many experiences, from the mundane, such as eating a bowl of noodles, to the life-altering, such as giving birth to a child, are difficult to describe in ways that are fully adequate. The difference with violence is that the ethical stakes of speaking or not speaking about it are much higher. If we cannot describe what it feels like to have the hiccups, that is one matter. If we cannot tell our best friend that we have been raped, or that we keep having vivid nightmares of a murder we have witnessed, that is quite another.

The rape example is important because it brings us to two important obstacles to speech in the face of violence that should be addressed individually. The first are codes of social propriety. As I discuss in chapter 4, the initial feminist discourse on rape that emerged at the end of the 1960s carefully delineated the social obstacles that discouraged women from speaking out about sexual violence, including codes in the most literal sense, such as laws that made it impossible for women to testify in court without having their sexual histories reviewed. There also were, and still are, informal codes that make it uncomfortable and extremely difficult for women to speak openly about the violence they have suffered, not least the awareness that in speaking about such crimes they will contribute to the sexualization of their bodies, a phenomenon that, up to a certain point, women learn to bear. Such codes of propriety regulate how and to what extent we speak about violence all the time. After September 11 many felt the force of those codes with new urgency. Where one lived, whether any of one's loved ones or even acquaintances had died: such distinctions regulated how and in what ways people felt authorized and able to speak about the events. Unspeakability served as a useful rubric under which to gather the various social *and* phenomenological aspects of the event that made discussion of it feel at once compulsory and inadequate.

Also important are the obstacles to speech that stem from psychic trauma. The long history of theories of trauma, reaching back to the first cases of "railway spine" in the nineteenth century, shows that speech is one of the many human modalities affected by psychic shock, which the medical establishment eventually came to recognize as the source of pathology. Trauma theory, the interdisciplinary nonclinical work that has made trauma a key topic in literary studies (among others), has tended to focus on this symptom at the exclusion of any others, often making trauma equal to speechlessness and vice versa. But whatever the overemphasis on this aspect of trauma and the indifference of these theorists to features of trauma such as disassociation and hyperarousal, it has long been noted that many people who experience extreme violence have difficultly speaking about it. Many victims of trauma have described feeling a compulsive drive to speak about their experiences and having difficulty finding a receptive and sympathetic listener. Work by neurobiologists has located changes in brain activity that occur under conditions of extreme stress, although the links are not, at least at this point, causal. The best that can be said is that such findings "indicate PTSD patients' trouble putting feelings into words are reflected in actual changes in brain activity."[44] However important and potentially useful such studies are, they don't demonstrate that violence or traumatic experiences are unspeakable, nor do scientists have a good empirical basis yet to account for cultural differences in brain activity. It is worth noting that muteness, once a prevalent symptom of shell-shocked soldiers, is rarely seen in combat veterans these days, which would indicate that our responses to trauma are historically and culturally inflected. All of this suggests that while there may well be some yet-to-be-explained obstacles to certain kinds of speech attendant upon the experience of trauma, claims about the unspeakability of violence tend to issue not from carefully evaluated scientific evidence but from some combination of personal conviction, theoretical commitment, common sense, and popular sentiment. And it is to the literary forms in which these claims are made that *The Prestige of Violence* is addressed.

zembla in the
new york times

PALE FIRE'S HISTORICAL VIOLENCE

In an unusually lyrical moment in Vladimir Nabokov's *Pale Fire*, Charles Kinbote offers a paean to the near magical powers of the written word. Having just been handed, albeit temporarily, the manuscript of the poem by John Shade, Kinbote rhapsodizes:

> We are absurdly accustomed to this miracle of a few written signs being able to contain immortal imagery, involutions of thought, new worlds with live people, speaking, weeping, laughing. We take it for granted so simply that in a sense, by the very act of brutish routine acceptance, we undo the work of ages. . . . What if we awake one day, all of us, unable to read? I wish you to gasp not only at what you read but at the miracle of its being readable. . . . Solemnly I weighed in my hand what I was carrying in my left armpit and for a moment I found myself enriched with an indescribable amazement as if informed that fireflies were making decodable signals on behalf of stranded spirits, or that a bat was writing a legible tale of torture in the bruised and branded sky. (289)

This passage is perhaps best known for the (here elided) admission that Kinbote is a poor poet, which critics have cited as proof that he can *not* be the author of the entire poem, and that he *is* the likely author of the weak alternate lines he half-heartedly flogs in the commentary. For my purposes, this passage is important for the way it affirms the capacity of language to bring us into contact with a real that is constituted in and through violence. Although Nabokov famously asserted in "On a Book entitled *Lolita*," that "reality" is "one of the few words which mean nothing without quotes," I will aim to show that *Pale Fire* assumes the presence of an ultimate, rather than contingent, reality.[1] Kinbote, it turns out, will be disappointed when he does read the draft manuscript of the poem, but the novel *Pale Fire* aims to deliver something not too far off from Kinbote's ecstatic hope.

The primary move made by Kinbote here is an exultant celebration of the power of language to make new worlds and communicate existing ones, thereby revivifying our contact with the everyday reality around us. Language here is not the corrupted code in which inessential social knowledge is looped in an empty cycle of self-reference and validation, but a miraculous conduit to the real. For Nabokov, here as in his other works, there is no meaningful distinction between successful linguistic art and the richness and rawness of reality; if anything, literature is more likely than mere experience to get one into contact with the real. As in *Lolita*, where Humbert Humbert's virtuoso prose attempts to elide but succeeds—when read carefully—in revealing his cruelty, so here language is ultimately more a medium of revelation than obfuscation.

Through Kinbote Nabokov at once rejects the notion that language blocks our access to the real, and suggests, albeit indirectly, of what stuff the real is made. Reading is as amazing, Kinbote tells us, as if writing and reading were capable of revealing the reality of worldly torture and otherwordly suffering. Torture, regicide, bruised and branded skies, and the inevitable arrival of a bigger and more competent assassin: these are the realities that Kinbote suggests we should see shadowing the miracle of ordinary written communication (301).

While I have attributed these views to Nabokov, this vision of a normally hidden reality that is all but wholly constituted out of horror might be taken only as further proof of Kinbote's paranoid derangement. As such it would constitute a challenge to, not an endorsement of, the prestige of violence. The violence on which Kinbote harps in his constantly reiterated and presumably unwarranted fears of assassination is relentlessly associated with delusion and disconnection from reality. Yet I will suggest that as a whole, *Pale Fire* insists upon both the primacy of violence *and* the privileged role that literary language plays in revealing it. Kinbote is delusional, *Pale Fire* suggests, and yet his madness still appears to be a symptom of the real violence set in motion by revolution. This madness is not merely akin to Nabokov's art, but is its internalized correlate.

Before proceeding further, some minimal recapitulation of both the book's plot and the main terms by which it has been interpreted by critics may prove helpful. The novel takes the form of a posthumous critical edition of a long poem entitled "Pale Fire" by the poet John Shade. Sandwiching the poem is the foreward, and then the commentary and index, of the eccentric scholar who has gotten hold of the manuscript, Dr. Charles Kinbote. We learn early on from Professor Kinbote that Shade was murdered, although we do not initially know anything further about the crime. By the time we finish the text, we likely do not know what to think. But we *have* learned the following: that Kinbote claims to be the exiled king of a (perhaps real) country called Zembla and that he believes himself to be under threat from the Soviet-backed extremists who ousted and now want to assassinate him; that he believes Shade was killed by an assassin who was in fact attempting to murder him; that most everyone else believes that Shade was killed by an escaped lunatic who was institutionalized by the Judge whose house Kinbote has been renting. Over the course of commenting on the poem, which concerns primarily the poet's preoccupation with death and immortality in the aftermath of his daughter's suicide, we also learn that Kinbote had believed the poem was about him and his lost kingdom and that he is terrifically disappointed when he discovers that it is not. Finally, we are led to suspect (although here the evidence is carefully buried in the index and in other small details) that Kinbote is not who he pretends to be: he is an unpopular, homosexual, and delusional Russian American scholar named Professor Botkin.[2]

All of this puts the reader/critic in a peculiar position, for even if we are convinced that Kinbote is really Botkin (as I am, for instance), the novel we are reading and the character that is actually drawn for us is that of Kinbote: both must somehow be sustained. Just as most critics think Kinbote is really Botkin, nearly all readers come to realize that Shade's killer is in all probability Jack Grey, a deranged escapee from a mental hospital seeking revenge on Judge Goldsworth, Shade's neighbor, who sent him away. But not all critics have read the novel this way. One critical camp has it that no murder takes place at all, and the whole text is just John Shade's strangely Nabokovian literary creation.[3] Still more dizzying is the theory that Kinbote is the creator of all of *Pale Fire*.[4] Given the degree to which *all* these readings bracket the novel's violence with deflating skepticism, *Pale Fire* would seem to entail a robust refusal to award any prestige to violence.

But to the extent that Nabokov smuggles both contemporary geopolitics and his own autobiography into the novel we are invited into a chain of associations and substitutions in which language—especially Nabokov's literary language—is made directly *from and out of* the losses wrought by violence. Shade transmutes the death of a small bird, of his parents, his aunt, and his daughter into poetry; Botkin, in his madness, transforms his unknowable but seemingly tortured past into the vivid political drama of Charles Xavier. Both characters make artful "pale fires" of their suffering, fires that also reflect the suffering of their creator. Nabokov's own losses of father, brother, language, and homeland are repeatedly copied, burlesqued, and elided in the events that befall his characters.[5] Zembla itself encodes an important reference to the nuclear history being made throughout the period just prior to and including the novel's publication. All these losses and sorrows, from the accidental death of a bird to the alienation of the outcast, serve as pale fires of, and surrogates for, the luminous real of violence. Where later texts examined in this book insist upon the incapacity of language to articulate the violence that constitutes their notion of the real, in *Pale Fire* the former is the primary ambassador for the invisible, ever-presence of the latter. What we have is language and, when it is good—when it is art—its miracles maintain an authentic relationship to the pain, suffering, loss, and violence that inspires it. Thus, by virtue of the distinction that Nabokov's novel draws between high art and everyday speech Nabokov is able to preserve a conduit between language and the real. Language does not represent violence, but it does transform, transfigure, and transcend it.

What I aim to reveal, then, is an episode in the uneven development of a set of ideas about language and violence. My argument is not that Nabokov's views about language and violence are broadly representative of the period; his body of work and his biography are far too idiosyncratic to bear such a claim. But I do want to suggest that *Pale Fire* in particular can be coherently placed with a historical narrative such that certain features of this remarkable text anticipate and illuminate the direction of some important writing that follows. *Pale Fire* brings the specific contours of what I am calling "the prestige of violence" into focus and renders the coterie consensus on the subject that emerges in later years considerably clearer.

I also hope to make a more local intervention by suggesting that Nabokov's work is far more engaged with and conditioned by the political world than the criticism of it has tended to suggest. Partly because Nabokov's reputation was made and solidified during the height of the cold war, direct critical attention to it has only recently come into play. Nabokov, who came from an aristocratic family that opposed bolshevism, repeatedly claimed—in *Speak, Memory*, *Strong Opinions*, and other *belles lettres*—that his fictional world-making exempts him from the vulgar tyranny of mere historical givens. He has in turn been consistently read as the high priest of the high style, the aesthete who stares down history through the sheer brilliance of his imagination.[6] This image has been sustained even in the face of fictions that clearly subvert the posture of mandarin indifference. Criticism of Nabokov's challenging multilingual work has generally stayed within a small sphere of erudite specialists, well-trained in various subjects that are central to his work (such as nineteenth-century Russian prosody, French literature, and, more recently, lepidoptery) and deeply committed to biographically-based criticism, but at times resistant to readings that run counter to the author's self-understanding. By contrast, I read *Pale Fire* as a meditation on the proper relationship between the reality claims of the political and those of the aesthetic. Whereas Nabokov has long been read as insisting on the latter at the expense of the former, I aim to show a complex interdependency, one in which aesthetic value cannot be separated from the violent political realities it triumphantly overcomes and whose energies it gathers for itself in the process.

Although at some moments those energies seem to derive solely from the Russian past, *Pale Fire* insists that the cold war admits no zone of safety. As the Cuban Missile Crisis confirmed the very year that the novel was published, the conflict between the United States and the Soviet Union created a global vulnerability that was felt in the United States with particular force in the fifties and early sixties. *Pale Fire* confirms that you can find the violence of history anywhere, even in New Wye, and not just because indigenous madmen and suicides proliferate: émigrés, both brilliant and deranged, are tossed onto college campuses just as nuclear fallout spreads into the Midwest from the Soviet Arctic and Pacific atolls. The authors of novels studied in later chapters of this book respond in complex ways to the sequestration of military conflict during the later years of the cold war by reimagining their own lack of direct experience of it as a form of higher access. *Pale Fire* speaks eloquently of a different and earlier moment, one in which it is far less clear that some parts of the globe will fare better than others.

"A BIGGER MORE COMPETENT GRADUS": ZEMBLA, THE COLD WAR, AND NUCLEAR FALLOUT

> Oh, I may do many things! History permitting, I may sail back to my recovered kingdom, and with a great sob greet the grey coastline and the gleam of a roof in the rain. I may huddle and groan in a madhouse. But whatever happens, wherever the scene is laid, somebody, somewhere, will quietly set out—somebody has already set out, somebody still rather far away is buying a ticket, is boarding a bus, a ship, a plane, has landed, is walking toward a million photographers, and presently he will ring at my door—a bigger, more respectable, more competent Gradus. (301)

Nabokov wrote in his diary that the missing page number on the final entry of the index was evidence that Kinbote took his own life.[7] Regardless of whether we think that such extra-textual explanations are admissible, we might still want to understand the source of suicidal despair Kinbote expresses throughout the text. It was probably not caused by the loss of a kingdom, but it also could not have emerged in a historical vacuum. What, if not the loss of the Zembla he claims to have fled, has so deranged his mind? Although we are not given anything substantive, we are given some hints. Where Kinbote gives us a king in a Ruritanian Romance, Nabokov hints at a lonely émigré and a lost, pre-Soviet world. Much like Nabokov himself, we can presume that Botkin has lost the Russia of his youth.

In that sense, Kinbote's fantasized loss of Zembla is the product of both Botkin's and Nabokov's loss of Russia. This is both the loss of a homeland upon emigration and also the earlier loss when Russia became part of the Soviet Union. Zembla is both an art-effect and symptom: where Nabokov has made novels out of that loss, Botkin/Kinbote makes delusional footnotes. But in addition to figuring the loss of Russia, the geopolitical position of Zembla as construed by Kinbote structures it as a Soviet satellite state; Nabokov goes to considerable lengths to explicitly establish the USSR as Zembla's interfering and powerful neighbor. Indeed, if we strip away all of Kinbote's self-serving bluster about the perfection of Zembla's prerevolutionary taxation and sexual mores we have an entirely credible tale: the ruling powers of a small state of geographic significance are overthrown and put under Soviet influence. Though we might deem this scenario fantastic, fear of its occurrence certainly shaped U.S. foreign policy for quite some time. Finally, Zembla's name, usually read as a clear signal of the place's pure fictionality, also refers to the USSR and in ways that bring the geopolitics of the early sixties to the fore. Steven Belletto has recently pointed out that Novaya Zemlya is not just the name of a place on the world map that fell under Soviet control, but the site used by the Soviet Union, along with a facility in what is now Kazakhstan, for many of their nuclear tests: "[D]uring the late 1950s, Novaya Zemlya did not merely correlate to the icy land evoked by Swift and Pope, it was also a far-off place with a very particular political importance: the site where the Soviets tested their atomic bombs" (765–66).[8]

Although Belletto himself does not pursue his insight too far in this direction, it places Zembla at the very heart of the cold war. In the years between 1949, when the Soviets conducted their first successful atomic bomb test, and September 24, 1963, when the Limited Test Ban Treaty was approved by the U.S. Senate, both the political stakes of the arms race and the public health consequences of nuclear testing were very much on the public mind. These were years, Paul Boyer has argued, marked by a spasm of public opposition spawned by reports that nuclear fallout from aboveground testing was both ubiquitous and dangerous.[9] As the title of David Bradley's 1948 bestseller indicated, there was *No Place to Hide*. By 1958 the Department of Public Health had begun to monitor the nation's milk supply and by 1959, according to Paul Boyer, "a full-blown fall-out scare gripped the nation" when *Science* published the results of a Columbia University study that demonstrated a sharp rise in the levels of strontium-90 in the bones of children. In addition, *The Saturday Evening Post* published "Fallout: The Silent Killer" (82–83), also about strontium-90. By 1962, the year of *Pale Fire*'s publication, strontium-90 was shown to exist at vastly higher levels in the teeth of babies born after 1957.

Nabokov was in the process of composing *Pale Fire* during these years; Brian Boyd dates Nabokov's initial inspiration and preliminary work on the book to 1956 and 1957, with the bulk of composition occurring from late November of 1960 to early December of 1961. And although Boyd is utterly uninterested in such details, it is clear that Nabokov was attentive to contemporary politics, especially Soviet-American relations, during this period. Letters from the author to Katharine White and Harold Ross of the *New Yorker* in 1951 refer to an article Nabokov hoped to write on the subject. Ross, in turn, assures Nabokov that the only thing that could preclude the article's publication is "the dropping of an atomic bomb that would put us out of business."[10] As Ross's joke suggests, the nuclear testing that the Soviets did in Novaya Zemlya and at the Semipalatinsk Test Site from the late 1940s onward was of monumental importance: the period was marked by a series of unexpectedly early successes from the Soviets in matching and even exceeding the United States, from its explosion of a multistage hydrogen bomb in 1955 to its launch of Sputnik in 1957. The power of the Soviets to initiate or retaliate in nuclear kind dovetailed rather neatly with fall-out fears. Both dramatically heightened Americans' sense of vulnerability: they could suffer as the intended targets of nuclear warfare or as unintended victims of a toxic global scourge.

Nabokov eventually abandoned the article he broached with Ross and White, but *Pale Fire* provides further evidence that Nabokov's invocation of the nuclear resonance of the name Zembla is not just accidental. The link between Zembla and Novaya Zemlya is made explicit in what must be one of the least explored corners of this painstakingly deciphered novel: Kinbote's commentary to line 949 of Shade's poem. In it he veers off into a long digression about Gradus's first morning in New York, part of which is taken up reading two days' worth of the *New York Times* abandoned on the benches of Central Park (274–75). If we follow in Kinbote's footsteps and look up the editions of the *New York Times* that he cites we enter into a surprisingly dense and intricate entanglement in a historical and political world whose constitutive element is violence. It is clear that Nabokov spent quite a bit of time reading through these editions of the paper and mining them for material. Everything from tiny two-line classifieds to the major news articles of the day are reworked, referenced, or quietly winked at in *Pale Fire*. For his part, Kinbote tells us at the end of the passage that he researched these editions, thus nominally explaining—or revealing—how he managed to achieve the level of detail offered.

Although the list of headlines provided by Kinbote sounds ridiculously Kinbotean, many of them have been pulled from the paper unchanged.[11] Among the items that Nabokov inserts into the novel is the headline "2 Octogenarians Hail Soviet Fair" and the assertions by a reviewer of Scandinavian tourist books that "the fjords are too famous to need description, and . . . all Scandinavians love flowers." Material that we might assume to be perfect examples of his diseased auto-historicism turn out to be barely altered historical artifacts. Kinbote's farcical scene of an international picnic can be found in the *Times* where a now-Swedish "moppet" and her Japanese friend exchange farewells in their native languages. A description of Queen Elizabeth rubbing her eyes and nose under the watchful eyes of observers is not a Zemblafied fantasy of royal scrutiny but a carefully extracted sample of the *Times'* international coverage.[12] I take this section to impinge upon the critical debates about Zembla's status insofar as it reminds us that our most casually invoked standards of plausibility fail to account for the weirdness that occurs every day as catalogued by the most respectable authorities.

But the most significant article for anyone looking to explore the political and historical valence of Zembla is the first article cited by Kinbote, which in *Pale Fire* reads: "Hrushchov (whom they spelled 'Khrushchev') had abruptly put off a visit to Scandinavia and was to visit Zembla instead" (274). The equivalent article in the July 21 edition of the *New York Times* confirms that Khrushchev had in fact "abruptly put off a visit to Scandinavia" citing "the 'anti-Soviet' atmosphere prevailing" in Sweden, Denmark, and Norway.[13] More important is the reason the visit was postponed. Toward the end of the first and then into the second page of the article, the author provides more background. The anti-Soviet atmosphere decried by the Kremlin in notes sent to the Danish, Swedish, and Finnish embassies is traced by the author to a statement made by Sweden's foreign minister following a proposal by Khrushchev for a halt to nuclear testing in the area. The minister is reported to have pointed out that the Soviets were the only ones in the area with nuclear weapons and that everyone's energy would be better spent trying to prohibit such weapons outright. And where were such weapons being tested in the immediate area? In Novaya Zemlya, of course.

What, exactly, should we make of this, beyond noting that it confirms that history and politics matter to the novel? Given that so much of *Pale Fire*'s comic energy comes from the absurdity of Kinbote's cloak and dagger Zembla stories in an American college town, the allusion seems to suggest that while the character of Kinbote's paranoia is misplaced, the deathly danger that drifts to the United States from Zembla—Kinbote, readers will recall, drifts onto U.S. soil with the help of a parachute—and Novaya Zemlya is indeed real. As the aftermath of the American nuclear tests on the Marshall Islands made clear, the ash released by nuclear tests into the atmosphere could travel far from its remote place of origin and was in the process of irrevocably entering the bodies of organisms from the simplest to the most complex.

The nuclear testing signaled so lightly but definitively in the name of Charles Kinbote's kingdom encodes a model of how the violent potentialities of warfare are both contained and diffused: the test sites in Novaya Zemlya are secret, remote, and geographically contained, but the tests conducted there result in the spread of deadly fallout. The fallout instantiates in concrete terms the invisible diffusion and perpetuation of violence that occurs in much more subtle and abstract ways throughout the novel. The metaphorical usage of the term fallout, whose use first appeared in a 1954 *Time* magazine article that attests to the "fall-out of fear and worry" that the hydrogen bomb tests in Soviet Siberia generated, helps us make sense of the world of *Pale Fire*, one in which the dead come back as ghosts, in which birds are "slain" by immobile panes of glass, and in which even sweet-tempered old poets are not safe from the madmen in their midst.

SECRETARIES AND FATHERS, POETS AND WAXWINGS: *PALE FIRE*'S "ACCIDENTAL" VICTIMS

> Personally, I have not known any lunatics; but I have heard of several amusing cases in New Wye ("Even in Arcady am I," says Dementia, chained to her gray column). (237)

The same issues of the *New York Times* that refer to a postponed visit by Krushchev to Sweden contain an article not cited within *Pale Fire* but deeply relevant to it. The front–page article from the July 21 edition is headlined "State Bar Urges Major Change in Statute on Criminally Insane," and reports on the support of the New York State Bar Association for a change that would allow for more lenience toward the mentally ill by bringing standards of criminal insanity in line with those of modern psychiatry.[14] While the then-current law based responsibility on the defendant's ability to know that the act was wrong, the new statute would allow the defendant to escape punishment if, despite knowing that the act was wrong, he was unable to resist the impulse to commit it. At the close of the article the journalist provides some context for the legal issues at stake. The current law was based on a definition of insanity drafted in England in 1843, when a mentally ill Scotsman named Daniel M'Naghten attempted to assassinate Prime Minister Sir Robert Peel, but failed when he mistook the P.M.'s secretary for his prey and shot him instead. M'Naghten heard voices telling him to kill Peel, believed that Peel was a demon leading a conspiracy and suffered from a severe sense of persecution, all of which contribute to the current consensus that M'Naghten suffered from schizophrenia.

That the article is relevant to *Pale Fire* seems undeniable. It looks, that is, like an analogue to the murder of Shade. But perhaps even more importantly, the article *and* Shade's murder recapitulate the death of Nabokov's own beloved father, mistakenly killed when trying to shield his friend from an assassination attempt. Nabokov alludes to this "accidental" murder in one of the most striking moments in his autobiography, *Speak, Memory*. Nabokov describes the fear that consumed him when he learned that his father had challenged a journalist to a duel. After an anxious ride back from school, young Vladimir discovered that the duel had been cancelled due to the journalist's contrition. Describing the wave of elation he felt at that moment he tells us that "ten years were to pass before a certain night in 1922, at a public lecture in Berlin, when my father shielded the lecturer (his old friend, Milyukov) from the bullets of two Russian Fascists and, while vigorously knocking down one of the assassins, was fatally shot by the other." "But," he assures us, "no shadow was cast by that event upon the bright stairs of our St. Petersburg house; the large cool hand resting on my head did not quaver, and several lines of play in a difficult chess composition were not yet blended on the board" (193).

The strangeness of that insistence is characteristic of Nabokov's riddle-making. To contend that a later event did not cast a shadow on an earlier event as it was experienced is to make a case that hardly seems to need making. It is fair to assume that the majority of readers do not believe in the kind of prophetic retrospection the passage asserts through denial. The only reason the connection would be made is that both events have been textually coordinated by Nabokov himself in the writing of the chapter. Here Nabokov is very much the divine author invoked by Shade at the close of canto three, a member of the unseen "they" who "[coordinate] these / Events and objects with remote events / and vanished objects" (63).

Yet just as the shadow of his father's death is/is not cast over the moment of the cancelled duel, so too is it cast/not cast over the whole of *Pale Fire*. In the opening lines of his poem John Shade speaks of a bird that, mistaking the reflection of the sky in a window for the sky itself, is killed as it flies into the glass. Taken as a poignant accident, the bird's death is perfectly suited to the poem's subject matter and tone, in which the vicissitudes of life and death in the pastoral world of a countrified academic enclave are charged with a homely grandeur. Yet for all the controlled pathos of the moment, the language is sinister. The rhetoric of the bird's death—its slaying—leads us stealthily outside the boundaries of the poem, into a world of betrayal, conspiracy, and assassination that mark Kinbote's commentary and Nabokov's shadow-(not)casting autobiography.

Keeping the acquired symbolic freight of the term "shadow" in mind then, its presence in the opening of the poem is both odd and resonant. John Shade opens the poem with an explicit identification with the bird ("I was the shadow of the waxwing slain"). The initial purpose of that shadowy identification is to allow Shade, at the moment of the bird's death, to take over its perspective. From this vantage point, liberated from the earth by his wings, the identification allows Shade to anticipate the transcendent author-god who appears in canto three and four, with whom the poet is explicitly allied. But the identification with the bird is also an anticipation of his own death that recalls the epigraph from *Speak, Memory*. Shade prophesies his own death, poetically recognizing that his future death cast a shadow on the death of a bird that occurred many months earlier.

The specific cast of that prophecy is made even more troubling by the fact that this poetic vision, which is both prophetic and retrospective, explicitly engages the rhetoric of political violence. The Shadows, according to Kinbote, are a group of Zemblan "extremists" formed with a special purpose: "to hunt down the King and kill him"(150). Kinbote claims that John Shade's murder was committed by one of them. And regardless of what we believe, Shade's death at the hand of a Shadow is oddly undeniable; despite the fact that Kinbote anxiously reveals a competing explanation that most readers will find more plausible, the regicidal plot is the only story that is fully narrated in the course of the novel. The opportunity to engage in hermeneutic anachronism—seeing "Shadows" in prior "shadows"—is akin to answering the question of whether a "shadow was cast" à la *Speak, Memory*.

Once the shadow of Shade's murder has been cast onto the bird's death, every aspect of that death is transformed, whether by paranoia, genuine evil, or both. If we affirm that shadow, we find Shade claiming to be "the shadow of the waxwing slain" as if he, and not the windowpane, were its cause of death. The *falseness* of the azure shades into the duplicitous and not the merely mistaken, while the presence of the term *slain* comes into especially sharp focus. The use of the word *slain* to describe the waxwing's accidental death is a provocation, although a subtle one. If birds are slain by windows then the possibility of accident is all but eliminated. It is as if Kinbote's paranoia has seeped into the poem, permeating its most innocent moments and insisting that there are no accidents, only obscurely willed and sinister acts masquerading as contingencies.

However, it is *not* Kinbote who thinks the waxwing has been slain, but John Shade. For the most part, Shade is preoccupied not with violence per se, but with death. Death and the hope he maintains for some form of life after death is his main theme. It is signaled in his poem in the dead bird, the suicide of his daughter, and the constant mortal threats of illness and old age that have claimed his parents and the beloved aunt who raised him. By the end of the poem, Shade has come to terms with his lack of certainty about life after death. Whatever order, meaning, and pattern that he had hoped could be recuperated from life through immortality, he now locates in art, or more specifically, poetry. This is addressed most directly and famously when he discovers that his ostensible proof of the hereafter—a near-death vision of a fountain he thought he shared with a stranger—was based on a misprint. Shade exultantly epiphanizes:

Life everlasting—based on a misprint!
[. . .]
But all at once it dawned on me that this
Was the real point, the contrapuntal theme;
Just this: not text, but texture; not the dream
But topsy-turvical coincidence,
Not flimsy nonsense, but a web of sense.
Yes! It sufficed that I in life could find
Some kind of link-and-bobolink, some kind
Of correlated pattern in the game,

Plexed artistry, and something of the same
Pleasure in it as they who played it found. (63)

Shade dismisses the afterlife as an irrelevant distraction from the sources of meaning to which we have access. It is enough that we have intertextuality, a collectivity of texts in which we can make and find a universe of patterns. Shade clarifies in Canto Four "And if my private universe scans right, / So does the verse of galaxies divine / Which I suspect is an iambic line" (69). Shade is insisting upon a dependent relationship between his pattern-making and the meaningfulness of the world at large without specifying the causal mechanism. While Shade has given us every reason to believe that he knows himself to be subject to a world not at his command, his theory of "combinational delight" lends him enormous control; whole galaxies are tuned to his rhyme. While Kinbote imagines that the world revolves around his persecution, Shade's suggests that the world relies upon his prosodic success.

But of course, Shade turns out to be wrong. At the close of the poem Shade proclaims that he is:

[R]easonably sure that we survive
And that my darling somewhere is alive,
As I am reasonably sure that I
Shall wake at six tomorrow, on July
The twenty-second, nineteen fifty-nine (69)

In the face of Shade's divine versifying—in which he casts himself as "one who plays the game" and thus as the primary author of his own future—he incorrectly prophesies his own short-term survival. Instead Shade is felled by Jacob Grey, who personifies the mad force of violent contingency that is loose even in bucolic New Wye.

ELECTRICITY, FIRE, AND LIGHT: LOSS, PERSISTENCE, AND RADIOACTIVE HALF-LIVES

How much more intelligent it is—even from a proud infidel's point of view!—to accept God's presence—a faint phosphorescence at first, a pale light in the dimness of bodily life, and a dazzling radiance after it? (227)

The nuclear allusion in the name of Kinbote's kingdom, in addition to signaling the political and historical world outside of *Pale Fire*'s superficially hermetic text, also gives us a way to think about the metaphors of light at a useful distance from those of theft, which, given the allusion to *Timon of Athens* in the novel's title, are so relentlessly linked to it.[15] Fallout from nuclear testing, after all, is contaminated by the radioactive energy that is commonly understood as an invisible form of light. *Pale Fire*'s countless verbal cousins of its title phrase certainly cannot be equated with the decaying half-life of an unstable atom, but the metaphor is nonetheless useful to keep in mind: many of the novel's "pale fires" speak far more eloquently of the ongoing dissipation and circulation of historical violence than they do of borrowings and thefts.

Professor Kinbote, to prepare his readers for the tale of his escape from On-hava, offers a brief primer on Zemblan geography and topography: "Several trails cross the mountains at various points and lead to passes none of which exceeds an altitude of five thousand feet; a few peaks rise some two thousand feet higher and retain their snow in midsummer; and from one of them, the highest and the hardest, Mt. Glitterntin, one can distinguish on clear days, far out to the east, beyond the Gulf of Surprise, a dim iridescence which some say is Russia" (138). As Michael Wood memorably quipped, "I wonder what the others say."[16] But given that, at the time of the novel's publication, Russia had not existed for decades, Kinbote's equivocation reminds us of both the losses wrought by revolution and their ongoing reverberations. Or, to put it in a less lyrical vein, the absence of Russia is here a kind of presence, and one intimately tied to the violence of history's ongoing convulsions.

The association of the title phrase with loss and persistence is especially apparent in the explicit linking of the novel's "pale fires" to its ghosts. In an excerpt from Hazel's diary of a ghost-watching episode, the specter appears to her as "a roundlet of pale light" and then as a "luminescent circlet" (188). Later in the same note, Kinbote reprints a poem by John Shade in which the dead live on in street lamps and lightbulbs. "The dead, the gentle dead—who knows? / In tungsten filaments abide" (192). Concluding this strange note in which ghosts appear as light and vice versa, Kinbote says enigmatically: "Science tells us, by the way, that the Earth would not merely fall apart, but vanish like a ghost, if Electricity were suddenly removed from the world" (193).[17]

As bizarre as Kinbote's assertion sounds, it provides a model of how violence at once is and is not present in the text. Particularly important is Kinbote's idea that without electricity, or what can be read backwards through Shade's quoted poem as light, the world would "vanish like a ghost." Such a vanishing is not as complete as it sounds at first. Kinbote tells us that without light the earth would vanish only to return—to haunt us—as a roundlet of light. The thing we have lost is indistinguishable from the phantom that returns.

This weird logic is confirmed in a belated gloss to the episode, indexed by Kinbote to line 230, in which the shade of Aunt Maud was believed to have returned to the Shade house soon after her death. Hazel appears to have thought the ghost was her dead Aunt Maud. Kinbote disagrees, and suspects that the ghost is an imposter, a spirit far from home looking to trick the inhabitants into providing shelter. Kinbote suspects, in short, that this ghost is much like Kinbote himself: he too is trying to make a surrogate home for himself in unfamiliar surroundings, attempting to enlist others in drawing the falsified connections. Faced with Kinbote's seemingly unwarranted dismissal of the former Aunt Maud as the ghost, the reader is in the same position as those who think the light across the Gulf of Surprise emanates from a ghostly Russia. That is, we are insisting upon the persistence of that which our eyes tell us is long gone.

We are thus left with a new way to read the "pale fire" of the novel's title. It should not be regarded simply as literary shorthand for the devious games of plagiarism, impersonation, and hidden authorship that have preoccupied critics, but as a figure for the way in which violence and loss persist and are renewed. The verbal linking of the dim light visible from the shores of Zembla to the pale fire of the novel's ghosts allows us to see the way whatever kinds of distortion might be signaled by the novel's pale fires, the persistence of what has been lost, of the original object being reflected, remains. In both places pale fire comes to stand for the lingering traces of losses endured, and still ever-present. Russia and Zembla lost to revolution, an aunt and daughter to suicide, father and fatherly poets to botched murders: all these beloved entities lost to cataclysm somehow still remain. The signs of their persistence constitute the real to which *Pale Fire* insistently points us.

SECRET PASSAGES: REVOLUTION AND THE REEMERGENCE OF THE REAL

> Certain creatures of the past, and this was one of them, may lie dormant for thirty years as this one had, while their natural habitat undergoes calamitous alterations. . . . The death of Oleg at fifteen, in a toboggan accident, helped to obliterate the reality of their adventure. A national revolution was needed to make that secret passage real again. (128)

While neither Shade's artistic megalomania nor Kinbote's persecution fantasies are validated, the vulnerability of both men to the contingencies of history is the basis for the transcendence of historical violence upon which art in *Pale Fire* depends. In one of his longer excursions into his past, Kinbote tells readers of a secret passage he discovered not once, but twice in his life. The passageway, surreptitiously built to allow his late grandfather, Thurgis the Third, to travel to the dressing room of an actress in the Royal Theater with whom he was involved, ultimately provides Kinbote's means of escape from the castle. Yet both times it is revealed, the gift of its appearance is causally linked to the deaths— near, accidental, and premeditated—that take place around him. In beginning the note about his rediscovery of the secret passage, Kinbote explains that as a child one day he was looking for "an elaborate toy circus encased in a box as big as a croquet case" that he and his expected friend had played with during a previous visit (124). That toy had been "the gift of a foreign potentate who had recently been assassinated" (124). Searching for this toy in his grandfather's closet he finds, in addition to a copy of *Timon of Athens*, a hidden door to a secret underground passage that he and his friend Oleg subsequently investigate. Just as the tunnel had originally been constructed to allow Kinbote's Uncle Thurgis his amorous trysts, the exploration of the tunnel by Kinbote and his friend leads them to previously unknown sexual delights. But soon after this erotic encounter, young Kinbote suffered a grave bout of pneumonia and his friend Oleg died; as a result, Kinbote surmises, he forgot about the tunnel's very existence.

Under threat from the extremists who have imprisoned him, Kinbote recovers his memory of the forgotten passage. As the passage cited in the previous epigraph tells us, "a national revolution was needed to make that secret passage real again" (127–28). The losses of the past are recuperated, paradoxically, through the cataclysm of revolution. While revolution and violence are not exactly synonymous, for Kinbote the King they might as well be; he narrates the revolution in Zembla as a successful coup d'etat and attempted regicide. But beyond Kinbote's certainty that he is personally being singled out for assassination are an array of hints and references to death, violence, and their shared ability to activate reality.

While through much of his commentary Kinbote's past seems to be all but bursting from him, his story of the passage takes us to one of the few places where recollection is labored and the past must be reconstructed. Long buried by the experience of illness and the loss of his friend, the secret passage was not so much forgotten by him as it was in a state of hibernation. The key to the reactivation of this memory is the threat of violence. Kinbote's aside about the source of the toy circus, a detail that initially seems included merely to whip up the small potatoes of Zembla with the glamour of world intrigue, is far more eloquent when examined in relation to Kinbote's rediscovery of the passage. Just as the gift of the assassinated leader initiates the sequence of events that lead to the discovery of the passage, its rediscovery will depend upon the threat of imminent harm. While the whole episode underscores the fragility of life to violent exigencies, that same violence also helps to excavate that which it hides. Crucially, that "reality" is both secret and subterranean, and is rediscovered only under pressure of the dangers from which it provides escape.

In *Speak, Memory* we find a similar secret passageway that leads, at least initially, to escape. In this work of autobiography, Nabokov describes a striking episode in his father's political career:

In the winter of 1917–18, he was elected to the Constituent Assembly, only to be arrested by energetic Bolshevist sailors when it was disbanded. The November Revolution had already entered upon its gory course, its police was already active, but in those days the chaos of orders and counterorders sometimes took our side: my father followed a dim corridor, saw an open door at the end, walked out into a side street and made his way to the Crimea with a knapsack he had ordered his valet Osip to bring him to a secluded corner and a package of caviar sandwiches which good Nikolay Andreevich, our cook, had added of his own accord. (177)

There is much in this passage that bears comparison to *Pale Fire*. Clever Odon has a fairly dull counterpart in reliable Osip (and both are alphabetically reminiscent of Oleg), although some of the weird flashiness of Kinbote's escape emanates from those caviar sandwiches. The knapsack resembles the absurd red get-up of the king, especially when we picture Nabokov senior in all his reputed elegance. And while he escapes through nothing more banal than an open door, the "dim corridor" he must traverse to reach it is a restrained version of Kinbote's dark underground passage. The dim passage, sketched within *Pale Fire* with much adolescent jocularity as a figure for anal sex, also recalls the memory of Nabokov's gay brother Sergei who died while imprisoned in a Nazi concentration camp. Nabokov recalls in *Speak, Memory* his shame at having revealed the secret to the family, but he is otherwise barely a presence in Nabokov's autobiographical writings.[18]

Violence hovers ominously in the shadows of all these passages. If we follow the story of Kinbote's escape and the similar tale of Nabokov's father, the power of revolution that Kinbote says was needed to "make that secret passage real" appears to be part of a larger truth about our ability to evade history and its violence. Ultimately, however, it appears that one can only outrun violence for so long. Even if you escape the assassination planned for you, you are likely to be caught in the crossfire of another. Thus, V. D. Nabokov escapes from the "already active" police force that captures him, only to be killed in the attempt on his friend Milyukov. Shade's "reasonable" certainty about his short-term survival proves wrong. Sergei was released after a few months by the Gestapo but was rearrested two years later and brought to the camp where he died.[19] Kinbote may have escaped one plot on his life, but he waits for an assassin even if he turns out to be an authorial creator. Finally, Zembla's name hints at the violence of history that is now stalking us all: the "pale fire" of nuclear radiation that spreads across the globe in the form of fallout, and which serves as a kind of hidden shorthand for the cold war as a whole. Yet there is compensation for the ubiquity of death and the relentlessness of revolution: it is that such violence is the very engine of art. Its revelatory energies have been captured in the novel precisely insofar as it appears to be elided, transformed, and transcended.

> But of course, the most striking characteristic of the little obituary is that it contains *not one reference* to the glorious friendship that brightened the last months of John's life. (101)

Consider three seemingly unrelated moments in *Pale Fire*. In the above epigraph, Kinbote draws his reader's attention to an obituary of John Shade. The next two are extracts from Kinbote's demented and self-serving index to the poem he has just edited: "*Kinbote, Charles, Dr.*, . . . his contempt for Prof. H (not in Index)" (309). "*Shadows, the,* a regicidal organization which commissioned Gradus (*q.v.*) to assassinate the self-banished king; its leaders cannot be mentioned, even in the Index to the obscure work of a scholar" (313). These quotations might be said to offer a parody of the reading I am putting forward. In my analysis *Pale Fire*'s attempts to deflate and deny the deathly violence that constitutes it marks its importance to the text. But I want to insist that my point is less an example of the first quote than it is a species of the latter two: it is not the *total* absence of any reference to violence that marks its importance, but the text's inability to actually leave out that which it insistently protests does not matter.

Despite the stridency with which *Pale Fire* insists that political violence is nothing but a fantasy, political violence remains as that which underpins the novel's value: it is against the horrific reality of death and violence under tyranny that the value of art becomes visible. Transforming the real of death and violence into something else—that is, into the real of literary art—*is* the project of the novel. Kinbote's delusions indicate not that the apparently grandiose and constitutive violence of the historical world is a phantasm, but that Nabokov's art and Kinbote's delusion are two routes to accessing and transforming the shimmering mystery to which violence brings us. Side by side, they disclose with an eloquent compactness a violence that, the novel suggests, cannot be apprehended directly, but whose centrality, importance, and even "reality" is preserved by art nonetheless.

Art is not a glorious private reality that renders one insensible to death and violence as it is in Nabokov's *Invitation to a Beheading*, nor does literary language need to be dismantled, broken, or stripped of meaning in order to achieve union with the sublimity of violence, as in the novels by other authors explored in subsequent chapters of this book. *Pale Fire* aims to create an art that attains some of death's most impressive powers: its inexorability, its ubiquity, its transformative potency.

The inevitability of an otherwise inconclusive death is indeed the one thing that *is* clear from the novel's bewildering ending. Put another way, both death *and* continued existence are certain. Kinbote assures us that he is going to try to resist the impulse to commit suicide, that "he will continue to exist" although, perhaps in other forms. I quote the long but important ending of the narrative portion of the novel:

> I may turn up yet, on another campus, as an old, happy, healthy, heterosexual Russian, a writer in exile, sans fame, sans future, sans audience, sans anything but his art. I may join forces with Odon in a new motion picture: *Escape from Zembla* (ball in the palace, bomb in the palace square). I may pander to the simple tastes of theatrical critics and cook up a stage play, an old-fashioned melodrama with three principles: a lunatic who intends to kill an imaginary king, another lunatic who imagines himself to be that king, and a distinguished old poet who stumbles by chance into the line of fire and perishes in the clash between figments. History permitting, I may sail back to my recovered kingdom, and with a great sob greet the gray coastline and the gleam of a roof in rain. I may huddle and groan in a madhouse. But whatever happens, wherever the scene is laid, somebody, some-where, will quietly set out—somebody has already set out, somebody still rather far away is buying a ticket, is boarding a bus, a ship, a plane, has landed, is walk-ing toward a million photographers, and presently he will ring at my door—a bigger, more respectable, more competent Gradus. (301)

This part of the novel, then, ends with Kinbote's paranoid fantasy intact: an-other Gradus *is* coming for him even if the last one shot someone else. But Nabokov asks us to think about Gradus as a figure of Death itself; he comes for Kinbote as he comes—is coming—for all of us. Kinbote emerges here as simply one incarnation of an endlessly flexible life form. And yet the persistence and transformation that exists in the face of death's inexorability, previously associ-ated with ghosts and the afterlife, here is a kind of art-effect. Kinbote becomes reinvented as an inventive artist, indeed as a kind of purified version of Nabo-kov; that is, stripped of the notoriety and audience he gained from *Lolita*, but left with his core identity as an exiled (and of course heterosexual) artist who has suffered the same losses the author has encoded within the text. Indeed, the kind of art produced by such a figure is so powerful that a poet can perish in the clash between two figments. Just as the death of Nabokov's father can be redeployed as art, so art can generate its own death and thus match the power of violence.

monks and
"the mind of watts"

VIETNAM IN *THE CRYING OF LOT 49*

> Far from a sickness, violence may be an attempt to communicate. (84)
> "A Journey into the Mind of Watts" (1966)

> [O]r whatever it is the word is there, buffering, to protect us from. (105)
> *The Crying of Lot 49*

A few months after the release of *The Crying of Lot 49* and less than a year after the riots in Watts, Thomas Pynchon published an article in the *New York Times Sunday Magazine* entitled "A Journey Into the Mind of Watts," in which he posits the copresence in L.A. of "two different cultures: one white and one black."[1] The white culture, as Pynchon describes it, "belongs to the mass media. What is known around the nation as the L.A. scene exists chiefly as images on a screen or a TV tube, as four color magazine photos, as old radio jokes, as new songs that survive only a couple of weeks. It is basically a white Scene, and illusion is everywhere in it, from the giant aerospace firms that flourish or retrench at the whims of Robert McNamara, to the 'action' everybody mills long [*sic*] the Strip on weekends looking for" (35). Against the unreality and simulation that mark the white scene, "Watts lies impacted in the heart of this white fantasy. It is, by contrast, a pocket of bitter reality" (35). In Watts, "Everything seems so out in the open, all of it real, no plastic faces, no transistors, no hidden Muzak, or Disneyland landscaping or smiling little chicks to show you around. Not in Raceriotland" (35). Readers of *The Crying of Lot 49*—with its references to transistor circuitry, the defense industry, Muzak, and the Disneyland landscaping of the Fangoso Lagoons—can hardly miss the similarities between its world and the white fantasy Pynchon describes. If only, we might think upon reading this, Oedipa had done what Pynchon suggests that white Angelenos do, that is, "leave at the Imperial Highway exit for a change, go east instead of west only a few blocks, and take a look at Watts" ("Watts," 35), she might have been spared much confusion

and heartache. The novel might not have ended with an ambiguous hint at illumination, but with concrete knowledge of the reality that her fantasy world
was hiding from her: a world in which you might be brutally attacked at any
moment, either by the police or by your desperately poor neighbors. For Pynchon could not be clearer in this piece that, as he sees it, violence is the real
and whites live in a fantasy because they fail to recognize and appreciate that
violence.

Unfortunately, in Pynchon's view, the gap between fantasy and reality is surprisingly hard to bridge. The social workers in Watts, trapped within their illusions, are incapable of communicating with those they are supposed to help.
For what separates white fantasy from black reality is a radical gap in their understanding of violence:

> As for violence, in a pocket of reality such as Watts, violence is never far from
> you: because you are a man, because you have been put down, because for every
> action there is an equal and powerful reaction. Somehow, sometime. Yet to these
> innocent optimistic, child-bureaucrats, violence is an evil and illness, possibly be-
> cause it threatens property and status they cannot help cherishing.
>
> They remember last August's riot as an outburst, a seizure. Yet what, from the
> realistic viewpoint of Watts, was so abnormal? . . .
>
> But in the white culture outside, in that creepy world of pre-cardiac Mustang
> drivers who scream insults at one another only when the windows are up; of large
> corporations where Niceguymanship is the standing order regardless of whose
> executive back one may be endeavoring to stab; of an enormous priest caste of
> shrinks who counsel moderation and compromise as the answer to all forms of
> hassle; among so much well-behaved unreality, it is next to impossible to under-
> stand how Watts feels about violence. In terms of strict reality, violence may be a
> means to getting money, for example, no more dishonest than collecting exorbi-
> tant carrying charges from a customer on relief, as white merchants here still do.
> Far from a sickness, violence may be an attempt to communicate, or to be who
> you really are. ("Watts," 84)

Pynchon's point seems initially but then definitively *not* that whites live in a
different reality than blacks, one structured by a different set of material conditions and social relations. Pynchon eventually makes it clear that the violence
that structures life in Watts is *also* present in the white world. The problem
is that whites are unaware of the reality in their midst because their habitual
modes of communication obscure it.

Yet just as important here is the implicitly positive value Pynchon assigns
to violence. On the one hand, Pynchon seems to bemoan the white fantasy
because it renders whites insensible to racism and to the violence it spawns.
But beyond that, Pynchon seems to invite us to think of violence in terms that

would make us reluctant to find ways to reduce it. If violence is neither a sickness nor an evil, what then is it? This passage suggests that violence is at once the subject and the medium of communication at its purest and most transparent; words are obstacles insofar as they obfuscate the violence that subtends *all* social relations. This is made clear enough when Pynchon contrasts the "little man" who denies a black man a job by mentally assigning him the label of "'Bad credit risk'—or 'Poor learner' or 'Sexual threat'" with the cop who has the power to kill you: "it may get more dangerous but at least it's honest." Violence is the secret subtext of everyday conversation, the reality that the language of the white scene keeps hidden even from its speakers.

⌐⫟⌐

I take these reflections on Watts and the "white scene" to provide the beginning of an answer to the question posed in the second epigraph at the start of this chapter, which is also the central question of *The Crying of Lot 49*: What *is* the word there to protect us from? And how is it that "the word" performs such a "buffering"? *The Crying of Lot 49* answers the question by enacting the buffering. According to the logic of the novel, because its medium is the word, such an enactment is inevitable. Yet in spite of this obstacle *The Crying of Lot 49* establishes quite clearly what "it" is: a violence that emerges, despite the novel's legendary reluctance to affirm any ontology, as the primary substance of reality. Words buffer us from the transhistorical force of violence and death.

The Crying of Lot 49 addresses the conundrum posed so forcefully in "Journey into the Mind of Watts": How can violence be the reality that underlies the "white scene" if the white people are unaware of it? How can language be at once a fantasy that screens violence and a form of violence in itself? How does the reality of violence penetrate and even structure the fantasy? Unlike Watts, where violence is a palpable daily reality, the reality charge of violence is primarily present in *Crying* in its debased, phantasmatic, and satirical mode. In place of the brutality of white cops *The Crying of Lot 49* gives us the diffuse and abstract privations of a deracialized underclass and an array of allusions, major and minor, to historical violence: the brutal westward expansion of our nation's pioneers, Nazi genocide, the trenches of France, and a much older, now all-but-obscured European power struggle.

As in *Pale Fire*, *The Crying of Lot 49* seems on one level to associate violence with delusion. The novel focuses on the efforts of the heroine, Oedipa Maas, to determine whether what seems to be a secret centuries-old alternative postal service—called the Tristero—is a genuine world-historical secret or a joke staged by her now-dead ex-boyfriend, Pierce Inverarity. Pynchon's novel operates upon the principle that words do indeed prevent us from accessing a reality too dangerous to confront directly even as it nurtures skepticism about the independent existence of that reality. Yet in the end, that skepticism, which has been rightly acknowledged by critics as part of the novel's anatomization of paranoia, does not entirely hold up. Even if we think Oedipa *is* being paranoid and the revelatory truth is never going to come, that is not because there is no reality to be found, but because we are too profoundly boxed in by those buffering words. Or put another way, even if the Tristero is a figment of her imagination or a ruse set up by Inverarity, that which inspired it—a history of losses both major and minor, from the death of an alcoholic sailor to the attempted genocide of European Jewry—is undeniable.[2] Indeed, in Pynchon's novel, the absent reality of violence is the one thing that cannot be denied. Violence is the desideratum that sets in motion *Crying*'s considerable resources of skeptical deflation, but it is also reinvigorated by the novel's dizzying debunkings.[3]

Because the real is largely registered in *Crying* by either its absence or false presence, violence is continually being dematerialized. Violence is always happening somewhere else, in the distant past or future, or in a form so bizarre as to beg credulity. While this might seem to work against the installation of violence as the real, it in fact is the condition of its privileging. The apparent absence, immateriality, absurdity, and unspeakability of violence is offered by *Crying* not as the sign of its unreality but as the proof that the novel understands its own lack of access to it. For if, as *Crying* insists, our language is a form of buffering, and our daily lives are defined by that buffering, then nothing establishes and protects the reality of violence more than its failure to fully appear on the scene. The ongoing buffering of the word will itself come to look like the foundation of a purer and even more authoritative intimacy with violence.

I argue that *The Crying of Lot 49* constitutes Pynchon's attempt to establish a more robust claim for affluent white Americans on violence. Pynchon's novel insists upon the special kind of knowledge of violence that only those who never experience it directly can possess. This is accomplished primarily through a set of references to the urban poor and the Vietnam War. These are not invoked to establish any concrete connection between Americans and the war or between the affluent and the poor but to render such concrete connections irrelevant. What matters about Vietnam in *The Crying of Lot 49* is not that the local economy is being propped up by defense contracts, nor that Americans are already serving in the war, but that we might imaginatively engage with its violence and thus become the vessels for its preservation. By the same token, the marginal, the poor, and the black—those the text understands as "the disinherited"—are not to be communicated with through words or helped through political and social action.[4] Instead, *The Crying of Lot 49* asks us to see their marginalization as a willful act of collective withdrawal that is best registered, communicated, and preserved by the respectful inaction of the affluent.

Even as *Crying* presents itself as a novel-length exercise in, and experience of, the *absence* of reality, it also gestures at a solution to the problem of our linguistic existence: it imagines that there might be a kind of language that instantiates everything that words ordinarily hide, a language that is itself "whatever it is the word, is there, buffering, to protect us from" (105). Such language is gestured at throughout: in the awaited "Word" (as opposed to "the word"), in the unseen letters passed through the Tristero postal system, in the words written in a magical ink brewed from the bones of slaughtered soldiers, in the wordless keening signaled by the novel's multivalent titular gerund.[5] It is realized in the novel's carefully debased and parodic vernacular, in what Oedipa calls "the high magic of low puns." Such language can only stop serving as a buffer when it stops trying to mean, or when meaning becomes so oversaturated that it cannot be managed. When that happens, to quote Mucho Maas, Oedipa's husband, at his most deranged, "Everybody who says the same words is the same person if the spectra are the same only they happen differently in time, you dig?" (117). This allows Oedipa and Pynchon, both of whom are "unfit perhaps for marches and sit-ins" but perfectly trained to pursue "strange words in Jacobean texts" (83) to become the vessels through which the real of violence manages to pass.

My argument is similar, in conclusion if not in operation, to that of Stefan Mattesich, who argues that "the basis of any escape from Oedipa's tower, for any freedom from the malignancy of social power in late capitalist America, or for any implied redemption of agency, is precisely the novel's refusal to mean, its attempt to write the world in a language that undermines its own referential coherence."[6] Yet I also assert that the novel *seeks access to* the very violence that Mattesich understands to undergird social power. The novel is not just about escaping that reality but also about harnessing it for itself in a new language that has been purified of meaning in its encounter with violence. It seeks, in short, a kind of language that can "communicate" the truth that the mind of Watts already knows.

BONES AND BLANKS: THE LANGUAGE OF TRANSHISTORICAL VIOLENCE

> To give the spirit flesh. The words, who cares? They're rote noises to hold line bashes with, to get past the bone barriers. (62)
> *The Crying of Lot 49*

As Oedipa sits through her first, decisive meeting with Genghis Cohen drinking "*real* homemade dandelion wine in two neat glasses" (76, emphasis added), we might think that the term "real" signals only that the wine is not *fake* like so much else in this period of the ostentatiously ersatz. Yet this is "real homemade dandelion wine" not merely because it is really made of dandelions and really brewed at home by Cohen. If we follow the persistent logic of *The Crying* of *Lot 49*, it is real because it is the distillation of the dead, made from dandelions whose alembic was a corpse-strewn cemetery. These dead bodies and the reality for which they stand bring Oedipa to the threshold of a revelation whose truth is its wordlessness. This wordlessness in turn intimates and initiates the emergence of new, purified language of death.

As Cohen tells her, "I picked the dandelion in a cemetery, two years ago. Now the cemetery is gone. They took it out for the East San Narciso Freeway" (76). This piece of information triggers the following important passage:

> She could, at this stage of things, recognize signals like that, as the epileptic is said to—an odor, color, pure piercing grace note announcing his seizure. Afterwards it is only this signal, really dross, this secular announcement, and never what is revealed, during the attack, that he remembers. Oedipa wondered whether, at the end of this (if it were supposed to end), she too might not be left with only compiled memories of clues, announcements, intimations, but never the central truth itself, which must somehow each time be too bright for her own memory to hold; which must always blaze out, destroying its own message irreversibly, leaving an overexposed blank when the ordinary world came back. (76)

Much like Oedipa, the reader is meant to sense that there is a substantive connection to be grasped, but one that, as she approaches it, leaves only a blank space in her consciousness. That blank space initially appears to mask the truth toward which the ever-expanding network of the Tristero leads. The Tristero seems to be an entity whose history and current activity constitute a potential truth so great as to be unassimilable. Or rather, the novel suggests that either such a truth exists, or what looks like the traces of a hidden truth is in fact a bunch of meaningless hokum.

While most readers will come to believe that whatever blank Oedipa is left with does not mask a lost truth about the Tristero, there is sufficient evidence that *something* epiphanic is registered here. The epiphany is contained in the very dandelion wine that Oedipa is ingesting, a process that allows her to bypass any linguistic mediation of the reality charge contained in the traces of those dead bodies. Cohen notes that the now clear wine had once been cloudy: "You see, in spring, when the dandelions begin to bloom again, the wine goes through a fermentation. As if they remembered." What follows is: "No, thought Oedipa, sad. As if their home cemetery in some way did exist, in a land where you could still somehow walk, and not need the East San Narciso Freeway, and bones still could rest in peace, nourishing ghosts of dandelions, no one to plow them up. As if the dead really do persist, even in a bottle of wine" (79). In this sense, the "message" blazed out, that which is too bright for her memory to hold, is shown to have an alternate, even preferable, mode of communication: it is preserved and sustained in the physical chemistry of the wine. The wine—made from dead dandelions fed by dead bodies—has a "memory" all its own and is thus transferred to Oedipa without ever having to be routed through, and thus contaminated by, human consciousness.

The "truth" that Oedipa senses, which is the truth of the dead as they are ingested, is not just incidentally or accidentally supralinguistic. What occurs here unfolds according to an inalterable logic: the epiphany or knowledge is "too bright for her own memory to hold; *which must always* blaze out, destroying its own message irreversibly, leaving an overexposed blank when the ordinary world came back" (76, emphasis added). No matter how many times she is confronted with such revelation she never will grasp it, for to do so—that is, to render it in any kind of coherent, readable code—would be to destroy it. We have arrived at the fetish of the unspeakable: the presence of some kind of revelation is guaranteed, not by its content, but by the degree to which that content exceeds cognition itself. While I take the "ordinary world" to be roughly commensurate with ordinary language—all those buffering words—it is more, too. Pynchon goes so far as to suggest that it is not merely language proper that is overcome but any kind of semiotic code. "Odor, color," even the transcendent sounding "pure piercing grace note"—all these "signals" are "really dross" that announce the persistence of something real most powerfully through their failure to record it.

And yet, despite this quite radical rejection of any language or code and the concomitant privileging of the bodily, material apprehension of the reality of the dead, the passage, indeed Pynchon's novel as a whole, retains a powerful investment in and hope for language itself. The wine, after all, is a substance that at once repudiates language in favor of the material *and* serves to instantiate a newly purified and revelatory language in its stead. This is a language that somehow preserves that which is lost and thus makes the absent death of others a present reality for those who are alive. This preservation of the dead occurs in spite of its apparent implausibility. We know, after all, that the conditions Oedipa cites that would allow the dead to persist are not in place and are not likely to be in the future: the land is not going to return, at least not anytime soon, to a state in which "you could still somehow walk, and not need the East San Narciso Freeway, and bones still could rest in peace, nourishing ghosts of dandelions, no one to plow them up" (79). But in spite of how untenable such a return to San Narciso's former state seems to be, just that appears to occur. The state of near collapse, the disorientation in and from language to which Oedipa is brought in the final pages of the novel actualizes just such a transformation. It is in this state of near breakdown, bereft of all conceptual markers, that "San Narciso at that moment lost (the loss pure, instant, spherical, the sound of a stainless orchestral chime held among the stars and struck lightly), gave up its residue of uniqueness for her; became a name again, was assumed back into the American continuity of crust and mantle. Pierce Inverarity was really dead"

(147). San Narciso reverts to an earlier, almost primordial state, a state in which one *can* walk the earth and the dead *can* lie undisturbed. And in the process of becoming a "name" it is also reabsorbed into an organic planetary whole.

In a certain sense this passage tells us all we need to know about Oedipa's logomania and about our own: her obsession with the Tristero is an attempt to come to terms with the death of Pierce or—as the novel usually refers to him, as if trying to help Oedipa along—"the dead man." Both Oedipa and the reader are being asked to face the reality of death and yet, facing the reality of death in *The Crying of Lot 49* entails the transformation of death into something different than it initially appears to be. Just as the death of Pierce and the regeneration of the earth to a prior state are linked here, it is death that promises the reinvigoration of language throughout the novel. Sanctified and deathly worldlessness emerges as the ground upon which a new and newly authenticated language is born. In the passage about dandelion wine, while Oedipa is left with nothing but the dross of secular signification and a luminous blank, that blank is understood as the aftereffect of what was once some kind of "message." By the end of the chapter, that message comes to look like nothing less than the form of communication that the dead use to speak with the living.

The structure implicit in Oedipa's encounter with a truth that "must always blaze out, destroying its own message irreversibly, leaving an overexposed blank when the ordinary world came back" is all but identical to the physical event that immediately follows her experience. We learn that Cohen

> rolled over to her a small table, and from a plastic folder lifted with tweezers, delicately, a U.S. commemorative stamp, the Pony Express issue of 1940, 3c henna brown. Cancelled. "Look," he said, switching on a small, intense lamp, handing her an oblong magnifying glass.
>
> "It's the wrong side," she said, as he swabbed the stamp gently with benzene and placed it on a black tray.
>
> "The watermark."
>
> Oedipa peered. There it was again, her WASTE symbol, showing up black, a little right of center. (77)

The single word sentence reading "cancelled," followed as it is by the "switching on a small, intense lamp" is a physical replication of Oedipa's more abstract and ephemeral experience of the truth that is destroyed, overexposed by something so bright that the message is blazed out.

But whereas the illumination offered by the wine was displaced from the original scene, here revelation takes the form of the immediate appearance of a legible symbol. When Oedipa first heard about the dandelion wine, whatever illumination she received as she sipped it was that which came of being washed clean of language; that blank was only slowly and indirectly substantiated by the appearance in the clouded wine of the persistent dead. Here the process is rapid and compressed: through the confluence of blazing light and benzene, the formerly hidden watermark of the muted post horn appears. I take that benzene to be a correlate to the absent "message" borne by the clouded wine, for it is a substance that, combined with blazing light, allows that which would otherwise remain hidden, lost, or dead to become a present and all-but-concrete reality.

Because bones appear with such bizarre and confusing frequency in Pynchon's text, and because they are central to my reading, I want to pause in order to briefly summarize the chain of textual examples I will follow. The dandelion wine, as I have already argued, manages to communicate to Oedipa the deathliness it absorbed from the cemetery bones from which the flowers grew. Bones also appear as the ingredient in a special kind of cigarette filter. Inverarity "owned 51% of the filter process" of Beaconsfield cigarettes, "whose attractiveness lay in their filter's use of bone charcoal, the very best kind" (22). The importance of these bones is signaled for the reader when Oedipa wonders, creepily, "bones of what?" To these bones are added those that Oedipa sees in Inverarity's housing development, the "Fangoso Lagoons." The Venetian canals of Fangoso feature, among other sights for scuba divers, "real human skeletons from Italy" (20). It turns out that the bones used in developing the cigarette filters and those used decoratively in the canals at Fangoso come from the same place. They are the bones of dead American G.I.s who were killed in a massacre by a lake in Italy during World War II. Paralleling these bones from the *recent* past are the fictional bones that appear in a seventeenth-century revenge tragedy, *The Courier's Tale*, which Oedipa goes to see. In the play, a magical ink is brewed from the bones of a retinue of soldiers massacred by a lake in Italy. When the blood of one innocent character is mixed with the ink made from the bones of the innocent massacred soldiers, the ink suddenly transforms the letter it was used to write. The recitation of lies becomes instead a full account of the betrayal and brutality practiced by the man who wrote it.

The bones of G.I.s from Italy might seem to be relevant to Oedipa's revelations only because she is initially under the impression that the bones used in the cigarette filters and at Fangoso came from the same cemetery that fed the dandelions. A reader who thought that the point of *The Crying of Lot 49* was to invalidate not just the Tristero but any secret and labyrinthine truth beyond those wrought by ordinary global capitalism might argue that Oedipa merely forgets where she had heard about the cemetery and the freeway project, and that she then later mistakes the imperfect workings of her overstrained memory for lost revelation. But I want to insist instead that while Oedipa may very well mistake a banal mental misfire for something more significant, *Crying* suggests that, on another level, there remains something powerful to be gleaned among the connections. Like the "real dandelion wine," these "real human skeletons from Italy" contain something genuinely revelatory and transformative.

Such revelatory power does not inhere in the cigarette filters. Developed "back around the early '50's, way before cancer" (46), the filters, like buffering words, are supposed to protect the body from death, even if neither can ever hope to be ultimately successful. But the ink made from the fictional bones, from those that were fished out of a lake in Italy, promises a more revelatory contact with death and with whatever new language emerges from contact with it. To understand the nature of the promise held by these bones, we would do well to look at the long description of the performance of a revenge tragedy (written by the fictional Richard Wharfinger) that Oedipa attends. The scene is perhaps the novel's most extended digression-that-is-not-actually-a-digression. The first clue that there are clues here comes early on. The seventeenth-century audience for whom the play was originally composed is characterized as "so preapocalyptic, death-wishful, sensually fatigued, unprepared, a little poignantly, for that abyss of civil war that had been waiting, cold and deep, only a few years ahead of them" (49). Lest we miss the implication that the original and current audiences are much alike, only two pages earlier, in the passage that relates to the G.I. bones, we are told that the Italian seller's search for a buyer in the United States was spurred by "stories about Forest Lawn and the American cult of the dead" (47). Wharfinger's and Pynchon's audiences do not just have matching sets of bones but a matching investment in, and obsession with, death.

The play that follows is, like all revenge tragedies, exceedingly, ingeniously, grotesquely violent. As such, the genre seems an unlikely vehicle for the wedding of violence to unspeakability. As one scene is described, "for about ten minutes the vengeful crew proceed to maim, strangle, poison, burn, stomp, blind and otherwise have at Pasquale, while he describes intimately his varied sensations for our enjoyment" (53). Yet immediately following this baroque display of violence, we encounter another blank, one that recalls those associated with the wine and the illuminated stamp. Heading to the bathroom during intermission, Oedipa discovers that "the walls, surprisingly, were blank. She could not say why, exactly, but felt threatened by this absence of even the marginal try at communication latrines are known for" (53). Thus the blankness of the wall, bereft of all communication, is matched by that of Oedipa herself, stripped as she is of words to account for her foreboding.

This incident in the bathroom is quickly replicated in dramatic form in the play itself:

It is at about this point in the play, in fact, that things really get peculiar, and a gentle chill, an ambiguity, begins to creep in among the words. Heretofore the naming of names has gone on either literally or as a metaphor. But now, as the Duke gives his fatal command, a new mode of expression takes over. It can only be called a kind of ritual reluctance. Certain things, it is made clear, will not

be spoken aloud; certain events will not be shown onstage; though it is difficult to imagine, given the excesses of the preceding acts, what these things could
possibly be. (55)

Like the "sinister" bathroom walls that seem to be withholding communication, whatever silence holds sway here is deliberate: that which is not said is
not unspeakable but unspoken. By the same token, no direct representation
of events through staged action will occur either: "certain events will not be
shown onstage." We soon find out what is not being said or staged, however.
The word that is withheld, only to be uttered later in the play, is "Trystero" (57).
"What may be the shortest line ever written in blank verse: 'T-t-t-t-t . . . ,'" is
followed by the withheld staging of what we later discover is the brutal killing
of one of the characters, Niccolo, by a band of black-clad assassins who are the
living embodiment of that shadow organization. This murder takes place by the
very same lake (in a country that is clearly identifiable as Italy) where a retinue
of knight-soldiers mysteriously disappeared en masse decades earlier. Unlike
the other blanks we have discussed, this one is not constituted by a blazing
light, but by its absence: the stage goes black following the menacing entrance
of these "shadowy" figures (57).

Yet, as with the delayed message of the dandelion wine and the faster appearance of the watermark, the blank that appears to stand for the Trystero is eventually filled in. When Niccolo's body is found, in the letter he had been reading,
which was filled with falsehoods intended to deceive a third party, Gennaro,
the writing has been transformed into a vehicle of radical truth-telling:

> It is no longer the lying document Niccolo read us excerpts from at all, but now
> miraculously a long confession by Angelo of all his crimes, closing with the reve-
> lation of what really happened to the Lost Guard of Faggio. They were—sur-
> prise—every one massacred by Angelo and thrown into the Lake. Later on their
> bones were fished up again and made into charcoal, and the charcoal into ink,
> which Angelo, having a dark sense of humor, used in all his subsequent com-
> munication with Faggio, the present document included. "But now the bones of
> these immaculate / Have mingled with the blood of Niccolo, / And innocence
> with innocence is join'd, / A wedlock whose sole child is miracle: / A life's base
> lie, rewritten into truth. / That truth it is, we all bear testament, / This Guard of
> Faggio, Faggio's noble dead." (57–58)

It is worth thinking about how far this ink has brought us from those buffering words, or from the truth whose "message" had to be destroyed in order
to be preserved. What occurs here is the wholesale *rejuvenation* of language, a
return, in fact to the Word.[7] This is not just language that discloses truth, although it is that. Nor is it a kind of naming that goes on "literally or as a form of

metaphor." Even the literal, after all, is not identical to the thing itself. Here, the thing being disclosed and the medium of disclosure are brought miraculously together. This writing is not merely the writing of the body but the writing that the body makes at its most direct moment of contact with the real: it is the body during and after the moment of death. It is blood, bone, and cremation all at once. As such it is able, to quote from a different moment in the text, to "call into being the trigger for the unnamable act, the recognition, the Word" (149).

In a literal sense, the "Word" that is triggered miraculously into being, which was "probably for the original audience a real shock, because it names at last the name Angelo did not and Niccolo tried to," is "Trystero." Many critics have suggested that we need not credit this dramatic miracle by which the lies of ordinary language are transformed into a new language of truth-telling. And clearly Pynchon's tone here is parodic: he is having fun not only with any number of genres and historical narratives but with his own themes, subjecting them to comic deflation through stylized hyperbole. But to the extent that this trajectory—from lying buffering words to unspeakable or unspoken blank to, finally, redeemed language—is one that the novel repeats again and again, the parodic intent only goes so far. The reiteration of this same historical narrative of a massacre by a lake (one in the play, the other during World War II) in which the bones of the dead are subsequently left to decay suggests a historical narrative that will not go away, that keeps repeating itself until we are able to extract the proper "message" from its brew.

THE WHIMS OF ROBERT MCNAMARA: VIETNAM AND THE DEFENSE ECONOMY

One by one the glamorous prospect of annihilation coaxed them over. (128)

The Crying of Lot 49, published in 1966 (after excerpts appeared under different titles in *Esquire* and *Cavalier*) has come to seem very much a document of its time. It sketches an emergent counterculture that was just becoming more widely known, but it also has enough allusions to the kind of suffering that takes place in Watts that it has also been read by many critics as addressing an economic and social crisis signaled in the book by the use of the terms "disinheritance" and "exitlessness." Although specific causes are never identified, the "disinherited" in the novel appear as victims of a historically specific moment of American history. Some of them are black or Latino: the most memorable are the customers at the used car dealership where Mucho Maas used to work. But far more of them are white people who have peeled off from mainstream society for reasons that do not seem to have much to do with race and seem to be barely about class: they are Scurvhamites and members of death cults, they belong to Inamorati Anonymous and the Peter Pinguid Society.

Yet the subcultures to which the disinherited cling are also shown to be part of a transhistorical phenomenon, whereby the dispossessed find meaning and alternative to their subjection in the Tristero. The "800-year tradition of postal fraud" (79) functions as the novel's paranoid version of what it understands to be a transhistorical principle of violence and mayhem. In that sense, we might also say that whatever historical specificity accumulates around the narrative does so *in spite of* the fact that the past keeps repeating itself. This may explain why Patrick O'Donnell warns against "assuming there is any definitive connection to be made between 'fiction' and 'history' by comparing the novel— in the moment of its production—to the selected particularities of its cultural milieux."[8] However, I want to suggest that the singularity of the historical moment can be reconciled with its apparent collapse into the transhistorical real of violence. For even as *The Crying of Lot 49* establishes violence as the transhistorical substance of the real, it is also committed to the idea that contemporary *access* to the real is at once threatened and, at least potentially, heightened. The special threat and promise of the contemporary moment is articulated in relationship to the Vietnam War.

Although O'Donnell notes that the novel was published in the same year as the Manila Conference to highlight the irrelevance of such a correlation, the war plays a significant role in determining how access to violence in America is ultimately claimed in the text. The war appears in the novel but barely registers in the minds of most characters, and while the situation might have looked somewhat different by the time of the novel's publication given how quickly public awareness of the war turned to opposition, *Crying* appears to be interested in the war precisely *because* hardly anyone knows or cares about it. References to Vietnam in *The Crying of Lot 49* signal violence that is sponsored by the United States and yet is inscrutable to the people whose economic and social lives produce and require this violence.

Although the war is registered explicitly in the novel only in a reference to antiwar activity at Berkeley and to the attempt of an aerospace industry executive to imitate the self-immolation of a Buddhist monk (both of which I discuss in depth later on), Pynchon's awareness of and interest in Vietnam is certain.[9] Not only had he taken two years off from Cornell to serve in the Navy, but upon graduation he put his engineering degree to work as a technical writer for Boeing. Just as importantly, his "short story, but with gland trouble," as Pynchon wryly described *Crying*, was flanked by two massive novels, both of which are centrally concerned with industrial warfare.[10] Indeed, his encyclopedic masterwork, *Gravity's Rainbow*, is perhaps the most famous novel ever written about a single military technology.

These same factors make it less surprising that Pynchon refers specifically to Robert McNamara in his piece on Watts; it is worth pausing to return to what he actually says about McNamara and the California aerospace industry.

As Pynchon evokes it, that industry is associated with illusion: "[I]llusion is everywhere in it, from the giant aerospace firms that flourish or retrench at the whims of Robert McNamara, to the 'action' everybody mills long the Strip on weekends looking for" ("Watts," 78). But where in the aerospace firms is the illusion? The geographers responsible for coining the influential term "the Gunbelt" suggest in their study that its economic importance is nowhere more enduringly and substantially exemplified than in Los Angeles, home to "the greatest concentration of ultra-high-tech weapons-making capacity in the world."[11] While the foundation for the eventual prominence of Los Angeles firms was laid in previous decades by civic boosters and land speculators, it is in the immediate postwar years that Los Angeles's dominance was solidified. Although defense work is notoriously vulnerable to the expansion and retraction of which Pynchon complains, the years one assumes he is referring to were marked by the steady expansion and consolidation of both industrial production and research and development in the L.A.-area aerospace industry.

The reference to Robert McNamara and illusion may have more to do with the military paradigm out of which specific technological needs grew: "The essential feature of the mid-century military-political landscape was the Cold War—a type of strife radically unlike any other in history. Weapons for the first time were designed not to be used; they were sought for their preemptive value" (30). The cold war paradigm led technocrats like McNamara to anticipate being able to exploit the steadier rhythms of deterrence to maximize the efficiency of the procurement process. These expectations proved wrong as the Vietnam War "upset everyone's assumptions: here again was a hot war, but of a new kind, requiring that the army learn new guerilla tactics" (31). But whatever the war might have required for it to be won, it was largely fought by the United States from the air with aircraft and defense systems that were often made in the Los Angeles area by firms like Douglas and Lockheed.

The illusory nature of the aerospace industry might, then, have something to do with Pynchon's understanding of the gap between the idea of cold war, with its emphasis on deterrence, and its actual practice, which relies on L.A.'s military hardware. If that is the case, then the aerospace firms are like Watts: they are out in full view but somehow invisible, not least because the killing they enable occurs thousands of miles from home.[12] But if that's the case, Pynchon's own novel manages to further mystify the material and geopolitical implications of the industry. Yet The Crying of Lot 49 furthers the invisibility of Watts and of the material connections that tie Americans to the violence in Vietnam. By the end of 1963, fifteen thousand American "advisors" were in Vietnam and by the end of 1965, troop strength had nearly reached two hundred thousand. And although the war was not yet the object of widespread opposition stateside, the Gulf of Tonkin Resolution, passed August 7, 1964, at once brought attention to America's role in the war and cleared the way for more and more troops and matériel to flow into Southeast Asia.[13]

Even though *The Crying of Lot 49* refers explicitly to the aerospace industry and to the civil unrest in Vietnam, and even though it demonstrates a melancholy fascination with the urban underclass, it engages in a radical redescription of the nature of Americans' relationship to violence. Far from being instantiated in the production of weaponry either directly or through the "multiplier effects" that helped to produce California's postwar economy, Pynchon understands white Angelenos to be defined precisely by their utter distance from violence.

⌐⫫⌐

The most famous passage establishing the novel's interest in the war comes in Oedipa's account of the UC Berkeley campus:

> She came downslope through Wheeler Hall, through Sather gate into a plaza teeming with corduroy, denim, barelegs, blonde hair, hornrims, bicycle spokes in the sun, bookbags, swaying card tables, long paper petitions dangling to earth, posters for undecipherable FSM's, YAF's, VDC's [*sic*], suds in the fountain, students in nose-to-nose dialogue. She moved through it carrying her fat book, attracted, unsure, a stranger, wanting to feel relevant but knowing how much of a search among alternate universes it would take. For she had undergone her own educating at a time of nerves, blandness and retreat among not only her fellow students but also most of the visible structure around and ahead of them, this having been a national reflex to certain pathologies in high places only death had the power to cure, and this Berkeley was like no somnolent Siwash out of her own past at all, but more akin to those Far Eastern or Latin American universities you read about, those autonomous culture media where the most beloved of folklores may be brought into doubt, cataclysmic of dissents voiced, suicidal of commitments chosen—the sort that bring governments down. But it was English she was hearing as she crossed Bancroft way among the blonde children and the muttering Hondas and Suzukis; American English. Where were secretaries James and Foster and Senator Joseph, those dear daft numina who'd mothered over Oedipa's temperate youth? In another world. . . . They had managed to turn the young Oedipa into a rare creature indeed, unfit perhaps for marches and sit-ins, but just a whiz at pursuing strange words in Jacobean texts. (82–83)

Pynchon's spatial metaphor of "worlds," in which the sensibility of a waning period can persist and coexist with that of the present, gives us a way of reading both the buffering words and "whatever it is" they are protecting us from as inflected by historical circumstance. Implicit in the account of Oedipa's confrontation with the Berkeley counterculture is that her own historically specific background emerges as a kind of buffering. As she walks through but is still somehow sealed off—by virtue of her age and socialization—from the revolution, dissent, insurrection, and cataclysm that she believes is emerging on the Berkeley campus, Oedipa finds herself suited only to chasing down words. In this sense, while both the buffering and the cataclysm are variously understood as having a much more expansive historical reach, they are inflected here with a very specific historical valence. The fifties play linguistic buffer to the cataclysmic real being enacted on the Berkeley campus.[14]

And yet, even as that scenario links the fifties to buffering language and the sixties to that which is violent and thus real, what also emerges here is a particular kind of linguistic form characteristic of the sixties. In the early part of the passage the cataclysm of the sixties appears to be expressed in, and as, a series of unintelligible acronyms. As Sean McCann and Michael Szalay have argued about the same passage, the nature of the political organizations for which the acronyms stand is less important for Pynchon than what they can be made to symbolize as a mystified aggregate—the essentially libertarian politics of mystery—and what they can be construed to oppose—the straightforwardly political practices and goals of liberalism.[15] While their reading is enormously illuminating, I understand the politics of mystery to also work in service of the prestige of violence. These acronyms serve as a model of a new kind of language, one that would be much more than the "lies, recitations of routine, arid betrayals of spiritual poverty" (141) that make up ordinary speech. They embody the kind of "surprise" Pynchon hopes might rescue us from both the buffering and the exitlessness of America. The violence of the Vietnam War and the new linguistic forms that are its complement serve as an exit ramp into the violence that America at once commits and covers up.

For while those acronyms may not be all that important to Pynchon (or more precisely, Pynchon may have wanted to foreground the proliferation of acronyms rather than the specific political organizations for which they stood), they are nonetheless indispensable for understanding the nature of the novel's investment in violence as the source of the real. The acronyms stand for *Free Speech Movement, Young Americans for Freedom*, and *Vietnam Day Committee*, but I take the third organization and the war it was dedicated to protesting to be especially important. While in principle the cultural politics of mystery are large enough in the novel to encompass the Peter Pinguid Society, the Alameda Death Cult, and other crack-pot rightist organizations, the reference to the YAF gestures at a broader set of political concerns than will ultimately be pursued within the novel.[16] It is the Vietnam War, from the multifaceted violence of the conflict itself to the growing unrest in the United States among radicalized college students, that gives the novel access, directly and indirectly, to the violence that it equates with the real. The treatment of the Vietnam War is central to *Crying*'s understanding of both the historical specificity of its relationship to violence and the timelessness of the real to which it seeks access.

Other than the reference to the VDC, the most explicit reference to the conflict in Vietnam comes in the provocatively unlikely story Oedipa is told by a man she meets in San Francisco. He is a member of a group called Inamorati Anonymous, which aims to give aid to those suffering from "the worst addiction of all," love. This man tells Oedipa of the founding of the group by a former executive at the novel's aerospace firm, Yoyodyne, who, replaced by a computer, cuckolded by his wife, and uncertain whether to end his life, decides finally to "do the Buddhist monk thing":

> [One] day he noticed a front page story in the Times, complete with AP wire
> photo, about a Buddhist monk in Viet Nam who had set himself on fire to pro-
> test government policies. "Groovy!" cried the executive. He went to the garage,
> siphoned all the gasoline from his Buick's tank, put on his green Zachary All suit
> with the vest, stuffed all his letters from unsuccessful suicides into a coat pocket,
> went in the kitchen, sat on the floor, proceeded to douse himself good with gaso-
> line. He was about to make the farewell flick of the wheel on his faithful Zippo,
> which had seen him through Normandy hedgerows, the Ardennes, Germany,
> and postwar America, when he heard a key in the front door and voices. It was
> his wife and some man, whom he soon recognized as the very efficiency expert at
> Yoyodyne who had caused him to be replaced by an IBM 7094.... "I was about to
> do the Buddhist monk thing," explained the executive. (93)

I will return momentarily to a reading of this passage and what follows, but it should be noted at the outset that the self-immolation referred to here has had a surprisingly long, complex, and vigorous life in American literature.[17] The Malcolm Browne photo of Thich Quang Duc was the World Press photo of the year in 1963, and footage of the event was aired widely on television in the United States, Canada, and abroad. David Halberstam witnessed the event and wrote memorably about it, and it has been cited by a great many ordinary citizens to have been their first inkling that the growing conflict in Southeast Asia was both more violent and more politically ambiguous than they had previously imagined.

The monk's appearance here is probably the first in American literature and is certainly the first appearance in the work of a writer of any stature. Knowing the broader significance the image had in the United States is important, but that significance does not tell us everything we need to know because so much depends here on the radical decontextualization of the image. When the former defense industry executive shouts "Groovy!" upon seeing it, we know that what is at stake here is neither the complex religious and political context in which the self-immolations occurred nor the life the image was beginning to have in shaping American public opinion about the conflict in Vietnam. The executive's response emphasizes his total failure to understand what the event means in its proper context, and his subsequent imitation of the event underscores the radical disparity between his situation and that of the monk. Appropriately enough in a novel where awareness of the Vietnam War never becomes explicit among the characters, the passage seems to suggest that the horrifically sublime violence of Vietnam is utterly foreign to the buffered life of ordinary Americans under advanced capitalism and any attempt to replay such violence is sure to end in both failure and farce.

And yet the "joke" embedded in the reference plays upon both how poorly and how well the two men's situations mesh with one another. On the one hand, the monk's act of ascetic self-sacrifice hardly seems to fit the scene in which the executive hopes to replay it. But while there is a world of difference between a Buddhist monk's protest at his political and religious persecution and an executive's despair over being replaced by a computer, some kind of common ground is being explored. The executive's uncertainty about whether to kill himself is explicitly identified as a symptom of his complete psychic capitulation to and immersion in a corporate culture that has recently rendered him obsolete: "Having been since age 7 rigidly instructed in an eschatology that pointed nowhere but to a presidency and death, trained to do absolutely nothing but sign his name to specialized memoranda he could not begin to understand and to take blame for the running-amok of specialized programs that failed for specialized reasons he had to have explained to him, the executive's first thoughts were naturally of suicide. But previous training got the better of him; he could not make the decision without first hearing the ideas of a committee" (91–92). The mention of eschatology prepares us for some kind of comparison of religious viewpoints, and the fact that both men's specific personhood matters little to the larger system of order, devotion, and self-sacrifice is a joke not easily missed.

Yet the passage suggests other kinds of continuities as well. The list of milieux into which the executive's Zippo has followed him establishes a chain of lived experience whose jarring jump-cuts—from Normandy hedgerow to postwar America, for instance—establish rather than deny its historical authenticity. But unlike later American fiction in which the scarred and morally compromised Vietnam vet is a shadowy presence if not an actual character, Pynchon's novel crucially understands the place of the Vietnam War in America to be indirect, dematerialized, attenuated, and symbolic. The executive is not a soldier, not a general, not even a weapons-systems engineer; he is instead a businessman, a bureaucratic cog in the machinery of the military-industrial complex. Indeed, that is the only kind of American participant in the war the novel conceives of—no American soldiers seem to fly the planes or drop the weapons that the executive is distantly complicit in producing. To the extent that he positions himself as a potential victim through the monk he tries to emulate, the novel reveals his victimhood as a failed aspiration. That failure in turn seems to be bound up in his relationship to buffering words. His initial failure to make a decision about whether to "do the Buddhist monk thing" is traced to his immersion in a corporate culture that trades only in empty signifiers. The attempt at self-immolation is an attempt to escape the buffering effects of language and gain access through death to the very reality he has been indirectly producing.

That said, it is his *failure* to kill himself that eventually gives way to a revelation all but structurally identical to those set in motion by dandelion wine, benzene, and Wharfinger's magical ink. Unlike the ink with which the executive signs documents, the meaning of which he does not comprehend, the gasoline with which he tries to kill himself makes a hidden sign suddenly and mysteriously legible: "The stamps on some of the letters in his suit pocket had turned almost white. He realized that the gasoline must have dissolved the printing ink. Idly, he peeled off a stamp and saw suddenly the image of a muted post horn, the skin of his hand showing clearly through the watermark. 'A sign,' he whispered, 'is what it is'" (93).

It would be hard to locate a more forceful account of one kind of language being stripped away in favor of a more revelatory one. In place of the debased ink whose falsehoods, like those of Angelo's letter, are bleached away, we get truth in the form of a watermark. But whereas in the case of Oedipa's lost "message" any kind of information was dismissed if it seemed to participate in semiosis, here the sign of the post horn promises truth. The value of this sign is linked, much like the ink of Wharfinger's play, to the body; the watermark appears to be written upon his skin and as such is a kind of writing of the body. All that was wrong in the executive's identification with the Buddhist monk is redeemed by what comes of failure: the appearance of a revelatory sign. That sign is proof that he has absorbed the lesson that the man waiting on a street corner in Watts understood all along: that his lack of entitlement to a job is part and parcel of his place in a world where security and prosperity is an illusion and violence is what is real.

However, and precisely because this vision of reality is so intimately linked to the paranoid story of the Tristero, it cannot function as a fully successful instantiation of a new language. In the course of the novel, the Tristero, the post horn, and all the communication that passes through the alternate postal system function as *distorted* versions of the kind of language the novel seeks. The Tristero emerges as an excessively narrativized and ordered account of a much more diffuse, ephemeral, and multivalent principle of death, loss, violence, and destruction. What *The Crying of Lot 49* ultimately preserves of the Tristero is the brutal deathliness and loss for which it stands; it locates that deathliness and loss not in the black residents of Watts or in either the American or Vietnamese victims of the conflict overseas but in a character who serves as a proxy for both.

"HIS VIKING FUNERAL": THE DERELICT
SAILOR AND THE INDIGENOUS REAL

The figure of the Buddhist monk is not so much abandoned as located in a more plausible surrogate: a sailor whose fiery death Oedipa imagines during what critics refer to as the *walpurgisnacht* sequence of the novel. The larger sequence in which we meet the sailor narrates Oedipa's encounters with a wide cast of characters who live at the margins of society, far from the affluence of either San Narciso or the Los Angeles with which Oedipa is familiar. Having fled the sexual advances of one of the many men she has consulted in her efforts to learn about the Tristero, Oedipa wanders aimlessly around San Francisco by foot and by bus. It is in this section that both she and the reader confront something other than the white scene: Oedipa sees Mexicans, wanders through Chinatown, and rides "among an exhausted busful of Negros going on to graveyard shifts all over the city" (98).

This section is as close as Pynchon gets to representing the "bitter reality" found in places like Watts. One of the few moments in which the novel's attention rests on the black underclass for longer than a single sentence comes when Oedipa wanders into a laundromat where she saw the post horn symbol tacked up to a bulletin board. The laundromat is a place at odds with much of the section precisely because it is white, clean, and bright, where almost everything else she encounters is dark and dirty: "Around her the odor of chlorine bleach rose heavenward, like an incense. Machines chugged and sloshed fiercely. Except for Oedipa the place was deserted, and the fluorescent bulb seemed to shriek whiteness, to which everything their light touched was dedicated. It was a Negro neighborhood" (99). This sinister whiteness is like the sinister blank found on the bathroom wall during the production of *The Courier's Tragedy*, only here the whiteness is explicitly racialized. It is as if the laundromat is deeply complicit in the whitewashing of the Negro real, to some bleaching and blotting out of the knowledge that Oedipa seeks.

The racial specificity of this knowledge is eventually abandoned or, rather, transfigured into that of the sailor, who is soon found "shaking with grief" with "[b]oth hands, smoke white" covering his face (101). In the sailor we find the all-but-realized self-immolation of an American, though now in the figure of a truly dispossessed, if still white, member of the underclass. Unlike the symbolically bereft executive whose body is the temporary backdrop for a post horn that is held against his skin, this sailor has the sign literally tattooed upon his body. In an emotionally charged scene, Oedipa approaches the man, who asks her to deliver a letter, via W.A.S.T.E., to his wife. Although she insists that she cannot do so, she climbs the rooming house steps to the halfway point where he is huddled and holds him to her breast as he weeps. As she does so she has a premonition of his death by fire:

Cammed each night out of that safe furrow the bulk of this city's waking each sunrise again set virtuously to plowing, what rich soils had he overturned, what concentric planets uncovered? What voices overheard, flinders of luminescent gods glimpsed among the wallpaper's stained foliage, candlestubs lit to rotate in the air over him, prefiguring the cigarette he or a friend must fall asleep some-day smoking, thus to end among the flaming, secret salts held those years by the insatiable stuffing of a mattress that could keep vestiges of every nightmare sweat, helpless overflowing bladder, tearfully consummated wet dream, like the memory bank to the computer of the lost. (102)

And then:

So when this mattress flared up around the sailor, in his Viking funeral: the stored coded years of uselessness, early death, self-harrowing, the sure decay of hope, the set of all men who had slept on it, whatever their lives had been, would truly cease to be, forever, when the mattress burned. She stared at it in wonder. It was as if she had just discovered the irreversible process. It astonished her to think that so much could be lost, even the quantity of hallucination belonging just to the sailor that the world would bear no further trace of. She knew, because she had held him, that he suffered DT's. Behind the initials was a metaphor, a delirium tremens, a trembling unfurrowing of the mind's plowshare. The saint whose water can light lamps, the clairvoyant whose lapse in recall is the breath of God, the true paranoid for whom all is organized in spheres joyful or threatening about the central pulse of himself, the dreamer whose puns probe ancient shafts and tunnels of truth all act in the same special relevance to the word, or whatever it is the word is there, buffering, to protect us from. The act of metaphor then was a thrust at truth and a lie, depending on where you were: inside, safe, or outside lost. (104–05)

Unlike the rest of the city (or rather, the individual residents it figures) the sailor is not plowing the *safe* furrows, but furrows notable mostly for their "rich soils." The language of furrowing is returned to in the second passage, where the sailor's DTs are revealed as that which take him to those richer soils. Only now, those fresh furrows are recast as an "unfurrowing." The rich soil plowed by the sailor is reached only by the mechanical failure of the mind, cognition un-hinged by delirium tremens. Readers are then moved from the special knowl-edge the sailor has attained through personal dissolution to the eventual, even necessary, disappearance of that personal knowledge. Only now the disappear-ance of all that the sailor's consciousness might have held is transferred to the bodily fluids that are soaked up by the mattress, as if it is in those released fluids—tears, sweat, and semen—that his consciousness resides. We are being given exactly that which appears to be taken away; the "irreversible process" of death is shown to be anything but. For even as the passage insists upon death as a dramatic conflagration that erases any trace of those who once lived, death also functions, as in the dandelion wine, as a springboard for communion and persistence.

And yet, what might be most important in this moment is that the fiery death of the sailor *never happens*. The man's tragic but sublime immolation is only what Oedipa imagines will happen to him. This unrealized dramatic end is juxtaposed with another possibility, this one treated with far more skepticism: Oedipa imagines for just a moment that "she might find the landlord of this place, and bring him to court, and buy the sailor a new suit at Roos/Atkins, and shirt and shoes, and give him the bus fare to Fresno after all" (103). The tone of this fantasy tells us how implausible and even undesirable it is: surely a man with a "wrecked face, and the terror of eyes gloried in burst veins" (101) is not going to be truly helped by a fashionable suit. That this fantasy is misguided and even selfish is confirmed when the sailor drops her hand during the reverie. Oedipa herself was "so lost in the fantasy that she hadn't felt it go away" (103). We are thus invited to understand the novel's privileging of the fantasy of conflagration over that of direct charity to be somehow willed by the sailor himself.

A similar privileging of disappearance over social engagement occurs a couple of pages earlier, when Oedipa muses on the condition of the dispossessed and disinherited all around her, thinking: "Whatever else was being denied them out of hate, indifference to the power of their vote, loopholes, simple ignorance, this withdrawal was their own, unpublicized, private. Since they could not have withdrawn into a vacuum (could they?) there had to exist the separate, silent, unsuspected world" (101). After cataloging some of the psychological and institutional factors that produce social inequality, Oedipa concludes that the withdrawal of the disinherited into the private communication system of the Tristero is a freely chosen act. I have suggested that we should read the Tristero as a paranoid version of what is shown to be a more fundamental principle of violence and death. Thus Oedipa seems to be suggesting that the poor, the black, and the marginal voluntarily withdraw into the private fantasy of the Tristero as a way to cope with and make sense of their misfortune. In doing so, they assert some small measure of control and perhaps protect themselves, if only psychologically, from what they cannot fully escape anyway.

Regardless, that is the explanation Oedipa provides herself of why so many groups seem to use W.A.S.T.E. But the syntax of the passage is also strangely passive: the collective being described here does not actively *withdraw*; instead Oedipa notes *this withdrawal*. The last sentence is even more curious: the phrase "there had to exist" seems to attribute the imperative to a psychological need, but we cannot be sure at this point if the need is that of the disinherited or that of Oedipa and other affluent whites. In the end, *Crying* moots the distinction by suggesting that what is good for the goose is good for the gander: the sailor does not want a suit; he seems instead to want to disappear in a fiery conflagration. His disappearance allows for the preservation of some sphere that is "separate, silent and unsuspected." But instead of that being the conspiratorial realm of the Tristero, it is the realm of persistence through death. The sailor's special knowledge is at once produced by his imagined fiery death and crucially erased by it. Yet in being erased by it, it is also, curiously, transferred to Oedipa. For while she has a sudden epiphany about the "irreversibility" of death and all that will be lost when the man and the mattress burns, she also absorbs upon her breast the same primal bodily substances that seem to hold, if not consciousness, then something deeper and better of the person.

What is transferred to Oedipa through tears is also, on a different level, transferred to the reader through Pynchon's language, which records both the fact and substance of this loss, if not the precise quality of the hallucinations. The passage hints at the grounds upon which the dead will be preserved and by which language itself will be remade as something other than, or somewhat different than, an ordinary buffer. Like the political acronyms that proliferated on the Berkeley campus, once again linguistic possibility is located in the form of something that is not quite a word and where straightforward meaningfulness is compromised. The acronym "DT" of *delirium tremens* also stands for the time differential of calculus (dt), the significance of which emerges for Oedipa and the reader as she remembers a college boyfriend studying calculus: "'dt' God help this old tattooed man, also meant a time differential, a vanishingly small instant in which change had to be confronted at last for what it was, where it could no longer disguise itself as something innocuous like an average rate; where velocity dwelled in the projectile though the projectile be frozen in mid-flight, where death dwelled in the cell though the cell be looked in on at its most quick" (105). This change to be confronted is death itself: it is the missile-like projectile that brings death through large-scale violence and through the deathliness of cells gone malignant as they act upon a seemingly healthy body over time. The dt is also a sign drawn from the language of mathematics that allows or forces us to confront the reality of death. Indeed, the point is emphasized in the passage as the dt shows us something that the seemingly abstract operations of mathematical language deny through a false stasis. By holding the sailor and absorbing his tears Oedipa "knew that [he] had seen worlds no other man had seen if only because there was that high magic to low puns, DTs must give access to dt's of spectra beyond the known sun, music made purely of Antarctic loneliness and fright. But nothing she knew of would preserve them, or him" (105). This moment of the text is like the index entries of *Pale Fire* that list Professor Hurley only to amend them with the parenthetical (not in index). Oedipa may be telling us that no one else knows them, and yet she manages to have some access to what he knows without him ever telling her anything. His death by fire, however imaginary, completes the transfer of knowledge. Such a transfer is retroactively confirmed by Mucho Maas at the end of the novel, even if he is high on LSD at the time. In a line I quoted earlier in this chapter, Mucho declares, "Everybody who says the same words is the same person if the spectra are the same only they happen in a different time, you dig?" (116). The repetition of the word spectra takes us back to the time when Oedipa used that same term. We need not believe what Mucho says to see in his statement a confirmation that when Oedipa grasps the link between DT and dt, and when she receives the visceral impression of the sailor's suffering, that his knowledge is not nearly as vulnerable to total loss as she thought. She functions as the vehicle for its persistence, even though she has suffered none of his privations. Just as when Oedipa drinks the dandelion wine, this transfer is the novel's account of how it is that people who are only good at "pursuing strange words," who live in an illusory white scene, can still encounter the real of violence.

The novel's own equivalent to the DT/dt is, as many critics have pointed out, its general reliance on the "high magic to low puns."[18] Frank Palmeri analyzes the novel's linguistic play under the rubric of metaphor and argues that in the novel they function to "keep it bouncing" so that the Tristero can never mean just one thing. Similarly, Katherine Hayles argues that the effect of Pynchon's unstable metaphors is to suggest the arbitrariness of language and the provisionality of all comparisons. She also argues that "the text's desire to go beyond language, to reach a realm beyond time and space, may, like calculus, have deep connections with the desire to deny death" (117). Contrary to Hayles, however, I want to insist that the text's "desire to go beyond language" is realized in the effort to access a new language that is inextricably *linked to* death. Metaphor's importance to that project is its ability to bring language to the point of utterly arbitrary nonsense: the nonsense borne in and by language is its own holy deathliness, the thing that allows us to break through and from cognition into the reality of violence. This will be the authority of the buffering word and we do not have to go to Watts, or transform the society in which we live, to claim it.

The Crying of Lot 49 is, among other things, a story about the failure of liberalism. More disturbingly, it makes the failure of liberalism into a kind of ongoing victory for the real. This victory lies in the preservation of the real of violence, but also in the bloodless transfer of its authority and authenticity to those who are most insulated from its material threat. The novel uses the violence it knows is occurring both at home, far from the world of affluence and illusion it calls the "white scene," and in Vietnam, as a way to establish a connection for more affluent white Americans to the reality of violence. That connection is not realized in any material sharing of that violence. Rather, the novel converts death into a persistence that can be transmitted only through language utterly stripped of the power to communicate meaning.

americanizing vietnam in mailer's *the armies of the night*

"Fine," Metzger said, "and what next, picket the V.A.? March on Washington?
God protect me," he addressed the ceiling of the little theater, causing a few heads
to swivel, "from these lib, overeducated broads with the soft heads and bleeding
hearts. I am 35 years old, and I should know better."

"Metzger," Oedipa whispered, embarrassed, "I'm a Young Republican." (59)

The Crying of Lot 49

[H]ad fifty or a hundred thousand civilians ever assembled before in America for
a purpose remotely like this?: a symbolic battle which might have real broken
heads? (97)

The Armies of the Night

No terms are more central or contested in Norman Mailer's inspired work of
new journalism, *The Armies of the Night*, than "real" and its apparent opposite,
"symbolic." Indeed, the term "real" shows up in the online bookseller Amazon's
concordance of the one hundred most frequently used words in the book, at a
rate comparable to the words between, say, and look.[1] Initially the sheer repetition of the word seems like a mere verbal tic, for it often appears in a colloquial
sense as either a loose synonym for genuine or as an intensifying adverb. But
such uses, frequent as they are, tend to reinforce rather than dilute the force of
Mailer's more sustained and deliberate meditation on the real. The following
passage lets us see quite clearly how all these different uses of the term coalesce:

Liberal academics had no root of a *real* war with technology land itself, no, in all
likelihood they were the natural managers of that future air-conditioned vault
where the last of human life would still exist. Their only quarrel with the Great Society was they thought it temporarily deranged, since the Great Society seemed to
be serving as instrument to the Goldwater wing of the Republican party, a course
of action so very irrational to these liberal technologues that they were faced with

the bitter necessity to desert their hard-earned positions of leverage on *real* power in the Democratic party. . . . No, just as money was a concept, no more, to the liberal academic, and needed no ballast of gold to be considered *real*, for nothing is more *real* to the intellectual than a concept! (15–16, emphasis added)

While the term initially serves simply to emphasize that, to Mailer's mind, liberals had no substantial objection to "technology land" and that they were reluctant to give up the concrete and practical power they had acquired, this passage culminates in a return to his obsessive theme: the attenuation of reality by the relentless encroachment of abstraction and symbolization by liberalism. Unlike the liberals, nothing is *less* real to Mailer—or so he implies—than a concept. The real is to be located elsewhere: in the nugget of gold, yes, but even more so in the body engaged in a *real* war against technology land, which, amazingly enough, is best fought by writing a book.

The opposition Mailer sets up here between the real and its apparent foe, liberalism, is consistent with the arguments put forward in much recent work on Mailer and postwar liberalism.[2] Sean McCann has convincingly argued that all of Mailer's work, including *Armies*, is animated by a surprisingly consistent antiliberal republicanism. His argument accounts nicely for what I characterize as Mailer's preoccupation with violence as the source of reality by showing how, for Mailer, the "unifying force of war" and the "vitalizing" effect of conflict at once binds the nation together and sustains a more robust intercommunal personhood. My focus, however, is not on Mailer's political philosophy but the ways his text registers anxiety about, and attempts to correct for, the political geography of violence. As McCann astutely points out, Mailer decries the war in Vietnam, and imperialism generally, not because he recognizes the suffering of those abroad as that of fellow individuals who possess universal human rights, but because he believes that the perpetration of such violence abroad dissipates the energies that might more usefully be applied at home to bind the republic together.

Whereas McCann's analysis shows how the desire to "bring the war home" works in concert with Mailer's republicanism, I want to suggest that such a desire is not necessary to it. Plenty of republicanist thinkers show no such predilection for violence; Hannah Arendt's *On Violence*, for instance, published just two years after *Armies of the Night*, explicitly rejects violence in favor of the legitimate power that she understands to derive from the reasoned assent of the citizenry.[3] The desire to "bring the war home" then, can be understood as the logical outgrowth of Mailer's republicanism but it can also be untethered from his specific political perspective. Consequently, my argument will focus less on liberalism as the enemy of the real than on that which Mailer seems to despise about liberalism: its abandonment of the real in favor of "the symbolic." *Armies of the Night* describes America's corruption—moral, political, and spiritual—in terms of its immersion in the symbolic at the expense of the real, even as Mailer offers himself as at once exceptional and emblematic of the broader ills of the age. The very title of the book inaugurates this opposition. It initially looks like a question: is the March on the Pentagon a real battle, one being fought by an "army" in service of a larger war? Or is it merely a symbolic act and thus one that will leave us mired in the same liberal symbolic order that got us into a proxy war in the first place? The answer, it will turn out, is that the march is part of a real war, but it will become real through the work of Mailer's own literary labors. That is, Mailer's project is to actively transform the march into a real battle *through* his literary acts of symbolization, thus rescuing not just the public event, but himself and his work, in the bargain.

Throughout much of the book, especially in the first half, Mailer seeks a solution to the personal and national crisis of liberal degeneracy through macho adventurism. The new left promises to disrupt Mailer's own comfort and that of the nation by staging a symbolic act with the potential to burst through its own limits and become a "real" act. Yet this hope never bears fruit: Mailer understands adventurism to fail insofar as the march does not stop the war machine in its tracks or, alternatively, incite the state to full totalitarian repression, complete with concentration camps and indefinite detentions. But its failure is also importantly personalized; Mailer's arrest marks the end of his personal adventure and requires a redefinition of what will count as an adequate entrance into the real. Mailer's age, his ambition, his privilege, and his vocation as a writer rather than as a revolutionary or soldier, all render him unfit for the real battle and require him to recuperate something of value for the symbolic war.

By the end of the novel, the metaphor of the army is abandoned in favor of a group of figures whose heroism can instantiate a symbolism untainted by technocratic liberalism. He no longer refers to Union soldiers or trench-sodden G.I.s, but rather turns to the suffering of pacifist Quakers, some of whom are the very "lib, overeducated broads with soft heads and bleeding hearts" that Pynchon's Metzger and Mailer alike generally deride. It is in the suffering of these Quakers, who remain in jail long after Mailer has been freed and long after the protesters beaten by MPs have gone home, that Mailer is able to redeem nonviolence. The suffering of the Quakers in domestic prisons emerges as a solution to the dissipation of a properly American violence abroad. American imperial violence is brought home by being introjected as penance performed by the "burning" Quakers.

The pivotal moment comes when Mailer imagines the Quakers burning with a hunger strike–induced fever so hot that it produces visions of the marchers as "a column of Vietnamese dead, Vietnamese walking a column of flame, eyes on fire, nose on fire, mouth speaking flame" (287). In the symbology of *Armies*, the Quakers and the marchers are reimagined as the women and children being burned by napalm and as the self-immolating monks who fuse the symbolic and the real in their act of holy suffering. The mouth aflame is a symbol, but a special one: it symbolizes the merging of the symbolic and the real, speech and violence, word and body. This is at once a solution for the nation insofar as the Quakers bring violence home through their suffering, and for Mailer, whose writing is resacralized. Authenticated by its ability to speak for and through the suffering Quakers, *Armies of the Night* understands itself as that "mouth speaking flame."

"LIKE PRIMITIVE WRITING": LITERARY WORK AND THE SYMBOLIC

> No gun in the hills, no taste for organization, no, he was a figurehead, and therefore he was expendable, said the new modesty—not a future leader, but a future victim: there would be his real value. He could go to jail for protest, and spend some years if it came to that, possibly his life, for if the war went on, and America puts its hot martial tongue across the Chinese border, well, jail was the probable perspective, detention camps, dissociation centers, liquidation alleys, that would be his portion. (78)

As numerous critics remarked at the time of the book's publication, Mailer links his personal fate—as a man but even more so as an author—to the fate of the nation, and more specifically, to the march itself. In Mailer's telling, both he and the event are striving to become real and not merely symbolic. He tellingly parses the distinction between the two when recounting his drunken speech the night before the march: "'We are gathered here'—shades of Lincoln in hip-pieland—'to make a move on Saturday to invest the Pentagon and halt and slow down its workings, and this will be at once a *symbolic* act and a *real* act'—he was roaring—'for *real* heads may possibly get hurt, and soldiers will be there to hold us back, and some of us will be arrested'—how, wondered the wise voice at the rear of this roaring voice, could one ever leave Washington now without going to jail?—'some blood conceivably will be shed'" (47, emphasis added). Despite the fact that Mailer's account of the plan to invest the Pentagon cites a practical and explicitly nonsymbolic aim—that is, to temporarily interrupt the workings of the U.S. military—this is importantly *not* what will make the act real. Mailer, it appears, is in search of a violence untainted by instrumentality. He derides the old left in particular for their "sound-as-brickwork-logic-of-the-next-step" planning (86), preferring instead the "politics of mystery" that he as-sociates with the new left at its best. Instead, the potential for the march's "real-ization" lies in heads getting hurt, incarceration, and bloodshed. Only then can the act of "investing" the Pentagon be tallied as a real act. Here, the real is a kind of shorthand for the material and the corporeal, and is most keenly pres-ent when the body is under threat of violence. Will the event be real if the threat of violence or imprisonment does not materialize? Mailer thinks not. In *Armies of the Night* only violence can rescue the march and make it real. The distinction between the privileged realm of the real and the disparaged sphere of the symbolic is the fulcrum upon which the author's assessment of the event turns.

This value system appears not to have been in place when Mailer was first asked to take part in the demonstration. Irritated by a phone call from Mitchell Goodman asking for his participation in the upcoming events, Mailer reports that "he went on for a breath or two about the redundancy of these projects. When was everyone going to cut out the nonsense and get to work, do their own real work? One's own literary work was the only answer to the war in Vietnam" (9). The issue here is not that these activities are merely symbolic, but that they are not equally real. The various acts of civil disobedience and demonstration are redundant because they merely replicate the "real" solution to the war produced by writing. The realness of his writing is reinforced when he admits that he has not been getting nearly enough done recently: "Mailer began to realize that he had not done any real writing in months—he had been making movies—but then it didn't matter, he had done as much in the way of protest as anyone, his speech at Berkeley in 1965 had attacked Johnson at a time when lots of the mob now so much against the war were still singing 'Hello, Lyndon'" (9). Here, the naturalized metaphor—that of speech as a form of attack—is dissolved into literality. At this point in *Armies of the Night*, there is no salient distinction between an attack through words and a physical attack, between an antiwar movement pursued through symbolic means, and one pursued through "real" battle.

Despite Mailer's initial confidence about his work, it does not take long for him to begin worrying. Mailer's concern that the symbolic order will corrode the very substantiality of the real—much as the world of liberalism is slowly attenuating the nation's own grip on the real—starts to threaten the status of his own writing. The implication of his "real work," whatever its content, in the crisis of the symbolic is played out with particular vividness in a section of the text where, after praising the wild get-ups of the young marchers, Mailer suddenly turns condemnatory. Sounding very much like Frederic Jameson of *Postmodernism avant le lettre*, Mailer decries the danger to history that the young marchers embody and that their clothes exemplify:

> [S]till, there were nightmares beneath the gaiety of these middle class runaways. . . . The nightmare was in the echo of those trips which had fractured their sense of past and present. If nature was a veil whose issue had been ripped by static, screams of jet motors, the highway grid of the suburbs, smog, defoliation, pollution of streams, overfertilization of earth, anti-fertilization of women, and the radiation of two decades of near blind atom-busting, then perhaps the history of the past was another tissue, spiritual, no doubt, without physical embodiment, unless its embodiment was in the cuneiform hieroglyphics of the chromosome (so much like primitive writing!) but that tissue of past history, whether traceable

in the flesh or merely palpable in the collective underworld of the dream, was nonetheless being bombed by the use of LSD as outrageously as the atoll of Eniwetok, Hiroshima, Nagasaki, and the scorched foliage of Vietnam. The history of the past was being exploded right into the present: perhaps there were now lacunae in the firmament of the past, holes where once had been the psychic reality of an era which was gone. (92–93)

Mailer makes a fairly clear link between the aesthetic of pastiche that guides the marchers' sartorial choices with the threat they pose to history. Their clothing, "assembled from all the intersections between history and the comic books, between legend and television, the Biblical archetypes and the movies," is at least a symptom and perhaps an actual instance of the "history of the past being exploded" and of "the past being consumed by the present" (123).

Indeed, this is the danger Mailer goes on to spell out, and the terms of that danger require attention. The past is conditionally physicalized—"if nature . . . then perhaps history"—as a tissue, a term that ambiguously evokes both flesh and a more delicate, evanescent semisubstance. The ambiguous physicality implicit in the term "tissue" is then immediately denied: history is "spiritual, no doubt, without physical embodiment." But before that model can hold, Mailer introduces the possibility—signaled by "unless"—that history might be *literally* embodied in the genetic coding that determines the shape of all life. What I take to be especially important here is the way that this embodiment is then figured, through a casual simile, as "like primitive writing." This simile holds out hope that the reality of the past might not be consumed by the promiscuous symbolization that threatens it, that symbolization, in the form of DNA and primitive writing, might itself be a kind of corporeal "real." He tentatively proposes the possibility that this tissue has a physical location in the DNA of the human body. Those sequences determine height, blood type, or predisposition to various diseases, and thus are the writing of one's ancestors—the past embodied—upon and through the body. Like Pynchon's invocation of the codes buried in the fluids that stain the old sailor's mattress, the body here serves as a place where writing and language can be embodied and, thus, made real.

The ability of the body to perform an end-run around the more dangerous kinds of symbolization is displayed with some frequency in the text. Right at the point that Mailer is berating Mitch Goodman about the value of literary work, he stops himself to say that "Mailer had never had a particular age—he carried different ages within him like different models of his experience: parts of him were eighty-one years old, fifty-seven, forty-eight, thirty-six, nineteen, et cetera, et cetera" (9). Perhaps in keeping with the state of mind that allows writing to qualify as "real work" and as the "answer to the war in Vietnam," Mailer does not present this as a problem at this point. If anything, we are asked to see this as part of Mailer's richness as both narrator and "protagonist," even if this indeterminacy of age is also linked to the "erosions in his intellectual firmament" made by "whisky, marijuana, seconal and benzedrine" (5). But looked at in light of his sense of the past being endangered by the unmoored and gluttonous present, the plasticity of Mailer's felt age can appear a bit more dangerous. The deficiency that is implicit in this plasticity is confirmed upon his eventual arrest, an arrest that marks the climax of Book I and that Mailer has explicitly suggested is his primary purpose.[4] Describing his sensations at the moment immediately after his arrest, Mailer says: "He felt his own age, forty-four, felt it as if he were finally one age, not seven, felt as if he were a solid embodiment of bone, muscle, flesh, and vested substance, rather than the will, mind, and sentiment to be a man, as if he had arrived, as if this picayune arrest had been his Rubicon" (138). This sense of embodied stability, undermined only slightly by the "as if," is a hallmark of the real.

Here, indeed, we have the paradox of Mailer's situation in a nutshell. His celebration of the march, and the value he places on his own experience of it, is rooted in its capacity to be a battle in which bodily safety is at stake. The arrest here stands as a kind of surrogate for actual violence, demonstrating the ultimate control of the state over the individual's body. In the passage that serves as an epigraph to this section, Mailer sees a clear trajectory from this arrest to his eventual liquidation by the state in a concentration camp or other apparatus of state violence, and it is this proximity to the violence of the state that is capable of bringing him back to the core reality of his current age. Yet, as is clear enough to any reader of the text, Mailer is in no position to divest himself fully of the power of symbolization. Even at this fleeting moment of embodied realness, figuration is everywhere: the "picayune" arrest, which already names the arrest as trivial and worthless, draws on a regional metaphor that compares a Spanish coin (the evocatively named "half-real") to anything of trivial value; the reference to the Rubicon ironically compares his own arrest to the movements of Caesar.

This allusion to Caesar's Civil War also is bound up in the most prominent metaphoric schema in the text. Mailer uses the American Civil War as the ruling historical metaphor by which the current conflict is explained, both to himself and his readers. Again and again we are invited to see the October march on the Pentagon as yet another battle in that "real" war, a move that, ironically enough, has Mailer consuming the past for the purposes of the present. Only a page before Mailer decries the gluttonous past-eating maw of the hippie sensibility, he melds the peal of a present-day trumpet on the morning of the march with one that "went all the way back through a galaxy of bugles to the cries of the Civil War and the first trumpet note to blow the attack. The ghosts of old battles were wheeling like clouds over Washington today" (91).

The uses to which Mailer puts the Civil War hint at the central strategy of the text for making the march into a real battle. The key will be Mailer's concepts of the "moral ladder" and the "rite of passage." These concepts enable a series of symbolic substitutions that bring into being the very violence Mailer's concept of the real requires. They function to legitimize Mailer's own symbolic conflation of the Civil War with the civil disobedience in which he is participating, but they also enable other, more resonant substitutions as well. Indeed, these symbolic substitutions ultimately allow for the relocation of the conflict in Vietnam to America and the introjection of that far-off violence into the bodies of the penitent Quakers. Such substitutions ultimately allow Mailer to succeed where Pynchon failed: in *The Armies of the Night*, Mailer's Quakers manage not only to "do the Buddhist monk thing" but to do the Vietnamese woman, child, and soldier thing too. In this achievement of cosanguinity with the Vietnamese, the symbolic achieves an embodied realness that would otherwise be unattainable.

"BURNING CHRIST IN VIETNAM": PROXY WAR AND THE LOCATION OF VIOLENCE

In his sleep did Mailer think of his favorite scheme, of a war which took place as a war game? Of a tract in the Amazon, and three divisions of Marines against three divisions of the best Chinese communists, and real bullets, and real airplanes, real television, real deaths? It was madness. He could not present the scheme without exercising the audience—they were certain he had discovered the mechanism of a new and gargantuan put-on, no one could take it seriously, not even as a substitute for Vietnam. . . . You could use every argument, but it was useless because the guard didn't care. If he did, he would be at war against the cold majesty of the Corporation. (189)

I asserted earlier that the value Mailer places on violence, and his desire to conceive of the march as a real battle, is an index of his anxiety about the political geography of violence. Yet the easier explanation is that Mailer's valuation of violence merely reflects a well-documented personal preoccupation. Mailer was, after all, infamous for his obsession with machismo. Mailer's most famous essay, "The White Negro," celebrated the ability of the hipster to escape emasculation by connecting to the animalistic violence that Mailer located in black men. Stories of fistfights and head-buttings proliferate in the reminiscences by friends and acquaintances.[5] Mailer's personal obsession was such that the sound director from the last movie Mailer directed recalled his "perfectionist quest to capture the sound of a punch in the face": Mailer spent hours being recorded punching himself and the sound has since been used in many other movies.[6]

Yet it is also clear that Mailer's representation of the march, and his worries about the effects of American-sponsored violence abroad on the domestic body politic, resonated powerfully with the general public. Tuli Kupferberg ("the one who was morally superior to Norman Mailer" for, as Kupferberg puts it, "about five minutes") worries as he reflects back on the march that "the whole sixties thing was a media event. . . . I didn't really want to believe it. It wasn't uncommon that the media influenced plans for a demonstration, almost in the same way that *The New York Times* sets the agenda of American politics. . . . Real upsetting" (Manso, 464). What Kupferberg calls a media event Mailer calls a "symbolic act," but their concern is the same. Alan Trachtenberg, reviewing *Armies* in *The Nation*, is understandably charmed by the book given that he sees Mailer as "the most consistently radical of our major writers."[7] But the terms of his approbation are worth noting. The praise he offers echoes Mailer's obsession with the "real." First he suggests that "Mailer writes as if the techniques and faculties of fiction were invented for just such a penetration of real life" (701). For Trachtenberg, Mailer's penetration of real life is visible in his idea that the march may be the beginning of a long and increasingly real war: "War, as in the beginning of his career, provides him with ultimate metaphors for our collective life. He suggests that the battle begun on the mall may loom as large in our history as the Civil War (from which he draws many of his images in the text). It already appears that the lessons in courage won in Washington are leading to a widening of the tactics of resistance and calculated disruptions. Mailer's intimations may be prophetic" (702). In Trachtenberg's account, what starts out as a preferred metaphor, a stylistic tic, is on the verge of losing its figurative status: the left is becoming increasingly militant and civil war is all but here.

Even those who criticized Mailer attest to the way the book articulated a broader cultural fascination with violence. *Armies'* revolutionary impulse is what leads Trachtenberg to praise it as "a testimony to literary responsiveness and responsibility" (702) while Irving Howe thought that it was "an irresponsible book" (Manso, 467). Looking back from the mid-eighties on what he describes as a turn to authoritarianism in the student left in the mid-sixties, Howe says: "[T]he atmosphere of the time—the Molotov cocktail on the cover of the *New York Review of Books*, for example—you can't hold Norman responsible, but he didn't disassociate himself either. Some of us did, at considerable discomfort and pain, because it meant being isolated from the dominant trend in the intellectual world" (Manso, 468).

The extent to which Mailer's account of regenerative effects of violence were fully in line with "the dominant trend in the intellectual world" is also clearly attested to by the remarkable success the book enjoyed. *Armies* not only revived his career, which had flagged since the publication of *The Naked and Dead*, but it brought him to even greater heights of success. The book won the National Book Award and then the Pulitzer Prize. Even more importantly, it was met with acclaim even by those figures who shared none of his political enthusiasm for the increasing militancy and unpredictability of the new left. Glowing reviews appeared in *The New Republic*, the *New York Review of Books*, and the *New York Times*. In his long review for the latter, Alfred Kazin insisted that the book speaks to public feeling in a way the pacifist establishment failed to:

> The feeling of the American opposition today, publicly if not actually led by such pillars of the Protestant establishment as the Rev. William Sloane Coffin, Jr. and Dr. Benjamin Spock, is not merely that the American war in Vietnam is hideously brutal and wrong, that we have no right to be devastating this far-off country in the name of our theological anti-Communism, but that the political and moral sages who founded our culture have been succeeded by generals, politicians, executives, hucksters and "experts."
>
> Nothing is more likely to drive a brilliant scholar at MIT into a rage than the picture of ex-professor Walt Whitman Rostow of MIT conferring with his boss on just where to bomb the North Vietnamese. "They" have all the power, and "we" have just imagination![8]

As Kazin understands it, American opposition to the war in Vietnam does not so much decry the brutality of the conflict—a war that, like Mailer, he sees as geographically misplaced—as bemoan the fact that the opposition does not have access to firepower. The widespread appeal of violence in the period has been noted by Jeremy Varon, who suggests that violent radicals like the Weathermen and the more moderate wing of the peace movement in the United States shared a remarkable amount of conceptual ground.[9] This shared ground, he suggests, can be seen in the way that "reality" and the "real" were central to a range of vernaculars that privileged authenticity.[10] Varon goes on to argue that, across the left, to *be* real and to *understand* the nature of the real, and thus to be authentic, seemed to necessitate a stance of militancy.

In my reading, *The Armies of the Night* shows how the investment in violence is rooted in the geography of violence in this period. Mailer's worry that American violence is being at once criminally perpetrated and squandered abroad may look from a certain angle like grotesque adventurism, but he gives voice to a very common concern that the war being fought simply does not belong in Vietnam, that we have literally misplaced our war in Indochina. This view is in fact implicit in the characterization of the conflict in Vietnam as a "proxy war" for the conflict between the United States and either the Soviets or the Chinese, or both. In this scenario, the South and North Vietnamese are acting out a war and in possession of a violence that does not properly belong to or with them. Jonathan Schell, looking back in 1988 at the war and the long-form war journalism he published in the *New Yorker* in 1967 and 1968, suggests that this view of the war was implicit in constant talk about transferring responsibility for the war to the "Vietnamese themselves," talk formalized as Nixon's policy of Vietnamization years later.[11] In Schell's view, no one wanted to admit that the war "was not a quagmire into which the United States was sucked but an American quagmire—a quagmire of doubt and confusion regarding its power, its will, and its credibility—into which Vietnam was sucked" (24). Michael Herr, writing a decade earlier, locates the origins of the war in what he calls the "John Wayne wetdream" that made every American in Vietnam, soldier correspondent, or adviser, "a true volunteer."[12] Wondering, for example, how Khe Sahn became such an important site in the war, he asks, "Did it proceed from the filthiest ground-zero slit trench and proceed outward, across I Corps to Saigon and on (taking the true perimeter with it) to the most abstract reaches of the Pentagon? Or did it get born in those same Pentagon rooms where six years of failure had made the air bad?" (107). It may sound as if the first possibility would allow for a concrete, real basis for war in Vietnam, but as Herr sees it, the grunts are all too often living out the war as if it were a movie, albeit a more contemporary movie than that being played out by the older generals and pentagon technocrats. Indeed, much of *Dispatches* is made up of Herr's confessions that he came to Vietnam because he wanted to witness, if not take part in, that vitalizing American violence happening far from home. Supporters, opponents, and the occasional neutral observers often shared this base assumption: that the war in Vietnam was being fought for reasons that had more to do with the United States than with Vietnam.[13]

Mailer is clearly fascinated with the idea of a proxy war throughout *The Armies of the Night*. In fact, the concept is central to how he understands the conflict. In his long chapter entitled, like his most recent novel at the time, *Why Are We in Vietnam?*, he offers a number of answers. Although in many respects his answer is the same here as in the novel, his approach is far less oblique. His initial answer is that war in Vietnam is being prosecuted as a result of the Christian, capitalist, anti-Communist zeal of the WASP elite. But this answer is soon supplanted by a more speculative one about the needs of the collective American psyche: "We were in Vietnam because we had to be. Such was the imbalance of the nation that war was its balance. The burning of villages by napalm might be the index of our collective instability" (187). Vietnam becomes not a proxy for a conflict between competing states but a war for a mysterious alternative to corporate liberalism.

The degree to which this is a proxy war, one that has nothing to do with the Vietnamese, is revealed by the fantastic alternative to the war he imagines, and which I cite as an epigraph to this section: "In his sleep did Mailer think of his favorite scheme, of a war which took place as a war game? of a tract in the Amazon, and three divisions of Marines against three divisions of the best Chinese communists, and real bullets, and real airplanes, real television, real deaths" (189). At first it appears as if the fight between the South and North Vietnamese is really a battle between the United States and China, but Mailer ultimately suggests that this plan will not work because the real enemy that the Marines should be fighting is not Chinese Communism but the American corporation. Unfortunately, the corporation has made Americans too apathetic to fight the war they should or could be fighting against it.

As Mailer goes on to explain it, the contradiction between Christianity and bureaucratic technology has so riven the American psyche that brutality is the only tonic. The brutality in Vietnam supplies what "technology-land" is driving out: mystery. "America needed the war. It would need a war so long as technology expanded on every road of communication, and the cities and corporations spread like cancer; the good Christian Americans needed the war or they would lose their Christ" (189). While brutality initially sounds like a substitute (or proxy) for Christian mystery, the distinction between the two all but collapses. It is in the carnage of Vietnam that the need for mystery is sated with the blood of the Vietnamese, blood that is then mysteriously transubstantiated into the blood of Christ. As he puts in a speech he makes upon his release from jail: "You see, dear fellow Americans, it is Sunday, and we are burning the body and blood of Christ in Vietnam" (214).

In the previous passage, the victims of this brutality are the Vietnamese; the burning blood of Christ is actually that of the Vietnamese people. Mailer makes this clear when he notes the absurdity of "the American corporation executive, who after all was the foremost representative of Man in the world today, was perfectly capable of burning unseen women and children in the Vietnamese jungles, yet felt a large displeasure and fairly final disapproval at the generous use of obscenity in literature and in public" (49).[14] Although Mailer refers to the executive here as a representative of Man, his analysis invites us to read him as a stand-in for Americans more generally. This American fights against the corporation by killing Vietnamese civilians on the corporation's behalf.

But if Mailer asks us to rethink the Vietnam War as an essentially American war, he is still left with the problem that the violence is happening in Vietnam and to Vietnamese victims. *The Armies of the Night* will solve this problem by relocating the "burning of Jesus Christ" to America and in the bodies of suffering Quakers.

"MOUTH SPEAKING FLAME": RELOCATING VIOLENCE, RECUPERATING THE SYMBOLIC

A group from the Quaker Farm in Voluntown, Connecticut, practiced noncooperation in prison. Among them were veterans of a sleep-in of twenty pacifists at the Pentagon in the spring before. Now, led by Gary Rayder, Erica Enzer, Irene Johnson, and Suzanne Moore, some of them refused to eat or drink and were fed intravenously. Several men at the D.C. jail would not wear prison clothing.

Stripped of their own, naked, they were thrown in the Hole. There they lived in cells so small that not all could lie down at once to sleep. For a day they lay naked on the floor. For many days they did not eat nor drink water. Dehydration brought them near to madness. (287)

Quakers, pacifists, and women are all initially scorned by Mailer and seen as obstacles to the kind of violence to which he looks forward with both fear and excitement. At times, Mailer demonstrates his own cooptation by liberalism by acknowledging that "well, he did not wish to get Mace in his eyes" and "he was secretly comforted by the thought that there would probably be no violence today; even worse, he was comforted by the fact that the best police in Washington would be at the Department of Justice to maintain order" (56). The self-disgust these thoughts provoke in Mailer culminate in his assertion that he "realized he felt gentle—in fact, this morning, he felt like a damn Quaker, which was no way for a revolutionary to feel, unless he was—mark this conjunction—going to consort with pacifists and draft-card burners" (57). The conjunction he wants us to mark—"unless"—is notable because pacifists and draft-card burners are just the sorts of gentle nonrevolutionaries with whom Mailer is in fact consorting.

His desire to escape violence inaugurates a discussion about the psychology of moral action, one that culminates in Mailer's powerful concept of "the moral ladder." After Mailer "transgresses a police line" and lands in jail, he sees Tuli Kupferberg, cofounder of a countercultural garage band, The Fugs, named after the euphemism for "fuck" from Mailer's *The Naked and Dead*. Kupferberg is considering accepting a sentence of five days in jail because he does not think he should promise that he will not return to the Pentagon within six months.[15] Mailer reports that he "listened to him with a dull ear. He hated to become enmeshed in these unmanageable connections between politics and personal morality. To a part of him, Kupferberg seemed absolutely right" (195–96). Mailer then alternates between explaining why he wants to leave jail—primarily because he fears the violence of the state—and why Kupferberg's logic is not strategic.

As we might expect given Mailer's tendency to denigrate strategy as a remnant of symbolic politics, his refusal of Kupferberg's logic does not hold, and indeed, it serves as the springboard for his quite probing and resonant account of the psychology of moral inaction:

Seen from one moral position—not too far from his own—prison could be nothing but an endless ladder of moral challenges. Each time you climbed a step, as Kupferberg just had, another higher, more dangerous, more disadvantageous step would present itself. Sooner or later, you would have to descend. It did not matter how high you had climbed. The first step down in a failure of nerve always presented the same kind of moral nausea. Probably, he was now like people who had gone to the Pentagon, but had not chosen to get arrested, just as such people, at their moment of decision, must have felt sickened as all people who should have marched from Lincoln Memorial to the Pentagon, but didn't. . . . One ejected oneself from moral guilt by climbing the ladder—the first step back, no matter where, offered nothing but immersion into nausea. No wonder people hated to disturb their balance of guilt. To become less guilty, then weaken long enough to return to guilt was somehow worse than to remain cemented in your guilt. (195)

There is a kind of relativism here, but it is psychological not moral: no matter when you back down from your commitments, and such a moment is all but inevitable, you will feel as awful as you would had you taken no morally courageous actions at all. But the ladder as a metaphor nonetheless insists upon a kind of moral ascension. Where it leads, if you climb high enough, is to the "rite of passage."

The rite of passage is itself produced by an encounter with violence. In what Mailer says "came to be known as the Battle of the Wedge" (272), MPs brutally beat the demonstrators and "their women [sic]" (277), clubbing, kicking, and punching them before dragging them off to a paddy wagon.[16] The chapter begins with an invocation of "the Civil War glow of the campfire light on all those union jackets" (270) and closes this way: "They were down to four hundred demonstrators, a hundredth of the force which had come to the Pentagon— they were out on the cold exaltation of having survived, of having remained— they were therefore tempted to stay and stay, to stay to the very end. They were now engaged in that spiritual test so painful to all—the rite of passage. Let us ruminate with them and contemplate the dawn" (278). While up to this point Mailer has emphasized his own absence from the proceedings through a documentary style that we as readers are led to understand is in part necessitated from his absence—he is in jail and thus does not participate in the "battle of the Wedge"—he does claim to have a privileged relationship to the rite of passage that it produces.

That privileged relationship can be broken into many parts, but all those parts coalesce under the sign of the symbolic. Mailer's relationship to a rite, which he cannot by his own terms be said to experience, comes from the special nature of his literary work, and thus we are brought full circle to the early claim he made for its centrality. Right before narrating the brutality that ensues, Mailer says he must "relinquish . . . the conceit that one is writing a history" (254). This is because "the mystery of the events at the Pentagon can't be developed by the methods of the historian—only the instincts of the novelist" (255). The novelist is more capable because "the novel must replace history precisely at that point where experience is sufficiently emotional, spiritual, psychical, moral, existential, or supernatural to expose the fact that the historian in pursuing the experience would be obliged to quit the clearly demarcated limits of historic inquiry" (255). The "experience" is at this point left unspecified, although it soon becomes clear that Mailer is speaking of the experience of violence and the rite of passage to which it can lead.

"The experience" that constitutes this history is also, importantly enough, not attributed to any specific person or persons. And while the experience becomes interior because those who experience the Wedge are initiated into a rite of passage that is itself an interior experience, *that* experience of initiation is discerned by the instincts of the novelist. Mailer signals this clearly enough when he suggests that "we ruminate" upon the rite and "contemplate the dawn" with that hard core of remaining protesters. The rite of passage then is the product of violence, but it is in turn something that can and must be reabsorbed by and explained through the realm of the symbolic, where it becomes more generally available.

Finally, Mailer understands the rite as that which literalizes the connection he has been invoking all along of the march as a Civil War battle, only now it has also been attached to other places and times in American history "when men and women of principle manacled themselves to a lost and painful principle" (280). Mailer's own symbolic machinations, which were first speculative, have now, he insists, been literalized. His attempt to link the so-called battle of the Wedge to Gettysburg, to the Alamo, to "the Argonne, Normandy, and Pusan" is also a bit tenuous. Mailer acknowledges that the very rite he wants to assert participates in this chain of the real is "a pale rite of passage next to these, and yet it was *probably* a true one" (280).

In order to reach the "End of the Rite," which is the title of the penultimate chapter, and thus to reach a certainty that the rite has in fact been achieved, Mailer finds it necessary not only to leave the site of the battle of the Wedge but to leave America for Vietnam. Seeking a true end to the march and to the rite he turns to the small group of prisoners, mostly Quakers who remain in jail. They are symbolically linked not just to Christ but more indirectly to martyrs from a different tradition altogether. As they burn with fever in their cells, Mailer understands them as proxies for those whom he imagines appear in their visions. He asks, "Did they pray, these Quakers, for forgiveness of a nation? Did they pray with tears in their eyes in those blind cells with visions of a long column of Vietnamese dead, Vietnamese walking a column of flame, eyes on fire, nose on fire, mouth speaking flame" (287).

The mouth speaking flame, like the Viking funeral that consumes the myriad coded traces of the sailor in *The Crying of Lot 49*, is an icon of redeemed and real-ized symbolism. Language has been purified by fire, emptied of its descriptive content, transformed into a consuming and sacral experience of violence. This moment of conflation between Vietnamese and American dead, which occurs only at the moment when speech is transformed into the suffering and "speaking" of exquisite violence, serves as a powerful icon of the novel's recuperation of its own verbal resources. *The Armies of the Night* ultimately reconciles its commitment to the ultimate reality of unspeakable violence with its opposite claim: that "one's own literary work was the only answer to the war in Vietnam" (9).

This reconciliation is achieved by turning to Vietnam, the place where Mailer acknowledges that real violence is happening even as he makes it appear to happen somewhere else. Constructing a complex chain of associations that links actual and symbolic acts of "burning," the Quakers become both the women and children burning in Vietnam and the Buddhist monks who doused themselves with gasoline and set themselves on fire. Thus, in *Armies of the Night* Mailer understands his fellow activists to succeed where Pynchon's Yoyodyne executive failed: they manage to pull off "the Buddhist monk thing" even if real bodies are never really burned. The solution to the moral problem of Vietnam, and to our largely symbolic relationship to the real violence being perpetrated there, is the symbolic introjection of that violence into the body politic. Mailer's child-burning American is transformed from the agent of violence into the victim of it through the help of the novelist, who enables ecstatic access to the real. In this way, violence becomes mysteriously immanent precisely where its absence is most striking.

veterans of sex

FEMINIST FICTION AND THE RISE OF PTSD

Sometime in the night she had moved into the realm of miseries
peculiar to women, and she had nothing to say. (62)

   Play It as It Lays, Joan Didion

Much has been said about the cultural transformations that separate the sixties from the seventies. My own account aims to show how one rather narrow development over the course of a decade—the emergence, and eventual institutionalization in the 1980 Diagnostic and Statistical Manual of Mental Disorders (DSM–III), of what came to be known as PTSD—informed the way writers understood and described the centrality of violence to American life as the Vietnam War came to a close. The turn to the very different domestic problems presented by Vietnam Vets and sexually violated women gave feminist novelists in this period a means to continue, extend, and fundamentally transform the terms by which violence would be defined and revered.

This chapter offers close readings of two important feminist novels of the decade: Margaret Atwood's *Surfacing* (1972) and Marge Piercy's *Woman on the Edge of Time* (1976). Both novels are explicitly feminist texts, representing rape as not only a constant practical threat with which women must contend, but as constitutive of the operation of patriarchy. Since rape is revealed by these novels to be a feature of "normal" life for adult women, one might expect them to offer powerful counternarratives to the worried assertions in novels from the sixties that violence is always being suffered far from home and from the possibility of direct experience or discourse. Yet Piercy's and Atwood's fictions transform the figure of the woman who suffers violence at home into the figure of the traumatized warrior abroad. This attests, I will argue, not merely to ongoing fascination with the figure of the soldier in this period, but to the need to convert the violence of rape into something that is not just habitually unspoken, but essentially unspeakable.

These representations of women as soldiers are importantly tied to the complex history being made throughout the seventies regarding what will come to be known as Posttraumatic Stress Disorder. Writers in this period draw enormous inspiration from the work being done by clinicians on combat trauma. But where psychologists, psychiatrists, and activists were working to heal sufferers of trauma by bringing their experiences *into* speech, novelists of this period instead turned to PTSD to ratify their own investment in the unspeakability of violence. PTSD functions as a technology for reimagining suppressed speech about violence against women as the "unspeakable" violence of trauma.

THE INVENTION OF PTSD AND
THE FEMINIST CRITIQUE OF RAPE

As is now well-known, what we have come to know as PTSD was born between 1968 and 1980. The DSM-II is now infamous in the psychiatric community for having dropped the category of "gross stress reaction," leaving the veterans who returned distressed from their combat experiences with little in the way of compensable combat-related diagnoses.[1] Instead, these veterans could be diagnosed as having an adjustment disorder—such as an "adjustment reaction to adult life"—but more frequently they were classified as either psychotic or suffering from preexisting personality disorders. Paranoid schizophrenia with depression was the most common diagnosis that a soldier experiencing symptoms now classified as PTSD received. It was not until the publication of DSM-III in 1980 that this was redressed in the form of the newly coined term Posttraumatic Stress Disorder, which synthesized, regularized, narrativized, and institutionalized a heterogeneous set of symptoms and ailments that had under previous diagnostic regimens been known as shell shock, combat fatigue, gross stress reaction, and Post-Vietnam syndrome.[2]

The vast body of literature on trauma that sprang up in the seventies—and that has continued under the nonclinical, humanities-dominated field of trauma studies more recently—has presented the emergent diagnosis as an example of how medical truth will out. But a growing body of historians, sociologists, and anthropologists offer a different account. They argue, to quote Allan Young, that PTSD "is not timeless, nor does it possess an intrinsic unity. Rather, it is glued together by the practices, technologies and narratives with which it is diagnosed, studied, treated and represented and by the various interests, institutions, and moral arguments that mobilized these efforts and resources" (5). Young in particular asks us to see the reality of PTSD not as a medical fact that exists independently of individuals, but as one produced out of lived experience, of people's belief in it, and by "the personal and collective investments that have been made in it." This understanding of PTSD informs my own reading of how the nascent discourse of combat trauma is brought into the literary texts in question, where it is produced out of a complex and sometimes conflicting set of investments.

There is broad agreement on who the major players were in the creation of the new diagnosis and how it happened. PTSD emerged due to the tremendous effort of a coalition of Vietnam veterans, particularly those active in Vietnam Veterans Against the War (VVAW), and a handful of mental health professionals, especially Chaim Shatan and Robert Jay Lifton. This coalition was helped in the effort by growing public opposition to the war, which was itself spurred by journalism that revealed just how the war was being prosecuted. News of the massacre at My Lai, for instance, helped to substantiate the reports of one vet whose grisly tale was initially dismissed by his VA doctors as a psychotic fantasy.[3]

The DSM-III, in which the PTSD diagnosis first appeared, represented a radical departure from previous editions, due in part to the power its appointed editor, Robert Spitzer, had over the revision.[4] The controversy that arose within the American Psychological Association (or APA, the body responsible for producing the DSM) over the classification of homosexuality as a mental disorder in DSM-II led to Spitzer's eventual decision to turn the issue over to a vote. As a result, homosexuality was listed as a disorder in DSM-III only "if the individual experienced distress or dissatisfaction with being gay." This partial victory led many to conclude that "DSM-III should be completely redone" and that the process was now explicitly open to political pressure.[5]

During this period of intense activism and agitation, different narratives about the nature of the disorder were being circulated. These narratives drew from a number of different paradigms, ranging from the biochemical to the psychoanalytic. Despite the different assumptions built into these schools, all worked with a shared model of trauma. As Ruth Leys summarizes:

> The idea is that, owing to the emotions of terror and surprise caused by certain events, the mind is split or dissociated: it is unable to register the wound to the psyche because the ordinary mechanisms of awareness and cognition are destroyed. As a result, the victim is unable to recollect and integrate the hurtful experience in normal consciousness; instead, she is haunted or possessed by intrusive traumatic memories. The experience of the trauma, fixed or frozen in time, refuses to be represented as past, but is perpetually reexperienced in a painful, dissociated traumatic present.[6]

For most therapists working with veterans, the best chance for recovery was thought to lie in the narration of the traumatic event and its integration into normal memory.[7]

ᗞ𝓂ᵕ

Trauma was very much on the public mind well before the actual publication of DSM-III, at least in part because of the adjustment difficulties Vietnam vets faced upon their return home. Soon after Veterans rights groups succeeded in winning recognition by and change within the mental health system, the parameters of PTSD were expanded to include the trauma that might be suffered by abused children and raped women.[8] But while the feminist movement that brought rape into public consciousness did eventually play an enormous role in the history of PTSD, trauma as a term and area of focus was all but absent from the most seminal early feminist texts and activism on rape.[9] Instead, the feminist antirape movement focused on redefining rape as an act of patriarchal violence.[10]

Rape, as was the case with pornography in the 1980s, served as the central social problem to which feminist theorists and activists oriented themselves in the 1970s. Unlike the seemingly intractable problem of pornography, which split the movement into countless factions, rape was a problem that feminists were able to address with measurable success. Alongside the development of a *theory* of rape, which I will address briefly below, was the rapid and successful development of a whole network of support that was fundamentally different from what came before. Appallingly prejudicial laws were changed, which in turn led to a greater number of successful rape prosecutions; more sensitive procedures were implemented among law-enforcement and medical personnel; perhaps most strikingly, a network of rape hotlines were set up across the country that persists to this day. Much of this work, to draw closer to the point at hand, centered first and foremost on *getting women to speak about the violence of rape.* Whatever the sectarian disputes over the exact social and psychological mechanisms that kept women subject to patriarchal authority, feminists urged women to speak clearly and forcefully about that which a corrupt propriety had made all but verboten to articulate. Silence about rape was characterized as a symptom of tacit coercion that mystifies the fully articulatable mechanisms of oppression and repression.

The feminist critique of rape runs powerfully against the grain of the ideas about violence forwarded, albeit in very different ways, by Nabokov, Pynchon, and Mailer. In those texts, domestic access to the experience of violence is terribly limited. By contrast, feminist activists and theorists of the late sixties and early seventies, many of whom were disillusioned by sexism within the antiwar movement, argued that no aspect of life for women under patriarchy is free of this insidious violence: play, schooling, sex, work, childbirth, marriage, and illness are all shot through with the constant threat and privilege of male violence against women. The opening sentence of the New York Radical Feminists Manifesto insists that "rape is not a personal misfortune but an experience shared by all women in one form or another" and the authors go on to title a chapter of their antirape sourcebook with the credo that "Rape is Sexism Carried to its Logical Conclusion."[11] This logic, in which rape is not an aberration from but an expression of dominant sexual mores was brought to a wider audience in Kate Millett's *Sexual Politics* (1970) and Susan Brownmiller's *Against Our Will* (1974). Brownmiller's introduction ends with the (in) famous assertion that rape is "nothing more or less than a conscious process of intimidation by which *all* men keep *all* women in a state of fear" (15, emphasis in original).

But while the feminist analysis of rape placed violence at the center of women's experience, it also insisted on the fundamental *differences* between the experience and moral status of the male aggressor and that of the female victim, a distinction that PTSD, in subsequent years, tended to blur.[12] While certainly not all traumatized vets were "self-traumatized perpetrator(s)" of atrocities, much of the feminist work on rape of the period insists on the importance of moral distinctions that the naturalization of PTSD in our own time occludes. As Brownmiller's formulation suggests, the assumed pervasiveness of violence to women's experience entails drawing a sharp distinction between men and women, and even more so between soldiers and rape victims. Indeed, while Brownmiller makes no mention of trauma in her book, her chapter on Vietnam details the pervasive use of rape by American soldiers and the South Vietnamese forces against Vietnamese women. Susan Griffiths argues in "The All-American Crime," that "[t]he same men and power structure who [*sic*] victimize women are engaged in the act of raping Vietnam, raping black people, and the very earth we live upon."[13]

Thus while from our contemporary standpoint there is nothing remarkable in placing the raped woman and the Vietnam vet in the same category—that of trauma victim—the conflation was both more novel and more politically charged at the time. Especially in Atwood's text, as we shall see, the conflation of the raped woman and the traumatized vet registers at least in part the wrenching debates among feminists about the role women played in the more militant and violent wing of the antiwar movement.[14] Jane Alpert's repudiation of the radical left from underground (and her suspected cooperation with the government upon her capture) was just one of many events that divided feminists about the nature and extent of women's complicity in the patriarchal violence of the state.

My own reading suggests that the problem of female complicity in violence is indeed crucially at stake in the representation of women as soldiers in Atwood's and Piercy's texts. But in linking the two figures, these novels do not so much admit to women's complicity in male violence—in, to use Griffiths' terms, "the raping of Vietnam"—as to use emergent discourse of PTSD to reconfigure complicity with violence as a form of unspeakable knowledge of it.

"A LANGUAGE IS EVERYTHING YOU DO": AMERICANS, MEN, WOMEN, AND THE REALITY OF VIOLENCE

> It was all real enough, it was enough reality for ever, I couldn't accept it, that
> mutilation, that ruin I'd made, I needed a different version. I pieced it together the
> best way I could, flattening it, scrapbook, collage, pasting over the wrong parts.
> A faked album, the memories fraudulent as passports. (145)
>> *Surfacing*, Margaret Atwood

Margaret Atwood's second novel, *Surfacing*, published in 1972, is the story of the unnamed heroine who narrates, in the mostly present tense, her trip to the remote Quebecois village where she grew up in order to investigate the disappearance of her father. We learn over the course of the novel that her mother has recently died, that her other siblings have long departed, and that her father has continued to live on the small isolated lake island that was her eccentric English-Canadian family's home. The heroine is accompanied by her boyfriend Joe and an unhappily married couple, Anna and David. All of the characters are Canadians—David in particular likes to glibly denounce the Yanks whenever possible—and appear to live in an English-speaking Canadian metropolis, presumably Toronto. Joe and David teach adult education classes although Joe is also an unsuccessful ceramicist and David fancies himself a filmmaker.

There are essentially two threads to the novel: an exploration of the sexual politics of the two couples as they spend a few days in the heroine's rustic family cottage, and the heroine's attempt to solve the mystery of her father's disappearance. We see the rampant and repulsive misogyny of the self-righteously left-wing David. Anna is constantly being sexually degraded and belittled by her husband and is afraid to appear before him without makeup. The heroine has to fend off an attempted rape by the sleazy David and then another attempt by her emotionally stunted boyfriend, Joe. Both are dissuaded only when the heroine warns that she is likely to get pregnant if they proceed.

The story of the father's disappearance hinges upon a collection of drawings that the heroine initially thinks are signs that her father went mad before he disappeared. But she eventually comes to realize that they are drawings of ancient rock paintings that her father, a former geologist for a mining company, has been tracking in his retirement. Certain that she must follow the clues that her father left her, the heroine goes searching for the paintings, initially with her friends under the cover of a fishing trip and later on her own. She plunges into the depths of the water to locate these ancient drawings, which eventually serves as a metaphor and catalyst for the heroine's recovery of a sense of wholeness. While underwater, she becomes conscious for the first time of the trauma of her first love affair, which resulted in an even more traumatic abortion, and that of her first marriage, which ended in divorce and estrangement from both her child—now living with her ex-husband—and her own maternity. Soon after this discovery she escapes from her friends as they prepare to leave the island. After they leave, she sheds all vestiges of civilization: she wears no clothes, stays away from the house, and lives by hunting and foraging in the woods. Only after her return to a precivilized state is the heroine able to heal. The novel ends with her return to civilization with a more complete understanding of herself as a woman and, so she believes, as an expectant mother.

⁓

My reading of this novel (and my inclusion of it in a book about American fiction) runs counter to the premises of most scholarship on the novel, much of it produced by Canadians and within the context of Canadian studies. As Kiley Kapuscinski points out, "The publication of the novel in the early seventies during an era of centennial fervour and in the same year as *Survival* has prompted many critics to read *Surfacing* as a treatise that reflects Atwood's early critical work in urging the self-consciousness of Canadians and inciting them to acknowledge the heritage of victimhood that is distinctly their own" (105).[15] Kapuscinski offers an astute corrective to these readings, showing how Atwood dissolves the border that separates peaceful Canadians from violent Americans, and victimized women from victimizing men. My own reading aims to show how Atwood, like many American authors of the period, finds a solution to national anxieties about complicity in American violence in the figure of the traumatized Vietnam veteran.

Unlike her 1993 novel *The Robber Bride*, which tells the story of a Canadian woman who gets involved with an American war resister, the heroine of *Surfacing* is consistently figured as a traumatized American vet fighting a war that no one else realizes is still unfolding.[16] Vietnam, neither the place nor the war, is ever mentioned. Instead, the heroine thinks often of World War II: on the first page of the novel she recalls her childhood during the war, how she and her brother "sat with our feet in blankets, pretending we were wounded. My brother said the Germans shot our feet off" (4). Atwood's heroine emphasizes the absolute distance that separated them from the actual conflict. She thinks, "I had a good childhood; it was in the middle of the war, flecked gray newsreels I never saw, bombs and concentration camps, the leaders roaring at the crowds from inside their uniforms, pain and useless death, flags rippling in time to the anthems. But I didn't know about that till later, when my brother found out and told me. At the time it felt like peace" (14).

It is not accidental that her brother is the one who initiates her into knowledge of death, pain, and violence. This knowledge seems to belong to him both because he is a boy and because he almost drowned before our heroine was born. The heroine is a graphic artist, and one day she discovers in scrapbooks various drawings she and her brother made. Her brother's contain "explosions

in red and orange, soldiers dismembering in the air, planes and tanks," "fly-
ing men with comic-book capes and explorers on another planet," and "purple
jungles . . . the green sun with seven red moons" (90). By contrast the heroine
discovers that she drew mainly "ladies" and "ornately decorated Easter eggs"
populated by little rabbits: "All of the rabbits were smiling and some were laugh-
ing hilariously; several were shown eating ice cream cones from the safety of
their eggtops. No monsters, no wars, no explosions, no heroism. I was disappointed in myself: I must have been a hedonistic child, I thought, and quite
stodgy also, interested in nothing but social welfare" (90). The heroine then,
even as a child, was alienated from the elemental truths of existence; the novel
will allow her, finally, to correct the distortions bred by her conformity to the
rules of gendered propriety.

The heroine's obsession with "ladies" comes as a bit of a surprise, for the
heroine is conspicuously represented in terms of a wounded masculinity. She is
taciturn, hardy, and self-sufficient. Her suffering is very clearly represented as
a form of trauma. The most striking sign of her traumatic suffering are flashbacks and hallucinations of her ex-husband. During a hike she says, "We begin
to climb and my husband catches up with me again, making one of the brief ap-
pearances, framed by memories he specializes in: crystal-clear image enclosed
by a blank wall" (44). A page later, thinking briefly of her child (who now lives
with her ex-husband), she thinks, "It doesn't exist, because for me it can't, it was
taken away from me, exported, deported. A section of my own life, sliced off
from me like a Siamese twin, my own flesh cancelled. Lapse, relapse, I have to
forget" (45).[17] The cycle of repression and intrusive remembering, her regressive
identification with and disavowal of the lost child, her emotional numbness, all
will become "textbook" symptoms of PTSD.

Most importantly, the heroine lives in a state of wary vigilance, as though
she is a soldier heading into dangerous territory. As the heroine and her com-
panions approach her village she thinks, "Now we're on my home ground,
foreign territory" (7). This may be a reference to the fact that the village is
French-Canadian whereas her family was not, or it may be a reference to
the fact that her family did not live in the village proper but on a tiny island
nearby. The heroine, we are led to understand, lives in a landscape of total
alienation and internal exile, which is also a recasting of the American presence in Canada in military terms, and the heroine is part of a guerrilla opposition. There is the "innocent looking hill" under which the Americans used to
have "concrete bunkers and the ordinary soldiers in underground apartment
buildings" (5). Now, however, the American presence is felt mostly through
tourism. The heroine is constantly on the lookout for signs of the American
enemy, from flags rippling on speed boats to the too-well-pressed flannel
of the visiting fisherman. She and her friends even suspect that the tourism
holds a more sinister menace: a man representing the Detroit branch of the

"Wildlife Protection Agency" may turn out to be a CIA agent looking to exploit the island for espionage purposes.

In one of the creepier sections of the novel, the heroine takes her friends on what they think is a fishing expedition, but she plans to sneak off, dive, and locate rock paintings. After reaching another island by canoe they bushwhack through the brush and come upon a gruesome sight: a heron that has been killed, desecrated, and lynched. The heron surely calls to mind not only the murder of African Americans but, in this Canadian novel of 1972, the atrocities committed by American soldiers in Vietnam, and the link is made all the stronger by the danger and the trepidation with which the heroine moves through the woods. Approaching the site of the carnage she sees hidden in the brush "footprints, bootprints, in the muddy places. Two sets, they pointed in but not out: whoever they were, Americans maybe, spies, they were still in there." She even imagines that "from the rock where I washed the dishes I could see part of their tent, in among the cedars at the distant end of the lake: their bunker. Binoculars trained on me, I could feel the eye rays, cross of the rifle sight on my forehead, in case I made a false move" (119).

The deflating joke comes when they finally find the men who made the bootprints and they turn out to be locals. What the heroine thought was an American flag turns out to be a pennant for the Mets, and all the men present are fans. Indeed, these clean-cut Canadians at first assume that the heroine and her friends "were Yanks, because of the hair and all" (129). But this, in the end, does not really matter, as being American is something that afflicts Canadians too. At one point she thinks of herself and David as the particularly damaged ones, as those who commit atrocities, while later she declares "American, they are all American now" (173). America is a shorthand for the total system, political, sexual, and linguistic, in which the heroine is trapped: "If you look like them and talk like them and think like them then you are them, I was saying, you speak their language, a language is everything you do" (130). What this allows in the novel is not the disappearance of the menace, but the heroine's realization that being American is something that inheres in language itself.

Initially, at least, it seems as if this insidious Americanism afflicts the men in particular. David bullies Anna into allowing him to have sex with other women: "I shouldn't get uptight, he says jealousy is bourgeois, it's a leftover of the property ethic" (99).[18] Even Joe, a far gentler and more sympathetic character, aims to trap the heroine with the word "love," which—like the marriage license her previous husband insisted they acquire—destroys authentic feeling by trying to pin it down. American English, in other words, is the language of misogynistic patriarchy. After staving off the first attempted rape, David calls her a "tight-ass bitch." In response she thinks: "I could see into him, he was an imposter, a pastiche, layers of politic handbills, pages from magazines, *affiches*, verbs and nouns glued on to him and shredding away, the original surface littered with fragments and tatters. In a black suit knocking on doors, young once, even that had been a costume; now his hair was falling off and he didn't know what language to use, he'd forgotten his own, he had to copy. Second-hand Americanism was spreading over him in patches, like mange or lichen. He was infested, garbled, and I couldn't help him" (154). Her position is clarified after one of the characters accuses her of either hating men or wanting to be one. The heroine ignores the second charge, but as to the first she thinks, "It wasn't the men I hated, it was the Americans, the human beings, men and women both" (155). She wishes she could destroy them all instantly so that "there would be more room for the animals." Anna responds to her silence by calling her inhuman, and this is indeed what the heroine seeks to become. For in *Surfacing*, the opposite of being an American is not being a woman, but being an animal, being inhuman.

The process of "surfacing" or healing that the novel narrates for the heroine entails her finding a way out of human language and thus out of the system of oppression. She can only recover from the trauma of her abortion by passing, however briefly, out of civilization and its language. Only by following the orders of newly rediscovered ancient pagan "gods" is she able to return to a state of precivilized animality. By doing so, she can become fully human, which also means that she is no longer an American. But the physicality of the female animal can only be reached by traveling through the elemental materiality of the masculine soldier's body, a body whose authenticity is guaranteed by its encounters with violence.

The heroine initially thinks that she might, somehow, have seen her brother's drowning by looking through "the wall of the mother's stomach, like a frog in a jar" and bemoans the fact that this cannot be true: "I would have known things most people didn't" (28). Following the secret that she believed her father has left for her, she seeks the ancient rock paintings that she believes he discovered. Upon plunging deep within the icy lake, what she finds is not a painting but the presence of a dead thing, "a dark oval trailing limbs. It was blurred but it had eyes, they were open, it was something I knew about, a dead thing, it was dead" (143). What she encountered underwater, it turns out, was not her dead brother in a flashback or the drowned corpse of her father, which is found by others in the next chapter. What she sees instead is her aborted child, the one she "murdered" after her first lover (an older married art teacher) insisted she do so. Although she knows rationally that "they scraped into a bucket and threw it wherever they throw them," she envisions the fetus in terms of the animals her brother kept trapped (and that she once set free) in his wooded hideout. It is "in a bottle curled up, staring out at me like a cat pickled; it had huge jelly eyes and fins instead of hands, fish gills, I couldn't let it out, it was dead already, drowned in air" (144).

It is in this abortion that the heroine finally discovers the source of her trauma, which is also the source of her authenticity and thus the key to her eventual healing. Her father and brother lead her, finally, to the discovery of a female violence that she abhors, but that when correctly perceived, is the source of a new and authentic power: "It was all real enough, it was enough reality for ever, I couldn't accept it, that mutilation, that ruin I'd made, I needed a different version. I pieced it together the best way I could, flattening it, scrapbook, collage, pasting over the wrong parts. A faked album, the memories fraudulent as passports" (145). The reality, in other words, that she encountered through mutilating her unborn child had been falsified. Her trauma is revealed to her not only as a disorder of memory but as a model of the kind of art that she will abandon. For this art is, like the fragments and tatters of language that constitute David, falsely mired in a false language.

In its place will come a new art and a new relationship to language. Having found the "gifts" left by her brother and father she finally receives what is left for her by her mother. In another scrapbook she finds a picture she drew of "[a] woman with a moon stomach: the baby was sitting up inside her gazing out. Opposite her was a man with horns on his head like cow horns and a barbed tail" (159). At the time of its composition, she was the baby and she gave God horns because she had learned from her brother that the devil had them, and she figured God needed to be evenly matched. But now she says, "They were my guides . . . I had to read their new meaning with the help of the power: The gods, their likenesses: to see them in their true shape is fatal. While you are human; but after the transformation that could be reached. First I had to immerse myself in the other language" (159).

This new language is elemental and can only be learned when the heroine strips herself of every vestige of civilization, which she proceeds to do. First, she has sex with Joe, who had earlier only been dissuaded from coercing her by the threat of pregnancy. Now, while he utters in his inconsequential language that he loves her she "is impatient, pleasure is redundant, the animals don't have pleasure. I guide him into me, it's the right season" (165). She is a human animal, mating not loving, guided by a primal instinct to reproduce. After his ejaculation, she feels her "lost child surfacing" and "forgiving her." She plans to have the baby squatting in the woods where it "will slip out easily as an egg, a kitten, and I'll lick it and bite the cord . . . it will be covered with a shining fur, a god, I will never teach it any words" (165). With this knowledge, she strips herself of clothing, escapes her friends and the cabin, and proceeds to live on scavenged berries and roots, listening for the language of the gods.

She finally achieves the desired state of animality when she becomes a word: "In one of the languages, there are no nouns, only verbs held for a longer moment. The animals have no need for speech, why talk when you are a word. I lean against a tree, I am a tree leaning" (187). Importantly, to become a word is not, then, to become a thing, but to become the action in which you engage. It is only after becoming an animal who no longer understands French or English that she is able to return to civilization where she ponders the child she believes is growing inside of her: "But I bring from the distant past five nights ago the time-traveler, the primeval one who will have to learn, shape of a goldfish now in my belly, undergoing its watery changes. Word furrows potential already in its proto-brain, untraveled paths.... It might be the first one, the first true human; it must be born, allowed" (197–98). With what seems to be an echo to the "trembling unfurrowing of the mind's plowshare" that signals, in *The Crying of Lot 49*, the remaking of language according to the nonreferential workings of coincidence, the heroine's baby is *acquiring* language, but a language that is also somehow separate from the corrupt and falsified meaning of everyday speech. This baby heralds a new age in which humans are no longer Americans.

The very end of *Surfacing* entails a return to "ordinary speech." The heroine hears Joe, who has returned to the island in search of her (much as she searched for her father), and she realizes that "he isn't an American, he is only half-formed, I can trust him" (198). Her lover comes back; that is, rescued by his refiguration as another fetus. She realizes that "for us it's necessary, the intercession of words" (198), but she at least is fully in contact with the real that language hides. Yet that "real" takes place at a double remove. It is reachable only through her figuration as the soldier encountering atrocity in a foreign land and it is always, necessarily, unspeakable. The seemingly everyday bodily violence against women—iconically captured in the act of abortion—can be real only when it is rendered experientially and discursively absent.

"THE PAST IS A DISPUTED AREA": REVOLUTION AS TRAUMA

It would be hard to imagine a novel more explicitly hostile to psychiatry than Marge Piercy's 1976 novel *Woman on the Edge of Time*. In a prefatory acknowledgment, Piercy thanks not only the staff of the journal *Radical Therapy* but also members of the "Mental Patient Liberation Front" and the many past and present inmates of mental hospitals she interviewed. The book, now considered a classic of feminist science fiction, tells the story of Connie Ramos, a woman trapped within a cruel and abusive mental health system that is dedicated not to healing but to perpetuating social inequality. According to the novel, Connie's problems do not stem from trauma so much as from the systematic brutalization and dehumanization she has suffered as a result of being a poor, brown-skinned, Chicana woman. Plenty of terrible things have happened to her: she was repeatedly raped in Chicago; abandoned after being impregnated by an Anglo boyfriend; her first husband was murdered by the police; her next husband abandoned her; and her last, beloved, common-law husband, Claud, a blind African American pickpocket, died from the hepatitis he was injected with as part of a "voluntary" study he took part in as a prison inmate. Her first hospitalization occurred after she abused her daughter while high and grief-stricken after Claud's death. By the time we meet Connie, her daughter has been taken from her. She soon lands in the hospital after being beaten by her pregnant niece Dolly's pimp boyfriend during his attempt to force her to have an abortion. But these horrors are presented as traumatic for Connie only to the extent that she is given no room by the society she lives in to either mourn her past or gain control over her future.

The plot of the novel proper takes place during a long hospitalization. During this stay she makes extended contact with a woman from the future—specifically from the year 2137—named Luciente, learns about their wise and egalitarian society, and is enlisted in a war to preserve the very future from which Luciente hails from its dystopian alternative. To the extent that Connie is shown to be psychically damaged by her past, the short time she spends in the utopian future of Mouth-of-Mattapoisett allows her to grieve for her losses and regain the strength and self-control to participate in revolutionary struggle. She will never, we find out in the final pages of the novel, escape the psychiatric discipline that has entrapped her, but *we* know that she is no longer sick.

The novel's hostility to psychiatry is central to its understanding of the broader evils of capitalist patriarchy. Luciente, Connie's guide to the future, delivers one of many homilies that lays out Piercy's critique of modern psychiatry: "In your time the physical sciences had delivered the weapons technology. But the crux, we think, is in the biological sciences. Control of genetics. Technology of brain control. Birth-to-death surveillance. Chemical control through psychoactive drugs and neurotransmitters. . . . They had not even a theory of memory! Their arrogance . . . amazed me" (215, first ellipsis mine). By contrast, in the future, "madhouses are places where people retreat when they want to go down into themselves—to collapse, carry on, see visions, hear voices of prophesy, bang on the walls, relive infancy—getting in touch with the inner self and the buried mind. We all lose parts of ourselves. We all make choices that go bad. . . . How can another person decide that it is time for me to disintegrate, to reintegrate myself?"(60). In the utopian future then, to go mad is a valuable mode of self-knowledge and development. Indeed, madness allows the citizens of Mattapoisett to make contact with the presocial real of infancy, an experience that has maintained its value, apparently, even in this clear-thinking social order.

This beneficial, prelinguistic "madness" is targeted by doctors, who act as agents of a logocentric patriarchy: "Cold, calculating, ambitious, believing themselves rational and superior, they chased the female animal through the brain with a scalpel. From an early age she had been told that what she felt was unreal and didn't matter" (273). Piercy's image is perfectly in line with Susan

Brownmiller's conflation of an imagined scene of Paleolithic hunting with the hypothetical rape that is the founding act of a patriarchal order. The sexual component of this hunt by doctors is made explicit repeatedly in the text, especially in the mind-control demonstrations they perform with the libidinous Alice. And Connie herself makes the connection as she prepares for the surgery, already performed on a few of her friends, that will allow the doctors to control her through the implantation of a device that releases specific chemicals by remote control. She thinks, "Tomorrow they were going to stick a machine in her brain. She was the experiment. They would rape her body, her brain, her self" (271). Although Connie has experienced literal rape, it is the figurative rape of the surgery around which the novel is organized.

Unlike her best friend in the hospital, Sybil, who holds a Dworkian repulsion of sex, she asks, "Who wants to be a hole? . . . Do you want to be [a] dumb hole people push things into or rub against?" (78).[19] Connie and the novel are invested in maintaining the possibility of heterosexual sex that is both pleasurable and egalitarian, but insofar as Connie understands any violation of her body or mind as a rape, rape is established as *the* act of violence upon which female personhood hinges. As in *Surfacing*, the means through which the subjection of women by sex is connected to the figure of the Vietnam veteran is subtle. There is only one moment of direct reference: when Connie and another patient, Skip, talk of a Vietnam vet named Otis who has also been subjected to the evils of pharmacological control (276). Just as in *Surfacing*, the Vietnam veteran is invoked in order to fundamentally reshape what it might mean to be a warrior. In *Woman on the Edge of Time*, Connie's time spent learning about the beauty and wisdom of the future is made meaningful by her decision to fight in a war. This war has many fronts, but all are part of the fight against those who would seek to control the minds of human beings through technology. Thus Connie comes to see herself as a soldier in the war against the doctors and their mind-raping chemicals.

Connie is also fighting the foes of the future. As Luciente explains about the enemies they are fighting: "Now they have the power to exterminate us and we to exterminate them. They have such a limited base—the moon, Antarctica, the space platforms—for a population of mostly androids, robots, cybernauts, partially automated humans, that the war is one of attrition and small actions in the disputed areas, raids almost anyplace. We live with it. It's the tag end. We fear them, but we've prevailed so far and we believe we'll win . . . if history is not reversed. *That is, the past is a disputed area*" (259, emphasis added). We are able to see, directly through Connie, the world of the future enemy. Connie accidentally arrives in the bad future one day due to the unsuspected receptivity of a degraded human living on a platform the evil society has constructed on their toxic portions of earth. There Connie encounters a world where women are bred and operated on to be grotesque objects of sexual pleasure, with enormous breasts and feet so small that they cannot walk. The society is cruelly hierarchical, and leisure involves watching either ultraviolent snuff films or sentimental bodice-rippers.

The last and most important front is that which Luciente refers to at the end of the passage, and it is here, strangely enough, that the centrality of trauma to this antipsychiatric novel emerges most forcefully. The logic of trauma provides a model for understanding the crisis of temporality in which the characters are enmeshed. For as Luciente says, *"the past is a disputed area."* This is not, it should be clear, a dispute about how to *represent* the past, but about which among various possible pasts will become the past. That is, what future we come to inhabit will be determined by which past eventually wins out. The theory of time that undergirds this is not developed with any particular care by Piercy; the author, like the characters, does not yet understand how these temporal vectors work. But because the past is susceptible to being transformed in the future, its meaning is enormously consequential. This becomes clear during one of Luciente's many speeches on revolution:

> "Those of your time who fought hard for change, often they had myths that a revolution was inevitable. But nothing is! All things interlock. We are only one possible future. Do you grasp?" Luciente's hand became iron on her ribs, her voice was piercing and serious.
>
> "But you exist." She tried to laugh. "So it all worked out."
>
> "Maybe. Yours is crux-time. Alternate universes coexist. Probabilities clash and possibilities wink out forever." (169)

It is in this sense that trauma can be understood to undergird the central crisis of the novel. In his seminal book on PTSD the anthropologist Allan Young discusses what he calls the signifying power of PTSD. PTSD generates meaning about the nature of events by arranging them within a temporal scheme. This power derives in part from the way the disorder has been defined and the protocols for establishing its presence in patients. "The content of the patient's current distress, either his expressed emotion (grief, guilt, etc.) or his embodied distress, is projected back, over time, to the traumatic moment. In this way the projected distress infuses and connects the morally and experientially heterogeneous events . . . with a new and homogenous meaning."[20]

Or to put it another way, diagnosis of trauma aims to settle a dispute over the patient's past, which in turn transforms both the present and the future. Young's point is that PTSD provides a particularly expansive, powerful, and diagnostically flexible means to do this. His specific account of PTSD, which is only incidentally important here, points more broadly to the way trauma serves as an important conceptual source for Piercy's ideas about how our account of past events can transform the meaning of the present and future.

One obstacle to thinking about the disputed past as derived from ideas about trauma in Piercy's novel is that in clinical circles what is at issue is an individual's, not a collective's, past. And while this remains true among clinicians, as Young points out, the idea of trauma gains enormous momentum in this period and in the process is relentlessly collectivized:

> The pathogenic secret starts off in the nineteenth century as something located in the minds of individuals. Typically, it extends no further than the patient and the therapist. But in the 1970s, the pathogenic secret begins to enlarge, moving outward. At first, it is simply a matter of mental contagion: the secret replicates itself in the therapist's mind and in the minds of the patient's spouse and offspring. . . . The psychological pathology of the individual, the microcosmos, has a mirror image in the moral pathology of the collectivity, the social macrocosmos. The collective secret is a willful ignorance of traumatic acts and a denial of post-traumatic suffering. Patients are victims twice-over: victims of the original perpetrators and victims of an indifferent society. The therapeutic act of bringing the secret into full awareness is now inextricably linked to a political act. Vietnam War Veterans are the first traumatic victims to demand collective recognition, and they are followed by victims of other suppressed traumas, such as childhood incest and domestic rape.[21]

Young's historicizing gesture seems right, and is central to the notion of cultural trauma I discuss in my next chapter, on Philip Roth—although the collectivization of the idea of trauma looks quite different in *Woman on the Edge of Time*. The "secret" of the past in which Connie is living is the resistance of which she and others will prove themselves capable. This is because what a pathologizing psychiatric discourse calls trauma Piercy understands to be a form of authentic knowledge of violence and brutality from which the true revolutionary act can spring. It is through Connie's efforts that the novel looks forward to an as-yet-unrealized future when the past might be stabilized and the victory of the people of Mattapoisett assured.

Their victory can only come about by returning, as it were, to the figure of the soldier, only now he is a she and she is fighting a truly just war. Following her surgery, in which the chemical-releasing implant is inserted into her violated brain, Connie mentally travels to the future, only this time she is a combatant and her doctors appear on the side of the enemy. This conflation is not just symbolic but offered as real on any number of levels: not only does the battle point to one of those "alternative universes," but upon her finally waking from her time travels the frightened doctors decide to remove her implant. Thus Connie was literally fighting the war on two fronts at once.

It is during this section of the novel that Connie comes to see herself as a warrior. When the nurse compliments her on her docile behavior, saying

"You're doing much better. . . . Now you want to get better," Connie responds, "'Oh yes.' She forced a stiff smile. 'I want to get well now.' War, she thought, I'm at war. No more fantasies, no more hopes. *War*" (327, emphasis in original). Later, embarrassed by having begged her rich brother Luis to let her visit him during Thanksgiving, she thinks, "Claud would have stopped speaking to her if he'd heard that conversation; he'd have taken off in a shot. But it is war, she thought. I am conducting undercover operations. I am behind enemy lines and I must wear a smiling mask. It is all right for me to beg and crawl and wheedle because I am at war" (339).

The novel ends with an act of revolutionary violence. While Connie is never able to escape while visiting her rich brother, she steals a pesticide from the plant nursery where she briefly labors for him. Upon her return to the ward, she manages to slip the poison into the coffee pot used by the doctors. Upon doing so, she has these thoughts: "'I just killed six people,' she said to the mirror, but she washed her hands because she was terrified of the poison. 'I murdered them dead. Because they are the violence-prone. Theirs is the money and the power, theirs the poisons that slow the mind and dull the heart. Theirs are the powers of life and death. I killed them. Because it is war . . . I am a dead woman now too. I know it. But I did fight them. I'm not ashamed. I tried'" (364). She manages to kill four rather than six medical personnel, but that fact is still offered as a victory. This penultimate chapter thus ends on a note of resistance and struggle.

The novel, however, does not end here. The final chapter is a document entitled "Excerpts from the Official History of Consuelo Camacho Ramos." We learn that, like many Vietnam veterans before 1980, Connie was diagnosed as suffering from "Paranoid Schizophrenia, type 295.3" (367). In fact, Connie's transformation into a warrior is absent from the record as her crime was never suspected. This document merely takes us up to the eventual removal of the implant. The novel ends with the following neutral report: "There were one hundred thirteen more pages. They all follow Connie back to Rockover" (369). This record, in other words, is another version of Connie's past and thus of the disputed past that can change the future.

This is the strangeness of Piercy's novel: while it is explicitly dedicated to showing how the violence that saturates everyday life for the poor, the brown, and the female can be resisted, it moves the conflict into a place and time that our ordinary discourse cannot possibly articulate. Put another way, while it is true that Connie's violent resistance is one that takes place in the here and now—four stretchers do in fact pull away from the scene of the crime—that event does not register, and not just because she is never caught. Rather it is because Connie's war takes place in, to use Luciente's term, "a crux," in a place and time that is everywhere and nowhere.[22] Robin Silbergleid sees this as one of the novel's great achievements: the omniscient epilogue, in which Connie's acts of resistance are unknown, like the novel's larger subversion of "the linear, teleological impulse of the heterosexual romance," leaves "the reader free to imagine [Connie] roaming in Mattapoisett forever—outside narrative, outside time."[23] But such an escape is hard to square with Piercy's explicitly liberatory aims.[24] In *Woman on the Edge of Time* violence against women becomes most visible and open to resistance once it transformed into a war, but as a war it has the unspeakable and intangible status of a traumatic symptom whose authenticity will disappear if it is treated.

The figure of the soldier is deployed in both Atwood's and Piercy's texts to address the violence by which they are persecuted and in which women are complicit. The link between rape and military conflict initiates a potentially productive inquiry into the way patriarchal violence and nationalist violence meet, yet in the end violence as a political and material reality is utterly mystified. These novels depart from the more pragmatic engagement with violence developed in feminist theory to embrace an increasingly existentialized, and thereby politically diffused, model of trauma. As such they contribute to the ongoing cooptation of trauma for the shoring up of a national myth of victimization by a violence whose horror is its immateriality and whose authority is its inspeakability.

"words generally only spoil things"

FANTASY, TESTIMONY, AND TRAUMA
IN THE WORK OF PHILIP ROTH

In a vignette by David Sedaris entitled "Possession," first published in the *New Yorker*, the author tells of an apartment hunt that brings him to the Anne Frank House in Amsterdam.[1] The search only begins after David and his boyfriend, Hugh, discover that the wonderful place they currently rent will never be available for purchase because the landlord plans to pass it on to his two young daughters. Sedaris muses, in a gag that becomes poignant only in retrospect, "I kept hoping for a miracle. A riding accident, a playhouse fire: lots of things can happen to little girls" (100). It is while Hugh and David wait for their newly purchased Paris apartment to be renovated that they make a trip to Amsterdam, where David's buyer's remorse is compounded by the loveliness of the city. On their first day out they stumble upon the Anne Frank House, which David sees through the inappropriate lens of his only recently completed real estate odyssey. As he puts it: "on seeing the crowd gathered at the front door, I did not think, ticket line, but, open house!" (100).

Enthralled by its architectural charms, Sedaris soon constructs an elaborate fantasy of installing himself in the house. "I felt as if I had finally come home. A cruel trick of fate had kept me away, but now I was back to claim what was rightfully mine" (100). Although treated with a light hand, Sedaris's joke depends on our awareness that his perverse possessiveness of the Frank House is related to both the "normal" feelings felt by his fellow history tourists and to the monstrous thirst of the Nazis and their sympathizers for what was not theirs. Sedaris rather outrageously suggests that those who turned Anne and her family in to the Nazi authorities were likely motivated by the same lust to displace and possess as he is and that, by implication, the ticketholders are. What *they* are after, unlike Sedaris, is not the apartment, but Anne and the history that she has come to personify. As Sedaris sees it, the line between claiming that you have been possessed by history and feeling possessive is dangerously fine.

Sedaris's story may or may not encode a reference to Philip Roth's first Zuckerman book, the 1979 novella *The Ghost Writer*, in which the young novelist protagonist projects the ghost of Anne Frank onto a pretty European refugee named Amy Bellette in order to claim the moral capital that victims of the Holocaust have come to acquire. But whether or not Sedaris considered or was even aware of Roth's novella, his story is useful to look at alongside Roth's lengthy career. The desire to claim something that does not appear to rightfully belong to us—in Sedaris an apartment, in Roth a history of violent persecution—is at the center of a crucial shift over the course of Roth's career. This chapter aims not only to demonstrate the growing prestige of violence in Roth's work but to show how this privileging of violence is underwritten by a model of cultural trauma. I will do so by looking primarily (although not exclusively) at the place of the Holocaust in Roth's fiction. In the changing status of the Holocaust in Roth's work one can see with special clarity the increasing centrality of cultural trauma to his understanding of violence and American life. While he begins as a prescient critic of the notion of cultural trauma, he comes to embrace the idea with ever more vigor.[2]

✐

Roth's early work positioned him as a realist with a streak of absurdist humor. The stories collected within the covers of *Goodbye, Columbus* (1959) move between a careful anatomization and a comic heightening of the tensions, contradictions, and desires that structure the lives of increasingly upwardly-mobile and assimilated American Jews. The works that follow tilt first toward sober realism, as in his novels *Letting Go* (1962) and *When She Was Good* (1967), and then toward the manic hyperbole of *Portnoy's Complaint* (1969). *Portnoy's Complaint* was followed by a wild range of formal and stylistic experiments, from the political closet drama of *Our Gang* (1971) to the absurdist satire of *The Breast* (1972) to the metafictional games of *My Life as a Man* (1974).

My analysis of Roth's fiction begins with his work from the late seventies, when he settles into a set of formal techniques and thematic concerns that remain in place for decades to come. It ends by looking at his remarkable novel of 2004, *The Plot Against America*. During this period the David Kepesh character is largely abandoned and most of his novels feature writer-protagonists. Between 1979 (when the first of the Zuckerman novels comes out) and 2007 (when he publishes the last of them), all but three of his works feature protagonists named either Roth or Zuckerman—and one of those three features the titular Everyman who shares Roth's birthday and many other biographical details.[3] Yet for all the consistency of Roth's remarkably prolific career from 1979 to 2004, it is also marked by a striking transformation in his attitude toward and conceptualization of violence. Whereas Roth's early work is committed to a rigorously materialist account of the place (and the absence) of violence in American life, his later work increasingly emphasizes violence that is symbolic, psychological, immaterial, and counterfactual.

ANNE FRANK IN NEWARK: *THE GHOST WRITER* AND THE REJECTION OF CULTURAL TRAUMA

> In Europe—not in Newark! We are not the wretched of Belsen! We are not the victims of that crime! (106)
>
> *The Ghost Writer*

Long before Sedaris, Roth saw Anne Frank as an object of desire, as someone of whom we might want to take possession. His 1979 novella *The Ghost Writer*, which details Nathan Zuckerman's fantasy of marrying Anne Frank, came out just one year after full-blown Holocaust consciousness arrived in America. Henry Greenspan has given a nice summary of the range of events that point to the significance of 1978.[4] In that year alone the NBC miniseries *Holocaust*—viewed by between 100 and 120 million people—was aired, Jimmy Carter established the presidential commission on the Holocaust that would eventually oversee the creation of the U.S. Holocaust Museum, and the controversy over the proposed Nazi marches in Skokie, Illinois, unfolded. I cite these events to suggest the way that the story not only takes up Anne Frank as a way to address Roth's contentious relationship to his more conservative Jewish critics but also to draw attention to the dynamic interaction the novella activates between the Holocaust consciousness of the 1950s (the time in which the story is set) and the time in which it is written.[5] At a moment when the Holocaust is being integrated into the informal curricula of U.S. civil religion and formal curricula of public schools, Roth takes up Anne Frank not to question the identification of Americans with the Jewish victims of the Holocaust, but far more radically, to question the terms by which American Jews claim Frank for themselves.

The plot of the novella is this: the young writer Nathan Zuckerman heads to the secluded Berkshire home of a great Jewish writer named I. A. Lonoff, in flight from the first stirring of paternal disapproval over the alleged anti-Semitism of a story he hopes to publish.[6] There he meets a mysterious young woman named Amy Bellette, a refugee who, he learns over the course of his visit, is carrying on an affair with the married Lonoff. In a central embedded chapter entitled "Femme Fatale," we read what turns out to be the story Zuckerman writes that very night, but which, like so much Roth, is arrived at through such a digressively unmarked transition that we cannot initially be sure if what we are reading is Zuckerman's fantasy or not. It is only in the following and final chapter that it becomes clear that the previous chapter is something that Zuckerman has just composed.

Zuckerman fantasizes in "Femme Fatale" that the young woman living with the Lonoffs is none other than Anne Frank. In his account, she was mistakenly thought dead when in fact she ended up in a Displaced Persons (DP) camp; she then took on a new identity and eventually found her way to the United States.

One day she is stunned to read a reference in the newspaper to the publication of her diary and then witnesses its transformation into a national sensation. We as readers have already been alerted to the cultural significance and moral capital of Anne Frank in the world of Zuckerman's Jewish elders. In a previous chapter we encounter the novel's great comic set piece, a letter solicited by his father from the eminent Judge Wapter, who tries to convince Zuckerman of his moral responsibility as a Jew not to publish the story. In the course of the letter and its accompanying "Ten Questions for Nathan Zuckerman," the writer is simultaneously compared to Joseph Goebbels and encouraged to attend the smash Broadway production of *The Diary* so that he may absorb its moral instruction.

It is against this backdrop that Zuckerman's ensuing fantasy of marrying Anne takes place. For while Amy is presented as a wholly worthwhile object of erotic fascination, she becomes desirable only insofar as she can be transformed into Anne, and thus into a trophy of Jewish suffering. Zuckerman makes this entirely explicit when he apostrophizes: "Oh, marry me, Anne Frank, exonerate me before my outraged elders of this idiotic resentment!" (170). Zuckerman imagines that proximity to—or rather marital acquisition of—the moral capital acquired at the camps will allow him to reconcile with his father and show those critics who call him a self-hating Jew that he is in fact a better Jew than they will ever be. Ultimately, Zuckerman abandons the marital scenario, and instead, he describes his acquisition of moral capital through Anne in terms of the twinned ethical project of their writing. His narrative of Anne's anguished coming to terms with the fame of her book becomes indistinguishable from the story of his own struggle as a writer.[7]

In contrast to Zuckerman's eventual recognition of his bad faith investment in Anne Frank stand those who fail to see the gap that separates them from Anne. Anne-Amy notes in *The Ghost Writer* that "the superpractical achterhuis was now a holy shrine, a Wailing Wall. They went away from it in silence, as bereft as though she had been their own" (150). But as Roth's novel is at pains to remind us, Anne is *not* their own; the novel vehemently insists upon the gap that separates the life of Jews in postwar America from those of European Jews in the thirties and forties. After Zuckerman expresses his outrage at the letter he received from Judge Wapter, Zuckerman's mother says, "He only meant that what happened to the Jews"—I take the exchange that follows to be of key importance. He replies, "In Europe—not in Newark! We are not the wretched of Belsen! We are not the victims of that crime!" (106). To this his mother cries, "But we could be—in their place—we would be." In a final insistence on the difference between Newark and Belsen, Zuckerman says, "You want to see the physical violence done to the Jews of Newark, go to the office of the plastic surgeon where the girls get their noses fixed. That's where the Jewish blood flows in Essex County!" (106).[8]

As outrageous as the line is, it serves to encapsulate an alternative to the traumatic view of history that will emerge in later years to account for how the Holocaust might belong to American Jews. Roth's vision in *The Ghost Writer* is stubbornly materialist, and that materialist vision highlights the physical and historical distinctness of American Jews, most of whom emigrated to the United States decades before Hitler's rise to power. *The Ghost Writer* is perhaps a strange text to describe as importantly materialist. By virtue of its concision, it lacks the obsessively catalogued details that give readers of *American Pastoral*, for instance, a lesson in every aspect of glove-making. By virtue of its setting, primarily at Lonoff's home in the Berkshires, it is far from the lively locales where Jewish American life typically unfolds in Roth's work. And by virtue of its obsession with writers and writing, it is in many ways an inward-looking text.[9] But Roth's interest in this text on writing is the occasion for the careful scrutiny of the daily material existence that allows a writer to write. Lonoff's exasperated wife, Hope, describes it in excruciating detail: "If you dare change the *pepper* mill, he'll ask what's the matter, what was wrong with the old one. It takes three months for him to get used to a new brand of *soap*. Change the soap and he goes around *sniffing*, as though something dead is on the bathroom sink instead of just a bar of Palmolive" (174).

While Hope condemns this "religion of art" as a way of "rejecting life," it is nonetheless a *lived* life, however intolerable for her. As Lonoff describes it: "I turn sentences around. That's my life. I write a sentence and then I turn it around. Then I look at it and I turn it around again. Then I have lunch. Then I come back and write another sentence" (17–18). Zuckerman sees how this life of turning sentences around inflects every aspect of Lonoff's behavior. As Lonoff shows him how to work the record player, he says, "This, I realized, is the excruciating scrupulosity, the same maddening attention to every last detail that makes you great, that keeps you going and got you through and now is dragging you down" (73). The lesson Zuckerman learns over the course of this slim *bildungsroman* is about the actual lived experience—its ecstasies and its tedium—of an author he had previously worshipped in the abstract. Zuckerman learns about the physical life of a writer within an even greater intimacy in *The Anatomy Lesson*, which makes up the third part of the set of Zuckerman books collected as *Zuckerman Bound*. There the artist uncovers a new source for, and obstacle to, art: not sex, but pain, a pain that however mysterious in origin, is located in, and felt by, the physical body, a pain to which art must somehow respond.[10]

So while Roth complicates the strictly realist mode of his earliest fiction by entangling it in various metafictional frames, his vision of Jewish-American life and the larger history into which that life should be inserted is rooted in the lived particulars of American postwar affluence. Roth's fiction at this point is dedicated to lovingly chronicling every decadent feature of this historically anomalous Jewish life. His Jews are guilt-ridden and neurotic, but they are also well fed, secular, ambitious, increasingly cosmopolitan, and endlessly libidinous. It is precisely in these terms that *The Ghost Writer* invokes and then denies the grounds of cultural trauma. Whereas Cathy Caruth's theory requires, as I describe in the introduction, for us to recast the absence of American Jews from the scene of genocide as the ultimate act of witnessing that is the basis for their trauma, Roth's novella suggests that it is only because Zuckerman and others *are not* the victims of that crime that they seek so passionately to establish their claim to it. In this reading, the insistence that Newark is not Belsen goes hand in hand with a thoroughgoing inquiry into the motives—personal and communal, if not yet national—that pass themselves off as traumatic symptoms.

LEON KLINGHOFFER ABROAD: *OPERATION SHYLOCK* AND THE DANGER OF BEING A JEW

> Would Jews without enemies be just as boring as everybody else? These diaries suggest as much. What makes extraordinary all the harmless banality is the bullet in the head. (328)
>
> *Operation Shylock*

Operation Shylock has the distinction of appearing in the same year that *Schindler's List* became an international sensation and that the First Intifada came to a close with the signing of the Oslo accords. It tells us the surprising story of Roth's recruitment as a good Jew; that is, as a Jew who works with the Israeli secret police to track down Jews who are collaborating with the Palestine Liberation Organization (PLO). The plot of the novel is enormously complicated, but a short summary can communicate the most relevant particulars. The novel follows the author Philip Roth as he recovers from a disastrous reaction to Halcion following knee surgery. The drug precipitated a major psychic break, one in which he lost any coherent sense of self.[11] Upon emerging from that crisis into tentative health, Roth discovers that he is being impersonated by someone who looks just like him. This false Philip Roth, whom our Roth nicknames Moishe Pipik, is traveling around the world advocating for a new Diasporism. Jews, this false Roth preaches, must flee the second Holocaust that awaits them in Israel to settle in a new and more appropriate homeland in Poland. In the course of trying to reclaim his name and discredit the imposter, Roth meets and seduces Pipik's luscious gentile girlfriend, Wanda "Jinx" Possesski, and eventually embarks on a secret mission for the Mossad that is redacted from the final text of the novel we are reading.[12]

I will focus at length in a moment on the removal of the eleventh chapter of the novel (which, according to the Roth character in the epilogue, would have been the final chapter). That redaction is crucial to understanding the central-ity of violence in this novel, but its significance emerges against the otherwise maddeningly ambiguous politics of the book. Much of the novel is made up of rants both for and against Zionism and the Jewish state. Even more than is usually the case in a novel by Philip Roth, the author's political views are in-determinable; *Operation Shylock* constantly offers and then undercuts views of the conflict between Israelis and Palestinians. These speeches, from characters unhinged by passion, are at once lunatic and compelling; Roth seems anxious to have his characters make the most outrageous of claims with the greatest rhetorical force. But however interesting in its own right Roth's position on the Arab-Israeli conflict may be, my attention to the matter in what follows is in-strumental. My interest is not in joining the decades-long and ever-ramifying debate about Roth's attitudes regarding Jewish identity, but in showing how his use of both the conflict between Israelis and Palestinians and the Holocaust registers a deeply changed attitude toward the nature of violence and the use-fulness of language to represent it.

I have described *The Ghost Writer* as a skeptical, even acerbic, send-up of the motives, both personal and political, in which Roth believes that Jewish American piety about the Holocaust is entangled. Zuckerman's fantasized sense of intimacy with Anne Frank is revealed to be just that—a fantasy. But if that text offers a prescient critique of the idea of cultural trauma, it is a critique that Roth increasingly abandons. In *Operation Shylock* the space between what it means to be a Jew in Newark and a Jew in Belsen is in the process of collaps-ing. In the world depicted by *The Ghost Writer*, Anne Frank can only exist in America on Broadway or in the fevered imagination of Zuckerman. But in the world of *Operation Shylock*, Ivan the Terrible may have been living as an ordi-nary auto worker named John Demanjuk and the Jewish American business-man Leon Klinghoffer is not even safe from the PLO when he goes on a cruise. As the character Philip Roth writes in his notes to what he thinks is the mur-dered man's travel diary, Klinghoffer may have thought he was enjoying the "floating lockup" of a cruise, but he found out instead that "*there is no neutral territory*" (328, original emphasis).[13]

Roth repudiates the vision of Jewish American life offered in *The Ghost Writer* even more directly when the Roth character runs into an old friend from the University of Chicago, George Ziad. Back then Ziad had appeared urbane and apolitical; he is now an obsessively bitter anti-Zionist Palestinian.[14] He praises the representation of Jewishness offered in Roth's early fiction as part of a time when "Jews everywhere wished to be known for something more vitalizing than their victimization." Or as he describes it more fully: "Green lawns, white Jews—you wrote about it. You crystallized in your first book. That's what the hoopla was all about. 1959. The Jewish success story in its hey-day, all new and thrilling and funny and fun. Liberated new Jews, normalized

Jews, ridiculous and wonderful. The triumph of the untragic. Brenda Patimkin dethrones Anne Frank. Hot sex, fresh fruit and Big Ten basketball—who could imagine a happier ending for the Jewish people?" (132). As Ziad sees it, Roth's fellow Jews have become intoxicated with an alternate account of themselves. The Six-Day War initiated a "cynical institutionalization of the Holocaust" that serves to "establish Israeli military expansionism as historically just by joining it to the memory of Jewish victimization" (132). While this is not exactly Roth's position in *The Ghost Writer*, it is not too far off either. "Hot sex, fresh fruit and Big Ten basketball": such are the terms by which Roth still understands Jewish life in 1979. But from *Operation Shylock* forward, Roth is no longer so sure that this is the real story. Ziad's elegiac celebration of Roth's former narrative of Jewish triumph is the novel's own ironically elegiac acknowledgement that fresh fruit and hot sex are not nearly as significant as Roth once thought. Instead, the Holocaust and its ever-ramifying effects stand at the center of a newly globalized Jewish identity. America's and Israel's destinies are inextricably entwined and both are caught in what appears to be the still-unfolding history of Jewish persecution.

This is all but explicit in *Operation Shylock*, where the passions of sex and art that occupied his early work are no longer enough. Reading what he thinks are Klinghoffer's diaries, Roth makes a note that asks, "Would Jews without enemies be just as boring as everybody else? These diaries suggest as much. What makes extraordinary all the harmless banality is the bullet in the head" (328). This casually direct assertion of the value, importance, and interest that violence lends those who suffer it comes at a crucial point in the character Roth's adventures in Israel. He acknowledges the prestige of violence not as he or one of his literary doppelgangers are trying to write a novel or get a blow job, but as he sits in an empty classroom in Jerusalem after having been abducted by two thuggish agents of the Mossad.

Roth was abducted, we discover, because the Mossad wants him to go on a special mission for them: he will continue to pretend to be a proponent of the Diasporism that was espoused by his impersonator. In doing so he will get George Ziad to introduce him to Yasir Arafat and to the shady, unknown Jews who are funding the PLO. Initially, Roth refuses and this refusal marks the end of the "novel." But in the epilogue that immediately follows Roth explains that he has removed the final chapter that he had written detailing his time in Athens and beyond with the PLO's Jewish backers. This redaction is odd because, before Roth agreed to participate in the mission, both he and the Mossad agent speculate that the literary value of the mission is its biggest potential draw. Having completed the mission, Roth asks himself in the epilogue, "[B]ut why *did* I do it?—given all the risk and uncertainties that exceeded by far the dangers of the unknown that adhere to writing—and enter into that reality where the brutal forces were in combat and something serious was at stake" (358). This is a question that supplies its own answer. The question is not why he did it *given* that he would have to enter a reality of brutal forces and serious consequences but *because* he would. *Operation Shylock* suggests that the need and the desire to enter that reality was reason enough. After all, what makes Jews interesting, according to an earlier formula, is the risk of getting a bullet in the head.

That the experience is its own reward goes some way toward explaining how it is that Roth, who has made a career out of refusing to respect communal taboos, would agree not to publish part of his work.[15] *Operation Shylock* frames the issue in a long speech given by the Mossad agent, known to Roth as Smilesberger, who recruits him. Smilesberger proclaims himself a follower of the Chofetz Chaim, a nineteenth-century rabbi from Poland who promoted the concept of *loshon hora*, or forbidden speech. These laws "forbid Jews' making derogatory or damaging remarks about Jews, even if they are true. If they are false, of course it is worse" (333). The jauntier translation of *loshon hora* provided by Smilesberger—"Words generally spoil everything"—even serves as the title of the epilogue in which Roth explains his decision to withhold his account of the adventures for Mossad.

⌒*ff*⌒

Although *Operation Shylock* is structured by its withholding of any representation of the intelligence mission—whose concrete threat allows Roth to escape the merely imaginary "dangers of the unknown" that he normally faces as a writer—it does not commit fully to the value of unspeakability. I say this not merely because the novel insists that the chapter was only withdrawn, not unwritable. The novel also celebrates the value of a category of writing that has become explicitly associated with trauma studies and its promotion of cultural trauma: the testimony. In an informal sense, the novel is stuffed with testimonies of a sort: every crank on the street seems to have a personal story to tell. But more than that, the novel is filled with the testimonies of Holocaust survivors. These testimonies are offered informally throughout the novel, but even more importantly, they are offered in court at the trial of John Demanjuk.

In her 1992 book *Testimony: Crises of Witnessing in Literature, Psychoanalysis, and History*, Shoshanna Felman proclaimed that "testimony is the literary—or discursive—mode *par excellence* of our times and . . . our era can precisely be defined as the age of testimony."[16] As Felman defines it, testimony occupies a strange middle ground between speech (or writing) and act.[17] The paradigmatic examples of testimony in her book are found in the Video Archive for Holocaust Testimonies at Yale University, although her use of the concept is expansive enough to include texts that are usually classified within traditional genres like poetry, memoir, and the novel. Felman can help us understand the significance of testimony in Roth's work because she articulates directly some of the implicit assumptions about the power and effect of testimony at play in Roth's text. Of particular importance for understanding testimony in Roth is Felman's notion that Holocaust testimonies manage to be linguistic acts that are also importantly supralinguistic. Testimonies "do not simply report facts" (7), nor do they offer "a complete statement, a totalizable account" of an event that Felman understands "exceeds any substantialized significance" (5). In this sense, testimony is an exception to the rule that "words generally spoil everything," but only because the words in testimony do not act like normal words.

Even more importantly, a testimony is, in Felman's opinion, the occasion for an encounter that allows the event or events being testified to pass from the person who gives the testimony to the person who listens, watches, or reads it. We see this when Felman reports her testimony (the characterization is her own) of what happened to the students in her graduate seminar at Yale when they watched the videotaped testimonies of men and women who had survived the Nazi death camps. After viewing the tapes "the class broke out into a crisis" that was anticipated by one of the survivors, who had worried aloud about the effects of the Holocaust on "the generations to come" (47). Citing her own testimony/lecture to her class in the wake of their "crisis" Felman asserts "the significance of the event of your viewing the first Holocaust videotape was . . . something akin to a loss of language, and even though you came out of it with a deep need to talk about it and to talk it out, you also felt that language was somehow incommensurate with it" (50).

There are several elements of this (in some quarters, infamous) passage from Felman that illuminate both *Operation Shylock* and the novel to which I turn next, *The Plot Against America*. After listening to a lengthy courtroom argument about the testimony of Eliahu Rosenberg, a survivor of Treblinka and a witness at Demanjuk's trial, Roth comments on both the lawyer's and the judge's failure to understand its significance. Rosenberg is being queried about a discrepancy: while he has identified the defendant as the sadistic prison guard for whom he was forced to work cleaning out the crematoria at Treblinka, a written account he composed and handed over in 1945 offered a first-person account of Ivan the Terrible's death during an insurrection. Rosenberg explains that although he used the first person in the written testimony, he had only reported what his friends had told him and what he wanted to believe was true. In the novel, Roth does not understand why the judge and the lawyer harp on Rosenberg's use of the first person. He thinks:

> The man is not a skilled verbalist, he was never a historian, a reporter, or a writer of any kind, nor was he in 1945, a university student who knew from studying the critical prefaces of Henry James all there is to know about the dramatization of conflicting points of view and the ironic uses of contradictory testimony. He was a meagerly educated twenty-three-year-old Polish Jewish survivor who had been given paper and a pen . . . where he had written not a story, strictly speaking of

his own singular experience at Treblinka, but rather what he had been asked to write: a memoir of Treblinka life, a collective memoir in which he simply, probably without giving the matter a moment's thought, subsumed the experiences of the others and became the choral voice for them all. (*Operation Shylock*, 294)

At its most basic, Roth's point is that the apparent discrepancy between Rosenberg's written testimony and his oral testimony is actually a sign of the reliability of both. The distinction he draws between the professional and the amateur writer is only emphasized by Roth's elegant formal analysis of Rosenberg's writing. While we might admire the professional writer, more important is that we see the special ability that Rosenberg has to testify not just for himself but for a collective, and to do so in a way that establishes commonality. "The ironic uses of contradictory testimony" is what Roth himself learned, at least in part, by studying James in the 1950s, a skill he passed on to his fictional double in *The Ghost Writer*. But Rosenberg is able to do something that in *Operation Shylock* comes to seem far more important: he testifies to the collective experience, desires, and beliefs of the camp inmates. Roth eventually makes explicit the value he attaches not just to Rosenberg's testimony but to Klinghoffer's diaries as well: "All this writing by non-writers, I thought, all these diaries, memoirs, and notes written clumsily with the most minimal skill, employing one thousandth of the resources of a written language, and yet the testimony they bear is no less persuasive for that, in fact it is much more searing, precisely because the expressive powers are so blunt and primitive" (298). Nonprofessional writing, because it lacks self-consciousness, because it is artlessly straightforward, can have the bluntness, the affecting directness that for Felman elevates the testimony above mere speech. Unlike Roth's own writing, which is deceptive, the testimony of the nonwriter has the power to "sear," to mark those who hear or read it. Like Felman's, Roth's testimonies seem to have the power to make singular experiences available to a larger community.

What these testimonies communicate is "the incredible drama of being a Jew" (329) under threat: "Without the Gestapo and the P.L.O., these two Jewish writers [Frank and Klinghoffer] would be unpublished and unknown. Without the Gestapo and the P.L.O. any number of Jewish writers would be, if not necessarily unknown, completely unlike the writers they are" (329). And while much of Roth's elevation of testimony occurs at the expense of artful writers like himself, this last formulation pulls Roth into the fold. *Operation Shylock* constitutes an act of self-definition by Roth at odds with his early career. Staring at the now unfamiliar Hebrew letters on the blackboard of the school—where he waits after being abducted to find out who intends to do him harm—he tries to divine the long-term consequence of those miserable hours he spent at Hebrew school preparing for his bar mitzvah. His answer? "Why, everything—what came of it was everything!" (312). Even if we readers assume that the mission for the Mossad is no more true of Roth's real-life experience than were the alternate lives he sketched for Portnoy and Zuckerman, that Roth is inescapably subject to the centuries-long Jewish history of persecution is *Operation Shylock*'s central insight.

VON RIBBENTROP IN THE WHITE HOUSE:
THE PLOT AGAINST AMERICA

> Turned wrong way round, the relentless unforeseen was what we schoolchildren studied as "History," harmless history, where everything unexpected in its own time is chronicled on the page as inevitable. The terror of the unforeseen is what the science of history hides, turning a disaster into an epic. (114)
>
> *The Plot Against America*

Roth's increasing insistence on a shared history and identity that unites all Jews—American, Israeli, or otherwise—leads him away, in *Operation Shylock*, from the material realities of Jewish American life in the age of American hegemony. But *Operation Shylock* can also be read as a fictional substantiation of that relationship that is, however surreal, rooted in some form of historical actuality. By contrast, *The Plot Against America* is counterfactual, but through it Roth continues and extends his case for the collective cultural trauma of Jewish Americans. Published in the aftermath of 9/11, the title seemed to allude as much to the political climate in which the novel was published as to the alternative American history it chronicled.[18] I return later to the contemporary implications of the novel but want to first attend to the explicit time and place of the novel, which is an alternative historical past in which the pro-Nazi aviator Charles Lindbergh becomes president and almost succeeds in permanently stripping the United States of its democratic institutions.

If in *The Ghost Writer* Zuckerman insists that we are not the wretched of Belsen, and if in *Operation Shylock* it suddenly matters that we could have been because we are still always in danger, *The Plot Against America* shows us that, in fact, we are. Newark, it turns out, was Belsen all along—we just did not know it. *The Plot Against America* provides a strangely structural assent to notions of trauma, particularly to notions of a peculiarly American trauma, which Roth's early work explicitly rejected. That rejection is, as with *Operation Shylock*, most immediately apparent in its treatment of the theme of anti-Semitism. If in *Operation Shylock* combating anti-Semitism necessitates going to Israel and pledging fealty to the Israeli state, in *The Plot Against America* that scourge can be fought at home. This is because, as the novel shows us, our fascism-hating country was only a hair's breadth from Nazism anyway. What brings Lindbergh to such political prominence and eventually to the presidency in the novel is a great unsuspected foundation of anti-Semitism that is only hinted at by fringe Bundists. Once FDR is out of the way it does not take much for the whole country to engage in a few dozen Kristallnachts of their own as pogroms break out across the country in any city with an identifiable Jewish population.

The novel appears to be an admission that the admonishing Jewish community of *The Ghost Writer* was right. When Judge Leopold Wapter asks in an absurd litany of "Ten Questions for Nathan Zuckerman: If you had been living in Nazi Germany in the thirties, would you have written such a story?" (102), we are meant to see the question as deeply misguided if not offensive. Newark is simply *not* Belsen. But if we return to this question having read *The Plot Against America*, Wapter's question no longer looks as easily dismissible. The difference between the two places turns out to have only *seemed* to be significant, when in fact it was thoroughly artificial. "Lindbergh's peacetime America" is described by the narrator of *Plot* as "the autonomous fortress oceans away from the world's war zones where no one is in jeopardy except us" (203). The point of this is that while Newark is not Belsen for gentiles, it might as well be for its Jewish citizens as they prepare to flee for Canada or risk being subject to an altogether involuntary and uncertain resettlement.

Astonishing though it may be, Roth manages to maintain moral authority over the Wapters of *The Plot Against America*, for as it turns out, such people end up being the biggest collaborators. The closest thing to the judge in this novel is Rabbi Lionel Bengelsdorf, the pretentiously erudite Jewish southerner who leads a large Newark congregation and becomes an advisor to President Lindbergh. The willingness of such hypocrites to ingratiate themselves to gentiles reaches its most monstrous form when young Philip's Aunt Evelyn, attending a White House event welcoming Hitler's foreign minister with her husband, Rabbi Bengelsdorf, enjoys an enchanted dance with Von Ribbentrop. The figures of courage and foresight in the novel include Roth's father and mother, but in general, the novel tends to identify an obsession with gentile mores and opinions as corrupt. Roth turns the concept of the self-hating Jew back against those who criticized *Portnoy's Complaint*, for in this novel you can tell a collaborator precisely by how much they want to perform Jewish respectability. Roth's own brother Sandy ends up using his drawing skills not to compose outlandish portraits of life inside Jewish Newark but to sketch the farm life of rural Kentucky and thus to become a collaborationist poster boy for the Lindbergh's "Just Folks" program, which sends Jewish teens on rural courses of de-Jewification.

While the Jewish characters in this novel are certainly scarred, wounded, killed, and individually traumatized by their brush with fascism in the novel, it is on the formal level that the trauma emerges most forcefully. When we are within the alternative history, readers understand that this story of homegrown Nazism and its traumatized victims is clearly demarcated as fictional. After all, we readers know Lindbergh did not become president, FDR did indeed win his last election, Walter Winchell did not become a presidential candidate or get assassinated or spark pogroms across the heartland. In the event that some reader does not know this, Roth provides extensive information in the appendix to the novel.[19] In this regard, the novel is a richly realized "what if?" which is what the author Roth insisted was his only aim in an essay he published in the *New York Times* about the book. However, this clear demarcation is importantly muddied toward the end of the novel, when we find out that Roth's outlandish alternative history dovetails seamlessly with the actual history of this period: events pick up right where they left off somewhere around January 1943 when FDR returns to the White House. But the dovetailing of possible history with actual history is not just represented by FDR becoming president again. Before we find out about this "happy ending," the narrator calculates that the assassination of Walter Winchell is the first such event, preceding the assassination of presidential candidate Bobby Kennedy by twenty-six years (272). I take this to be a significant move on Roth's part. Writers of alternative histories have to somehow reckon with what their narrative means for whatever time follows their account. Some evade the issue by leaving readers to guess but most have an entirely different future in mind for us. Their books show us how the whole course of history might have been changed had the events they describe played out. But this is not Roth's approach. Amazingly enough, American history picks up course and proceeds unchanged. Presumably, the realistic stories of Jewish American life told in *Goodbye, Columbus, Portnoy's Complaint, The Ghost Writer,* and *Operation Shylock* could occur as written.

What, then, are we to make of this perfectly encapsulated alternative past? Can it really be the case that this imagined spasm of fascism would not have made *any* difference to the future if it had occurred? While this seems implausible, I take Roth's insertion of this false history into our own to promote a vision of Jewish American cultural trauma that Roth had earlier rejected. That is, one way to read this rich and cryptic book is as a narrative of America's own traumatically forgotten past. It is as if we are being asked to accept that this outlandish story of the Nazification of America is our *true* past and we have suppressed any real knowledge of it because it is too painful. Here, instead of the trauma being entirely unspeakable, it is speakable only under the truth-telling aegis of fiction. The novel functions as an elaborate lesson in how we might come to understand that the implausible is in fact utterly plausible, that what seems like pure fantasy is nothing more or less than history at work.

The main lesson of the book is not the one that Herman Roth has long tried to impart to his children, that "[h]istory is everything that happens everywhere. Even here in Newark. Even here on Summit Avenue. Even what happens in his house to an ordinary man—that'll be history too someday" (180). Much of Roth's writing has indeed been dedicated to awakening readers to the importance of the lives of ordinary Jews in Newark. But *The Plot Against America* rewrites that ordinariness in ways that render it necessarily extraordinary. As young Philip comes to realize, "[T]he unfolding of the unforeseen was everything. Turned wrong way round, the relentless unforeseen was what we schoolchildren studied as 'History', harmless history, where everything unexpected in its own time is chronicled on the page as inevitable. The terror of the unforeseen is what the science of history hides, turning a disaster into an epic" (114–15). If history is, as Herman Roth declared, "everything," then surely it would not always be made up of "the terror of the unforeseen." The novel entails the equation of history and violence and the full elevation of that violence to the prestige other writers have long accorded it. History is most historical not when it concerns itself with family arguments about money and *shiksas* but when you are at risk of getting a bullet in your head or getting beaten, robbed, and burned alive in your car, as happens to Mrs. Wishnow, the Roth family's neighbor, after she is relocated to Kentucky. The history of Jews' successful struggle for material comfort and social acceptance is revealed as a falsehood, a narrative conceit and trick of retrospection. What really happened to us was a near genocide whose terrors we have been tricked into forgetting or not recognizing.

Mrs. Wishnow is important here, and she will bring us, at long last, to why it matters that Roth offers a traumatic view of history in which we can imagine that the Holocaust nearly happened to us. In the essay he wrote for the *New York Times* entitled "The Story Behind *The Plot Against America*," Roth elaborates on the "what if?" that prompted the novel and the pleasure he took in re-creating his parents as characters. He then goes on to explain what he believes is at the heart of the story:

> But the deepest reward in the writing and what lends the story its pathos wasn't
> the resurrection of my family circa 1941 but the invention of the family down-
> stairs, of the tragic Wishnows, on whom the full brunt of the anti-Semitism
> falls—the invention particularly of the Wishnows' little boy, Seldon, that nice,
> lonely little kid in your class whom you run away from when you're yourself a kid
> because he demands to be befriended by you in ways that another child cannot
> stand. He's the responsibility that you can't get rid of. The more you want to get
> rid of him, the less you can, and the less you can, the more you want to get rid
> of him. And that the little Roth child wants to get rid of him is what leads to the
> tragedy of the book.

Seldon, in other words, is like Israel in *Operation Shylock*: he is the responsibility you cannot get rid of and that, looked at from another perspective, you do not want to get rid of. In *The Plot Against America*, young Philip plays a major role in the Wishnow's relocation to Kentucky: he begs his influential Aunt Evelyn not to force their family to be relocated by Lindbergh's "Just Folks" program; she arranges instead for Seldon and his mother to be moved. This is a literalization of the Zuckerman's mother's point in *The Ghost Writer* about the Nazi death camps: "But we could be—in their place—we would be" (106). While the ultimate responsibility for the genocide is placed firmly in the lap of the perpetrators, the novel, like *Operation Shylock*, asserts the responsibility of American Jews for the suffering of others in order to claim the suffering as its own. In *Operation Shylock*, the Mossad agent known as Smilesberger taunts Roth for his blamelessness: American Jews have the luxury of not being responsible for the persecution of the Palestinians, but it is a luxury won by chance and one that no Israeli can afford. In *Operation Shylock*, Roth exchanges the luxury of blamelessness for the invigorating cocktail of complicity and victimization. In the allegory of *Plot*, American Jews are shown to have sold out their fellow Jews: Philip Roth and his family did not end up in Kentucky because someone else literally went in his place and this will be the source of Philip's ongoing trauma.

In a trenchant critique of the novel published soon after it came out, Walter Benn Michaels characterized the novel as shaped by "the utopian imagination of neo-liberalism" (299).[20] The novel's focus on the horrors of racism naturalizes the exploitation of the poor under capitalism. Its "victims are the victims of discrimination rather than exploitation, of intolerance rather than oppression, or of oppression in the form of intolerance" (297). My own reading suggests another way in which the novel occludes, distorts, and distracts from the political and economic realities that Michaels gathers under the rubric of neoliberalism. For while it is entirely true that *The Plot Against America* occludes the genocide of indigenous peoples and the horrors of slavery and converts American history into one about discrimination rather than exploitation, the novel also asks us to look away from the violence America was in the process of committing at the time of the novel's composition and publication.[21] Roth says he came upon the idea for the book in December 2000, but he was writing it as the public outcry (at least among professed liberals like Roth) grew about the rapid militarization of our response to 9/11, one which as of 2004 claimed the lives of many thousands of civilians.[22]

These victims are another thing we do *not* see when we think about violence primarily as something that happens to us in the form of a forgotten trauma, when we are traumatized not, as Vietnam vets often were, by what they did to others but by what we fantasize is happening to us. Indeed, the only contemporary parallel that is drawn by Roth is to the ongoing victimization of Americans by their fascist government. Roth insists that the novel is not a roman á clef about George W. Bush's plot to undermine civil liberties at home, but he then reverses at the end of the essay when he muses: "And now Aristophanes, who surely must be God, has given us George W. Bush, a man unfit to run a hardware store let alone a nation like this one, and who has merely reaffirmed for me the maxim that informed the writing of all these books and that makes our lives as Americans as precarious as anyone else's: all the assurances are provisional, even here in a 200-year-old democracy. We are ambushed, even as free Americans in a powerful republic armed to the teeth, by the unpredictability that is history."[23] Here Roth admits that he does draw some parallel between Hitler's plot (in which Lindbergh is largely a pawn) in the novel and the undermining of democracy that has gone on since 9/11 under George W. Bush. But what remains entirely invisible is not just the economic exploitation that underwrites neoliberalism but the military force used to maintain American power and secure goods and markets abroad. While Americans were losing their civil liberties, hundreds of Afghan and Iraqi civilians were losing their lives. But what matters far more than this in the novel is that we recognize the degree to which we are and have been ourselves under threat. That threat is utterly disconnected from the ongoing economic depredations of neoliberalism and the actual military aggression upon which it is still dependent. It does not matter whether we are really at risk of persecution by state-sanctioned terror or Islamic fundamentalism; what matters is only that we feel like we are. As Roth says of the threat posed by Lindbergh, which is, after all, the very germ from which the novel sprouts: "What matters in my book isn't what he does . . . but what American Jews suspect, *rightly or wrongly*, that he might be capable of doing given his public utterances, most specifically his vilification of the Jews, in a nationwide radio address, as alien warmongers indifferent to America's interests" (emphasis added). We need not subject our worries to scrutiny, need not look at them in light of the actual material and economic conditions in which we live. Instead, we are free to imagine ourselves traumatized by a past and present without ever acknowledging the actual perpetration of violence in our midst and in our name.

CHAPTER SIX

"the hammers striking the page"

DON DELILLO AND THE VIOLENT POLITICS OF LANGUAGE

I need the sound of the keys, the keys of a manual typewriter. The hammers striking the page. I like to see the words, the sentences, as they take shape. It's an aesthetic issue: when I work I have a sculptor's sense of the shape of the words I'm making. I use a machine with larger than average letters: the bigger the better. (117)
"An Interview with Don DeLillo"

FLASH
SSSSSSSSSS
BLOOD STAINEZAAC
KENNEDY SERIOUSTY WOUNDED
SSSSSSSSSS
MAKE THAT PERHAPS PERHAPS
SERIOUSLY WOUNDED (403)
Libra

The first of the above epigraphs comes from an interview given by Don De-Lillo soon after the publication of *Mao II*.[1] The aptness of the image of "the hammers striking the page" for DeLillo's body of work can hardly be overestimated. These aggressively hammering keys recall *The Names*, in which tools once used to chisel inscriptions into ancient stone are taken up by a murderous cult to shatter the skulls of their victims.[2] In these examples DeLillo gives words both the visual weight of sculpted matter and a weapon's ability to shatter other material objects. The second epigraph, one of four telegraph messages reproduced in *Libra* in the chapter entitled "22 November," brings those acts of making and unmaking together in a single moment. The novel insists that the assassination of JFK is the culmination of the paranoid narratives that incite Oswald and the other plotters, but the messages themselves function as visual rather than semantic objects that testify to the failure of language to represent the very violence it has unleashed. The telegraph messages *tell* us, mistakenly, that Kennedy has been wounded, but they *show* us that he has been killed.

Throughout DeLillo's four decades of writing novels, he has sought a language purified not just of plot but of meaning. Language is never more prized than when it appears as a sound and mark, when it possesses an inscrutable materiality almost equal to the violence it imitates. While Philip Roth's literary arc is marked by a transformative shift in his thinking about violence, Don DeLillo's oeuvre plays out as a series of variations on a set of propositions and ideas. The questions his novels pose go something like this: Does language protect us from death and violence or does it provide us access to it? Does the complicity of language in producing violence make it more or less likely to be able to represent it? Much as Pynchon worries in *The Crying of Lot 49* that language seals us off from the real of violence, DeLillo explores again and again how language is complicit in the production and the subsequent denial of this violent real. The clearest version of this account comes in *Libra* when a disgraced Secret Service agent who has hatched a plot for a failed assassination attempt on President Kennedy is shown ruminating on the matter: "A plot in fiction, he believed, is the way we localize the force of death outside the book, play it off, contain it" (221). Yet *Libra* also works to show how deeply the shattering violence that ensues is bound up *in* language. The same passage makes the opposite claim about plots. Here, violence is not staved off by plot but caused by it: "The tighter the plot of a story, the more likely it will come to death."

DeLillo's many novels, when read as a group, resolve this contradiction. The solution crucially depends upon no longer thinking about language in solely narrative or semantic terms. Once DeLillo develops an account of language that does away not only with plot but also with reference, language becomes the medium through which we can have the most authentic nonfatal encounter with the real possible. Although his abhorrence for violence is at once explicit and, I presume, sincere, DeLillo's conception of language does not move all but inevitably toward a deathly apocalypticism.[3] In what follows I will attend primarily to four novels by DeLillo: his first novel, *Americana* (1971), two novels from the middle period of his career, *The Names* (1982) and *Libra* (1984), and a more recent book, *Falling Man* (2007). The latter, like Roth's *The Plot Against America*, is a novelistic response to 9/11, and thus the book is a useful text through which to interpret the textual inheritance that shaped cultural responses to an event that is often described as having initiated a radical paradigm shift. I will argue that for DeLillo 9/11 was not the occasion for a radically new account of the relationship between violence and language, but rather, it provided the occasion a synthesis and robust redeployment of the ideas that he had spent decades developing. It also allowed him to reframe the problems of violence and language in a seemingly new political framework, one in which it is no longer Americans who sponsor violence abroad, but Americans who suffer it at home. Whatever complicity language retains in violence, it now comes to look like the complicity of the witness, not the perpetrator.

DEATHLESS DEATH IN *AMERICANA*

> Things become more real in proportion to the unreality of individual lives. The world has never been more real than it is right now.
>
> *Americana* (281)

Americana is many things: a road trip novel, a corporate farce, a portrait of an artist as a no-longer-young man, and a meditation on national identity. Its plot centers on one David Bell, a television executive who at the start of the novel has already clawed his way to the upper rungs of the corporate ladder. The rest of the book outlines his attempt to jump off that ladder, first by going across the country and making an experimental movie, and then by abandoning his artistic pretenses altogether and retreating to an unnamed island.[4] From the beginning, DeLillo suggests that language obscures, mystifies, and domesticates violence. David begins counting the number of people at a cocktail party, and he explains the activity this way: "Counting the house was a habit of mine. The question of how many people were present in a particular place seemed important to me, perhaps because the recurring news of airline disasters and military engagements always stressed the number of dead and missing; such exactness is a tickle of electricity to the numbed brain" (4). The media, of which David himself is a part, promotes a ghoulish fascination with death but also attempts to buffer us from its force by subjecting it to the pseudorational control of statistics. As such, it offers overall numbness and a light tickle instead of a shudder of horror. Contributing to the atmosphere of absent and dematerialized violence in *Americana* are the brutal boardroom politics and the war in Vietnam; David was exempted from conscription because of a trick knee and a spinal cyst, although he is by all reports an impressive specimen of American manhood.

Although deathliness is pervasive, the problem DeLillo identifies is that this deathliness is masked, hidden, and perverted. An anonymous executive on his floor sends around a cryptic memo that warns: "And never can a man be more disastrously in death than when death itself shall be deathless" (21). The quote, taken from St. Augustine's *City of God*, is perhaps an intellectual souvenir from DeLillo's days at Fordham, but the quote also works to reinforce the main theme of the novel: true life requires true death. A life without death—which is life that his been stripped of authenticating violence—is the very condition that the media conglomerates for which David is working threaten to condemn him.

If in later novels DeLillo suggests that language masks deathliness by producing specious meaning where there should properly be sublime nonsense, in *Americana*, at least initially, the problem is a *lack* of semantic correspondence between words and their meanings. David describes the fear that grows in him in response to the deanimalized violence of corporate life:

> As soon as fear begins to ascend, anatomically, from the pit of the stomach to the throat and the brain, from fear of violence to the more nameless kind, you come to believe you are part of some horrible experiment. I learned to distrust those superiors who encouraged independent thinking. . . . But I learned that new ideas could finish you unless you wrapped them in a plastic bag. I learned that most of the secretaries were more intelligent than most of the executives, and that the executive secretaries were to be feared more than anyone. I learned what closed doors meant and that friendship was not a negotiable currency and how important it was to lie even when there was no need to lie. Words and meanings were at odds. Words did not mean what was being said nor even its reverse. I learned to speak a new language and soon mastered special elements of the tongue. (36)

David's response to this language of unmotivated lying is horror; it constitutes something like violence, but we cannot name its threat. Unlike the gibberish, glossolalia, and incantatory brand names that will respiritualize language and death in later novels, in this first of DeLillo's novels, language without clear meaning is *bad*.

The problem is not confined to the corporate world. Bell thinks back on a conversation he had in his childhood in which his mother revealed that her obstetrician, Dr. Weber, raped her during gynecological exams. His mother has since died from untreated cervical cancer and her reluctance to seek treatment seems to derive at least in part from that abuse. She begins her revelation with the statement that, "[t]he minister and the doctor are at the heart of every community. . . . We've had doctors and ministers in our family practically all the way back to Jamestown" (139). The violence associated with Dr. Weber is, in the description that follows, not only extended to the minister but shown to have long since pervaded "the heart of the community." Bell himself strengthens the link between the two when he makes an abrupt transition from his mother's confession to the family minister. Reverend Potter, like Dr. Weber, called his mother "by [her] first name." Although he has committed no crime comparable to those of the doctor, Bell remembers the Reverend's pompous ineffectuality and the fact that, when he spoke "there seemed to be a curious disparity between the sounds he made and the movements of his lips; somehow they did not quite mesh. . . . It wasn't until years later, when I joined the network, that I found a term which perfectly described the way words issued from an unrelated mouth.

William Stockbridge Potter was out of sync" (141). Although Potter's verbal tic is not the same as the semantic irregularities of corporate speech, it is similarly tied to a complicity in the obfuscation of death. When his mother, seeking spiritual solace, tells Reverend Potter of her fear of death, he tells her to believe in "the power of laughter" and then congratulates himself on disproving the stereotype of High Church humorlessness. He represents another institution, this time the Episcopal Church, that condemns Americans to deathless life.

It eventually becomes clear that much of David's inner conflict is tied to his near-incestuous love for his mother and sister, both of whom he has lost, albeit in different ways.[5] Although he is still in contact with his boring sister Jane, David is distraught over his family's estrangement from his beloved and evocatively-named sister, Mary. We eventually learn that Mary escaped her dull suburban existence by taking off with a Mafia assassin. The movie David eventually makes includes a scene in which an actress playing Mary reads the lines David has written for her. Although this is David's version, there is little in the text to suggest that he is wrong, or that the larger vision informing his intuition is wrong. In Mary's monologue, her love for her mobster husband derives from his understanding of death: "We have learned not to be afraid of the dark, but we've forgotten that darkness needs death. They haven't forgotten this" (278). She admits that his understanding of and proximity to violent death, which he shares with his fellow Sicilians, is what she sought: "I needed death in order to believe that I was living, an atmosphere of death much more real and personal than anything the newspapers can offer. I didn't want him to get out of the business. I would have left him if he had" (279). However troubled we are meant to be by Mary's terrible honesty, the novel seems to endorse the view Mary attributes to her husband: "[D]eath is without meaning unless it is met violently" (280).

Ultimately, *Americana* commits to a kind of language that, like corporate speech, does not mean what it says, but, unlike corporate speech, does not hide death. DeLillo imagines a language that is deeply complicit with American violence and death but that no longer obscures that complicity. Just as in *Armies of the Night*, where Americans need the bloodshed in Vietnam because their own lives have been dangerously deanimalized, so *Americana* revolves around the recuperation of the authentically American violence only hinted at in the body counts from Vietnam. But unlike in *Armies of the Night*, where the violence of Vietnam has to be brought home, DeLillo turns instead to the indigenous violence of sex, to what he calls the "montage of speed, guns, torture, rape, orgy and consumer packaging which constitutes the vision of sex in America" (33).

Late in the novel, David is picked up hitchhiking by a rich cowboy named Clevenger who has offered him a job at the test track for tires and cars that he runs in West Texas. Along the way Clevenger tells a gruesome anecdote about a girl who kills herself after her parents punish her promiscuity by insisting that she shoot her dog. Having concluded his story with the delighted excla-mation, "that beats my meat!", Clevenger "howled then, the consummate reb yell, a two syllable sound that was hog call, battle cry, the bark of a saved soul at a prayer meeting" (364). This call, which combines a deeply American com-mercial jargon, religious ecstasy, and war whoop, means everything it says and achieves this oversaturation of meaning by having no semantic content. David understands this yell to mark the place literature cannot reach: "I didn't under-stand Clevenger. There were shades to him which dimmed what I kept expect-ing to find. Literature. The Movies." The call is an alternative to these forms and to their complicity in the obfuscation of death. This structure is replicated numerous times toward the end of the novel. Right after Clevenger's call, its structure is replicated by the incantatory list of "American names" recited by a xenophobic evangelical preacher (365). As if to immediately counteract the link between this kind of speech and any particular set of politics, the radio program is followed immediately by one from David's old friend, Warren, who provides his own litany of Third World revolutionaries (369).

It is against this inescapable but authentic violence that *Americana* tries to reconceive itself. Recovering from an orgy of sex, violence, and desecration that David gets drawn into at Clevenger's track before taking off, and having just escaped from a one-armed man who promises to sodomize him with his enormous cock, David comes to a self-realization: "I felt it was literature I had been confronting these past days, the archetypes of the dismal mystery, sons and daughters of the archetypes, images that could not be certain which of two confusions held less terror, their own or whatever they might become if it ever faced the truth" (377). *Americana*, like Bell's journey, this passage tells us, is about confronting the true violence of America, one that emerges from literary narratives but proves itself greater. Literature cannot do justice to the violence it spawns, although DeLillo will keep trying, and keep insisting on his failure.

A.E.I.O.U.: *THE NAMES* AND THE POLITICS OF LANGUAGE

"How is it so many people know three, four, five languages?"
"That is politics too," he said, and his teeth showed yellowish in the mass of hair. "The politics of occupation, the politics of dispersal, the politics of resettlement, the politics of military bases." (57)
The Names

In an early, first-page review of *The Names* from the *New York Times Book Re-view*, Michael Wood locates, "between the tidy scheme and the easygoing diffu-sion," something not truly other than language but that which usually goes by a different name: politics.[6] My reading of *The Names* aims to flesh out the ambig-uous connection Wood gestures at between the political concerns of the novel and its pervasive nonsemantic language. The plot of the novel centers on James Axton, a former freelance writer who has gotten a job as a "risk analyst" for a company that sells political risk insurance for multinational corporations. He divides his time between various locations in the Middle East and the subcontinent, where he does business, and Greece, where he has an office in Athens. Also in Greece are his wife Kathryn, from whom he is separated, and his son Tap. Kathryn and Tap live on an island where she works on an archeological dig for a humane and soulful expert in ancient alphabets, Owen Brademas. Tap is writing a novel based on Owen's Pentacostal upbringing on the American prairie during the depression. Much of *The Names* is made up of the cerebral conversations between Axton and his expatriate friends at drunken dinner parties, but the plot proper involves Axton's and Brademas's increasing obsession with an obscure cult that, the two discover, commit ritual murders when carefully identified victims wander voluntarily into a location with initials that match their own. Only when this pattern is realized does the cult set upon the victim with their iron tools, usually hammers.

The epigraph to this section comes from a conversation Axton has with a character I have not yet mentioned and concerns an aspect of the book I have not yet described. The man who insists that language is political is a Greek businessman named Eliades. From the beginning, Eliades is suspicious of Axton and tries to lure him into debates about the nature of U.S. power. By the end of the novel we are led to believe that Eliades is either a spy or a covert revolutionary and that he is involved in the shooting that wounds David Keller, an American banker and friend of Axton. Axton, for his part, learns only at the end of the novel that Eliades' suspicions about him were true: unbeknownst to him, the risk insurance company he worked for was a front for the CIA and Axton is left wondering whether the assassins had intended to kill him instead.

I will return momentarily to the political narrative in play here, but I want to pause for a moment on the character of Eliades. The importance of names can hardly be overestimated in this novel, and so it is noteworthy that Eliades is the only character whose *whole* name is carefully hidden from us. We meet the character Eliades, but there are also references to a Greek named Andreas. Although never clarified, an alert reader can deduce that they are one and the same: the man's full name is Andreas Eliades. Because the cult always murders people based on their initials, James starts noticing the importance of initials too, such as when he realizes while walking the hills that make up the city of Amman that he is approaching the hill known as Jebel Amman: "Jebel Amman/James Axton" (158). I do not want to connect Andreas Eliades' initials to a place but to a literary pun. For an author who has acknowledged the profound influence of James Joyce on his work, I take his initials to encode a reference to a famous pun from *Ulysses*. Andreas Eliades, in other words, is a latter day A. E., whose name Stephen Daedalus puns upon in order to acknowledge the immense literary and economic debts he shall never be able to fully repay. The implications of the allusion are complex. It takes up the cliché of the debt the Western world owes to Greek civilization and rethinks what kind of debt is owed and for what. Not only does the novel ask us to acknowledge that the sources of "our" civilization are much more geographically diffuse—spanning the Middle East, parts of Africa, and the subcontinent—it insists that in civilization itself lies the origin and continuing practice of barbarism.

Thus, while the characters in the novel constantly insist upon the radical difference between themselves and the cult, the novel refutes those claims and suggests there are important commonalities between these businessmen for multinational corporations and the cult members from whom they try to distinguish themselves. The cult does not just taint Owen Brademas, who becomes so close that he is unwillingly claimed by them as a member. James, too, can be seen as an unwitting and reluctant member. Although he satisfies his obsession with the cult through Brademas and through old friend and filmmaker Frank Volterra, James displays an immediate and natural understanding of the cult, divining first the logic of their ritual murder and then figuring out where they are and how they operate. As James speculates when he finds out that he has been working for the CIA all along, perhaps "those who engage knowingly were less guilty than the people who carried out their designs" (317). James may have thought he was merely engaging in small-talk with a bunch of apolitical businessmen, but it turns out he has been an active member of America's own murderous cult. For as James sees it, "If America is the world's living myth, then the CIA is America's myth" (317). While we might think that Axton's sense of guilt goes too far, DeLillo wants us to see that his prior willingness to engage in the kind of work he does, work that Kathryn thinks is politically and ethically suspect, is of a piece with the kind of cruelty that calls for committing murder in the name of linguistic symmetry. For just as the cult finds an unmatchable satisfaction on killing once the initials of place and victim have been correlated, so too does James's work revolve around identifying correspondences. In the midst of an argument with Charles Maitland, an engineer whose wife, Ann, has been having an affair with Eliades, the two men develop the following riff:

> "Weaving districts are becoming inaccessible. Whole countries in fact. It's almost too late to go to the source. It is too late in many cases. They seem to go together, carpet-weaving and political instability."
> We thought about this.
> "Or martial law and pregnant women," I said.
> "Yes," he said slowly, looking at me. "Or gooey desserts and queues for petrol."
> "Plastic sandals and public beheadings."
> "Pious concern for the future of the Bedouins. What does that go with?" (176)

James and Charles are not merely wittily demonstrating their intimate knowledge of the region, nor is DeLillo merely satirizing the kind of mathematical formulas that an insurance company might use to calibrate the risk of political instability. James and Charles are revealing how close the linguistic structures that constitute their own daily activities are to those of the cult. Even Rowser, James's boss, a man who, unlike James, does not think of the work they do as merely a job, responds to James's repetition of the phrase "war zone" with a comment that demonstrates his sensitivity to the nonsemantic, sonic pleasures of his own jargon: "It has a ring, doesn't it" (50). In *The Names* the distinction between a rational thirst for order and a spiritual appreciation of nonsemantic linguistic patterns cannot be maintained. One bleeds into the next and both are complicit in the production of violence.

That is not to say that the novel does not try to imagine an immersion in the materiality of language that would not be cruel. As James himself realizes on his final, long-delayed trip to Athens' most famous tourist attraction, "[T]he Parthenon was not a thing to study but to feel. It wasn't aloof, rational, timeless, pure. . . . It wasn't a relic species of dead Greece, but part of the living city below us" (330). Axton wants to think that the living city is itself sacralized by language, by the living speech of a polyglot humanity. Hearing the babble of the crowds, he thinks, "This is a place to enter in crowds, to seek company and talk. Everyone is talking. I move past the scaffolding and walk down the steps, hearing one language after another, rich, harsh, mysterious, strong. This is what we bring to the temple, not prayer or chant or slaughtered rams. Our offering is language" (331). To offer language as a sacrifice involves more than just speaking, more than just having small talk and conversation. It also seems to involve the shattering of language itself into its nonsignifying alphabetic parts. Thus, while DeLillo asks us to accept the intimate talk that binds humans together in fellowship as an alternative to what the cult and the CIA do, it is not clear that the difference between the two can be maintained. As Hungerford has pointed out, Tap's story of a character much like Owen Brademas, who tries but fails to speak in tongues, constitutes a literary practice that intervenes where religious experience is no longer tenable. As James sees it, Tap's misspellings "contain curious perceptions about the words themselves, second and deeper meanings, original meanings" (313). Even more important than those buried meanings is the crucially "inarticulate wish to delight me" (314) that James reads in the uncorrected mistakes. Instead of speaking in tongues, literature is renewed and remade by a child's untutored vernacular. But even Tap's writings can be tainted. His words, after all, are "mangled" like the corpses attacked by the cult. DeLillo's offering, in *The Names* and, as we shall see, in *Libra*, is a language that has taken on the sublime qualities of the shattered skull.

The heavy thudding surprise, the sudden insult. Even after you think you've seen all the ways violence can surprise a man, along comes something you've never imagined. How much force do bullets have to exert if they can hit a man in the chest and make his hat fly four feet in the air, straight up? It was a lesson in the laws of motion and a reminder to all men that nothing is assured. (188)

   Libra

If in *Americana* DeLillo seeks a language that admits and acknowledges its violence rather than hiding it, in *The Names* the complicity of language with violence is a problem that must be acknowledged and then mitigated as much as possible. In *Libra* DeLillo understands violence as that which surpasses and overmatches language. Although the novel follows *The Names* in showing how the human passion for pattern leads to murder, it departs from that text in suggesting that once violence occurs it cannot be recuperated by the language that released it. The assassination of President Kennedy, the violent event to which the novel is addressed, is presented as though untouched by the repetitive language that has percolated in its wake.

This description may seem odd given that *Libra*, more than any other DeLillo novel with the exception of *White Noise*, is so committed to demonstrating the power of language to structure, and even generate, reality. At many points in *Libra* it looks as though reality has become thoroughly textual, and nowhere more so than in the story of how Oswald becomes a "patsy." That story takes up much of the novel, and is told in alternating chapters; the first set, titled with a place name, provide a condensed biography of Lee Harvey Oswald starting with his years in the Bronx near where DeLillo himself grew up. The other set, with places and dates attached to each individual chapter, traces the emerging plot, among a group of anti-Castro former CIA agents, to stage a "surgical miss" on JFK. They want the attempted assassination to be traced back to Cuba so that the administration will recommit, in the wake of the failed Bay of Pigs Invasion, to overthrowing Castro.[7] From the outset, the initial plotters have the fabrication of a character in mind; they plan to "do the whole thing with paper. Passports, drivers' licenses, address books. Our team of shooters disappears but the police find a trail" (28). Even Oswald conceives of himself in fully textualized terms, making up his identity first by studying Marxist texts that he cannot understand and then by memorizing the Marine's manual left around the house by his brother. He later creates multiple pseudonyms built around elaborate linguistic games and forges documents that he then uses to establish his political credentials among competing factions and opposed political camps. Oswald's behavior reinforces the idea that there is no part of the self that is not subject to, and constituted by, the world of signs.

Yet against this insistence on the constructed nature of the world stands violence. It is the gruesome materiality of Kennedy's shattered body that ultimately reveals the limits of discourse, even if—as in *Americana* and *The Names*—language is dangerously complicit in the production of corpses. Appearing four times in *Libra* is this sentence: "There is a world inside the world" (13, 47, 153, 277).[8] While *Libra* contains a few other phrases that recur throughout the text, this phrase speaks directly to the model of the corporeal, nontextual real that *Libra* ultimately promotes, one in which the reality of violence is hidden by false discourse.[9] This reading of the phrase admittedly turns DeLillo's critique of paranoia against the text: at the most basic level, the phrase is used to show how Oswald and others think the world is keeping secrets from them.[10] But while on one level Oswald's search for occulted information is discredited, the reality instantiated by violence appears as something that is all too often hidden from sight. Real violence is the secret that language, as in *Americana*, keeps from us.

In making such a claim I am directly contradicting DeLillo's own account. In an essay entitled *American Blood*, DeLillo describes the assassination as that which has shattered reality, not instantiated it: "What has become unraveled since that afternoon in Dallas is ... the sense of a coherent reality most of us shared. We seem from that moment to have entered a world of randomness and ambiguity."[11] While this is a dubious, if pervasive, lapsarian myth, it suggests how it is that violence can at once disrupt our sense of reality, as DeLillo claims, and constitute it. The key is the adjective "coherent." The assassination in *Libra* is shown to have disrupted the coherence of a concept of reality that is now revealed to have been false. In its wake we are able to have a more authentic encounter with a sublimely incoherent real. "The world inside the world" signals this hidden but still intact reality that the assassination will bring to the surface.

The character Nicholas Branch, the CIA historian hired to write the "secret history" of the assassination, articulates the precedence that the gruesome materiality of violence takes over the documents and narratives that aim to illuminate it. Interspersed throughout the novel, these segments from Branch's point of view constitute a third temporal zone: the post-assassination present. While some critics have read Branch as a dupe of the Warren Commission, his point of view is consistently authoritative.[12] Having sifted for years through the documents regularly sent to him, Branch describes a shift in the archival material sent to him by the CIA curator. Along with photographs of shattered goat heads and of gelatin models of the president's skull, Branch receives

an actual warped bullet that has been fired for test purposes through the wrist of a seated cadaver. We are on another level here, Branch thinks. Beyond documents now. They want me to *touch* and *smell*.

He doesn't know why they are sending him this particular grisly material after all these years. Shattered bone and horror. That's all it means to him. There's nothing to understand, no insights to be had from these pictures and statistics, from this melancholy bullet with its nose leveled and spread like a penny left on trolley tracks. (How old he is.) The bloody goat heads seem to mock him. He begins to think this is the point. They are rubbing his face in the blood and gunk. They are mocking him. They are saying in effect, "Here, look, these are the true images. This is your history. Here is a blown-out skull for you to ponder. Here is lead penetrating bone." (299)

Against all those moments in which reality seems to be vulnerable to linguistic construction, the sheer physicality of the dead president's body suddenly shifts the balance. Ironically invoking the rhetoric of representation, Branch takes the Curator to be insisting that history cannot do justice to a past made up of shattered bodies. The assassination reinstates the primacy of material reality above and beyond its textual construction. And just as the president's body is penetrated by a foreign object, Branch experiences his once-removed encounter with the physicality of violence as analogously shattering. Destroyed along with his calm is his belief that his work as a historian should, or could, be accomplished. Confronted with apparent senselessness of a broken, opened body, Branch loses confidence in the possibility that the linguistic interventions of historical research and writing can recuperate the loss of meaning wrought by the assassination. In its insistence that violence stops the onslaught of discourse in its tracks, Branch's reaction to violence offers a *mise en abyme* of *Libra*'s own approach to the "shattered bone and horror" of Kennedy's assassination.

This becomes clear in the chapter in which the story of Oswald's desire for historic significance and the story of the agents' search for a patsy come together in a moment of bloody horror. Although narrative has brought the characters and readers to this moment of violence, the chapter in which Kennedy is killed is where plot falls away. The chapter entitled "22 November" is a meditation on the skull of the president. This chapter represents the climax of the novel but is formally different from it. While all the chapters of *Libra* are marked by small breaks, where the narrative makes a transition from one character to another, "22 November" is relentlessly disjunctive. Only twenty-seven pages long, it consists of twenty-seven short sections, the shortest of which is a mere thirteen letters ("HE LAAAAAAAAAA" [405]). Unlike some of the fractured chapters that focus on Oswald, the twenty-seven small sections move among the widest range of characters to be found anywhere in the novel. The narration rests for a moment, never to stop again, in the consciousness of various witnesses to the assassination, from invented characters to individuals identifiable from the Zapruder film and the Warren Commission. The effect is one of both disjunction and repetition as the same event is refracted through the minds of different characters.

These refractions have remarkable consistency, focusing as they do on the materiality of violence, specifically on the blood, bone, and tissue that leaks out from the body of the president. *Libra*'s concern with this matter has a folkloric resonance: Jacqueline Kennedy's attempt to retrieve fragments of her husband's skull and brain, visible in the Zapruder film, has long held a morbid popular interest. This moment is in fact narrated twice in *Libra*. In the section of the chapter that narrates the activities of the people inside the presidential limousine, Nellie Connolly notices that "the third shot sent stuff just everywhere. Tissue, bone fragments, tissue in pale wads, watery mess, tissue, blood, brain matter all over them" (399). Moments later she sees "that Jackie was out of the car, gone off the end of the car, but now was somehow back." Finally she hears her say, "I have his brains in my hand." Driving home this encounter with the broken body is the appearance of this same incident in the narration of another character. Agent Clinton J. Hill, who witnesses the assassination from his place on the limousine's left running board, notices that "[she] was trying to retrieve part of her husband's skull" (402).

The First Lady's attempt to retrieve the fragments are counterposed with the attempt of Bobby W. Hargis, who rode as a motorcycle escort, to avoid them: "He turned his body right, keeping the motorcycle heading west on Elm, and then the blood and matter, the unforgettable thing, the sleet of bone and blood and tissue struck him in the face. He thought he'd been shot. The stuff hit him like a spray of buckshot and he heard it ping and splatter on his helmet. People were down on the grass. He kept his mouth closed tight so the fluid would not ooze in" (399). Yet another of the sections deals with the reactions of a witness on the grassy knoll. Again the material effects of the assassination on the body of the president are the main focus: "The man in the white sweater, applauding, saw the stuff just erupt from the President's head. . . . Someone with a movie camera stood on an abutment over there, aiming this way, and the man in the white sweater, hands suspended now at belt level, was thinking he ought to go to the ground, he ought to fall right now. A misty light around the President's head. Two pink-white jets of tissue rising from the mist. The movie camera running" (400). The "stuff" that erupts from Kennedy's head, like the two "jets of tissue" that provide a ghoulish halo, are, on the one hand, part of the pattern through which *Libra* represents the assassination. Yet we are invited to read that pattern as the shattering of pattern itself. It is where we finally encounter the "world inside the world," the real that "coherent reality" normally manages to obscure. This should bring into focus for us that, unlike Branch, DeLillo *does* produce a text out of this blood and gunk. Branch's difficulties, and the novel's attempts to link its own narrative to them, look increasingly wishful. *Libra* develops an ingeniously flexible narrative of that assassination even as it asks to be read as an exercise in incomprehension. The novel insists upon the unrepresentability of violence against the evidence that is its own representation.

"SOMEONE FALLING. FALLING MAN.":
VIOLENCE AND THE ARTIST'S PERFORMANCE

> But this, what happened, it's way too big, it's outside someplace, on the other side
> of the world. You can't get to these people or even see them in their pictures in
> the paper. You can see their faces but what does it mean? Means nothing to call
> them names. I'm a name caller from before I was born. Do I know what to call these
> people? (64)
>
> *Falling Man*

Recalling not merely the diction but also the logic behind *Libra*'s insistence that "there is a world inside the world," *Falling Man* begins with this sentence: "It was not a street anymore, but a world, a time and space of falling ash and near night" (3). A man who has escaped from the collapsing twin towers on September 11, 2001, wanders away from the physical world of ash and night into the transformed world of New York. The plot of the novel centers on this man, Keith Neudecker, and on his estranged wife Lianne. Other important characters are their child, Justin; another survivor of the collapse of the towers, Florence, with whom Keith has an affair; Lianne's frail, urbane mother, Nina (who has died by the time the novel ends); and Nina's longtime lover, a German art dealer named Martin Ridnour. Martin's real name is Ernst Hechinger, and before he went underground, he was a member of *Kommune 1* in Germany and then in the Italian Red Brigades. Lianne's father killed himself long ago. Everyone in the novel is stunned by 9/11 and much of the text is spent attending to the strained conversations and odd behaviors that emerge in the aftermath of the crisis. Justin spends time with his friends scanning the sky for planes and trying to learn about the mysterious "Bill Lawton," who he believes—having misheard the name bin Laden when whispered by adults—is the mastermind of the destruction. Keith has his affair and becomes increasingly obsessed with playing poker while Lianne ministers to a group of Alzheimer's patients, encouraging them to write about the tragic events.

These closely intertwined narratives are joined by two other threads. The first is that of a performance artist—the most literal of the various falling men and women who inhabit the book—who uses a safety harness to stage impromptu repetitions of the "suicides" of those who jumped from the burning towers. This artist is assumed by characters in the novel to be drawing on a specific photograph that showed an oddly elegant and composed fall from the towers by an unknown man (221). This reference within the novel is to an actual picture taken by Richard Drew, which was itself the subject of an article in *Esquire*.[13] Although the photograph was published widely in the immediate aftermath of the event, soon after any publication of it was condemned as an exploitation of private horror. I will return to the performance artist at the end of this chapter, but there remains one more thread of the novel to delineate. Interspersed among the chapters that take place in New York is the story of one of the hijackers, Hammad: we first meet him in Germany as he is becoming radicalized. The astonishing final chapter of the novel, titled "In the Hudson Corridor," narrates first Hammad's experience in the airplane after the hijackers have taken it over and then switches upon impact with the building to narrating Keith's experience in the burning building. The novel thus completes a circuit as we end by more fully inhabiting the "world . . . of falling ash and near night" with which the text began.

ⁿ

Falling Man rehearses a number of the models DeLillo has developed in other novels to describe the relationship between violence and language. The main difference is that unlike in *Americana*, *Mao II*, or *The Names*, DeLillo no longer has to worry that violence is hidden from view: it is finally happening in New York rather than Vietnam, Beirut, or Abu Dhabi. And unlike in *Libra*, where Oswald's pathology exemplifies a national problem, in *Falling Man* the violence with which language is complicit seems to genuinely come from without. What remains consistent is that, as in the earlier novels, *Falling Man* explores narrative as an expression of the human need to control, structure, and ultimately stave off uncertainty, and promotes the aesthetic and ethical potential held out by language once it has been stripped of both plot and meaning.

In the novel's worst-case scenario, narrative is implicated in the atrocity that was 9/11. For Hammad, "The plot shapes every breath he takes. This is the truth he has always looked for without knowing how to name it or where to search. They are together. There is no word they can speak, he and the others, that does not come back to this" (176). Just as in *Libra*, "the plot" conflates the logic of conspiracy with narrative itself. And, again, as in *Libra*, wherein the plot provides Oswald with a sense of purpose and social standing, in *Falling Man* plots function in the same way across different cultures. They are stabilizing forces that offer certainty, structure identity, and foster connection to a select group of others. Although Martin/Ernst insists that we should look at the jihadists' thirst for plot within the specific political context of U.S. foreign policy and economic hegemony, the novel understands both Islamic terrorism and Martin's left-wing ideologies to be born of the same need for fellowship and order: "[T]hey're part of the same classical pattern. They have their theorists. They have their visions of world brotherhood" (147).

But while *Falling Man* acknowledges the general complicity of language in violence, and reaffirms that the West has its "own" terrorists, it also reframes the issue of complicity as that of the witness rather than the perpetrator. For while Hammad's vision of world brotherhood is murderous, DeLillo exposes its broader reach and effects. It is the master narrative that rules social relations in *Falling Man*: it connects not just Hammad to his fellow jihadists or Ernst to his old communards, but Keith to his poker buddies and Justin to his friends. If in some cases the plot that fosters community produces terrorism, it is also shown to be a necessary and inevitable part of the process of recovering from terrorism. Perhaps because the focus in the novel is on the victims of violence in *Falling Man*—unlike in *Americana* or *Libra*, where even peaceful Americans are implicitly seen as victims of their own murderous rapaciousness or paranoia—DeLillo emphasizes the therapeutic value of narrative, its ability to comfort. This is particularly clear in the descriptions of the poker games Keith has been playing for years with a group of buddies, one of whom he watched die in the towers. The narrator, focalized through Keith, says, "The cards fell randomly, no assignable cause, but he remained the agent of free choice. Luck, chance, no one knew what these things were. These things were only assumed to affect events. He had memory, judgment, the ability to decide what is true, what is alleged, when to strike, when to fade" (211). Like Hammad's plot, the poker game offers a satisfying illusion of limited agency, narrowing the scope of contingency and chance through the production of rules and procedures. Similarly, Keith engages in a series of physical therapy exercises that appear in the text as healing through their reimposition of an endlessly repeatable sequence: "[T]he wrist extension, the ulnar deviations. These were the true countermeasure to the damage he'd suffered in the towers, in the descending chaos. It was not the MRI and not the surgery that brought him closer to well-being. It was this modest home program, the counting of seconds, the counting of repetitions, the times of day he reserved for the exercises, the ice he applied following each set of exercises" (40).

Although Keith's desire for a sense of control is shown in these cases to be understandable as a response to his experience of calamity, the imposition of familiar narratives is not what the novel itself aims to achieve. The novel is clear that such circumscribed narrative games cannot tell us anything truthful about that "world of ash and night"; they can only give us temporary refuge from it. But unlike in *The Names*, in *Falling Man* the elimination of the narrative component, the stripping of language down to the meaningless matter of ritual incantation, is not a solution either. If anything, narratives in *Falling Man* seem to lead inevitably to the production of ritualized incantation. In Keith's earlier games, when his now-dead office buddy was still alive, the men engaged in a frenzy of delimitation, of tightening the plot. The men initially played many different kinds of poker but slowly whittled their play down to one game, five card stud. They banned food, then any alcohol that wasn't dark brown, then "sport's talk, television talk, movie titles" (99). This whittling down is itself associated with the calming pleasures of asceticism, self-denial, ritual, and rules—poker as spiritual discipline. And central to this discipline is the power of the word. As the narrator explains it: "[T]he dealer skimmed the cards over the green baize, never failing to announce the game, five card stud, even though it was the only game they now played. The small dry irony of these announcements faded after a time and the words became a proud ritual, formal, indispensable, each dealer in turn, five card stud, and they loved doing this straight-faced because where else would they encounter the kind of mellow tradition exemplified by the needless utterance of a few archaic words" (99). The narrative of the poker game here has the power to whittle the world down to ritual and in the process to strip language of both plot and meaning.

Falling Man is full of phrases like "five card stud," phrases that are uttered with gnomic intensity. A partial list would include "natura morta" (12), "organic shrapnel" (16, 66), "gentle fist" (40), "muzzle blast" (41), "Light-skinned black woman" (92), "died by his own hand" (169, 218), "unremarkable," and "infarct" (206). Although some of these words and phrases are first noted because of the complexities and paradoxes of meaning they contain, nearly all of them are offered as ritualized incantations. When Lianne thinks of the phrase "died by his own hand," she associates them with her father's suicide and calls them "beautiful words that had an archaic grain, Middle English, Old Norse. She imagined the words engraved on an old slant tombstone in a neglected churchyard somewhere in New England" (218). Similarly, Justin's attempts to speak only in monosyllables are characterized as "nearly ritualistic" (160).

These words do not fully realize the aesthetic ambition of *Falling Man*, but they are continuous with it. The aesthetic ambition of the novel is exemplified internally in the performance art of David Janiak, and it is realized in prose form in the final chapter of the book. Like Nicholas Branch in *Libra*, Janiak is an internal surrogate for DeLillo himself. But if Branch represents the failure of words in the face of Kennedy's corpse, Janiak's art serves a model for what DeLillo himself hopes to do. Much like the photograph of the unknown "jumper" by Richard Drew, Janiak incites anger, even outrage. Toward the end of the novel Janiak is found dead of natural causes, and Lianne, who saw him fall twice, tries to learn more about him. Her Internet search yields headlines like "MAYOR SAYS FALL MAN MORONIC" and old information about a symposium at the New School titled "Falling Man as Heartless Exhibitionist or Brave New Chronicler of the Age of Terror?" (220). This last satirical allusion to academia surely recalls the man who has written no less than four other novels about terrorism; that is, DeLillo himself. Also suggestive of DeLillo, who has been reluctant to talk to the media, is the fact that Janiak "said nothing about it when questioned by reporters after one of his arrests. He said nothing when asked whether anyone close to him had been lost in the attacks. He had no comment to make to the media on any subject" (222).

The David Janiak thread is, among other things, DeLillo's way of addressing in advance the charge, which he surely anticipated, that any literary treatment of 9/11 would be exploitative, in bad taste, or otherwise inappropriate. But while this may be one reason for Janiak's prominence in the text, the character also allows DeLillo to make a positive case for the role that literature can play in a world marked by violence. Unlike the ritualized language used by the characters of the novel, the art of the falling man, and by implication DeLillo's own art, promises to help New Yorkers process the sudden violence that has traumatized them. Lianne sees Janiak twice. The first time she sees him "there were people shouting at him, outraged at the spectacle, the puppetry of human desperation, a body's last fleet breath and what it held. It held the gaze of the world, she thought. There was the awful openness of it, something we'd not seen, the single falling figure that trails a collective dread, body coming down among us all" (33). The performance is like the repetition of trauma, one that might bring with it the opportunity to process the shock of the initial spectacle.

Yet if the falling man's art is the repetition of a traumatic event, then the trauma is located in the act of witnessing someone else's death rather than in being threatened with your own imminent harm. Indeed, the novel works to conflate Keith's experiences in the towers with the much more distanced acts of "witnessing" had by every TV viewer. In the final pages of the novel, where Keith's experiences in the tower are narrated, he repeatedly catches out of the corner of his eye the sight of bodies falling past his field of vision. After trying to save his friend, Rumsey, and then witnessing him die, Keith confuses that body with those he sees falling past the window. This moment reinforces the homology between survivors of the towers, like Keith, and those who saw falling men on TV or in photographs. Confronted by the performances of the falling man, all these witnesses are now collectively invited to confront a spectacle that they had been unable to process at the time.

Falling Man (and the falling man's art) is about the violence that you watch and about the kind of linguistic response that you might produce in its aftermath. The second time Lianne sees the falling man she sees him setting up his safety harnesses and this helps her to clarify what he is doing. She realizes that he is setting up his fall to be seen by the passengers of a passing train: "There would be those aboard who see him standing there and those who see him jump, all jarred out of their reveries or their newspapers or muttering stunned into their cell phones. . . . There was one thing for them to say, essentially. Someone falling. Falling man. She wondered if this was his intention, to spread the word this way, by cell phone, intimately, as in the towers and hijacked planes" (165). What she imagines him trying to produce is something that sounds very much like the ritualized language that she, and every other character of the novel, has been producing. To the phrases "organic shrapnel" and "gentle fist," we can add "falling man." If this language originally seemed, if not pathetic then tragically inadequate, its appearance here seems to require a reevaluation. Like DeLillo's impressive representation of what it might have been like inside the towers before they crumbled, the incantatory words uttered by the onlookers begin to look like the first step toward an authentic representation of violence.

The goal of all this seems in many ways similar to what we have seen in *Americana*, *The Names*, and *Libra*, but with some important shifts of emphasis. *The Names* is a political allegory about American power, a novel that worries about our fascination with violence and our failure to take responsibility for the violence that America sponsors abroad. In *Falling Man* there is no sense that this fascination must be purged or rehabilitated, just as there is only the barest and most depoliticized gesture at our complicity in the production of violence.[14] In the aftermath of an act of spectacular violence we can finally call our own, *Falling Man* focuses not on purifying language of its complicity with violence but on calibrating language to the sensitivities and needs of the American victim. Whereas in nearly all of his other novels, DeLillo interrogated the kind of American politics that would mistake the image of a catastrophe with the catastrophe itself, *Falling Man* draws on the spectatorial model of violence implied by the category of terrorism to recuperate for Americans an authentic experience of violence, one that dovetails with but also departs from his long-standing model of how literature might be related to violence. As Lianne says of the falls of the performance artist, "There was no photograph of that fall. She was the photograph, the photosensitive surface. That nameless body coming down, this was hers to record and absorb" (223). *Falling Man* aims to be that fall and we, merely by reading it, are the photosensitive surface that captures the indelible and undying image.

after the aftermath

AMERICAN FICTION SINCE 2007

In the concluding pages of *The Empire of Trauma*, anthropologists Didier Fassin and Richard Rechtman clarify their position on "the moral economy" of trauma, an economy in which compassion, insurance payouts, local and international justice, and reparations are all circulated. Although they insist that they "have not sought to discover whether trauma is real, or whether psychological treatment of it is a good thing," they do acknowledge that their work cannot and should not evade moral evaluation. Instead, they say:

> [O]ur task is not to distinguish between good and evil, but to critique the actual conditions that produce social realities. For example, to take the founding issue that led to the creation of PTSD as a diagnosis, we do not say there are "good" and "bad" victims and that the concept of trauma makes it impossible to distinguish one from the other (North American war criminals and the Vietnamese survivors of their massacres being essentially brought together in same psychic suffering). Instead we ask what the recasting of war crimes as traumatic experiences means for the perpetrators (social recognition and financial compensation) and for the American nation as a whole (reconciliation and redemption). For us, the critique of the ways in which victims and their causes are produced, which replaces judgments of the victims themselves and of the validity of their cause, is fundamental. (280)

I am fairly certain that in this book I have made the kinds of normative judgments that Fassin and Rechtman aim to avoid. Yet the inevitability of such judgments is something they themselves make obvious when clarifying the alternative. Instead of adjudicating between the competing claims of various groups they "examine what the failure to distinguish between them in the mental health system—or even beyond the medical context in popular use of the concept of trauma—obscures about social relations, historical realities, and political situations" (280). At the very least, Fassin and Rechtman imply, to gather all these very different groups into a single category entails some kind of failure and one that risks distorting or hiding important aspects of our political and social life.

Throughout this book I have examined a set of ideas that are intimately related to the concept of trauma. However, "trauma," although included within, fails to encompass the phenomenon I address. What I call the prestige of violence entails ascribing to violence a supralinguistic reality; trauma has offered one particularly fertile, influential, and pervasive theory of this model of violence, and one whose role in disseminating it can hardly be overestimated. But I hope to have suggested that literary accounts of the unspeakable reality of violence were circulating well before the rise of trauma as a key term of cultural analysis, and continue to do so independently of the label. Like Fassin and Rechtman, I want to suggest that understanding both the aesthetic forms that have disseminated these ideas and the social locations in which they have been most persuasive can clarify the "social relations, historical realities, political situations" that such ideas have habitually mystified.

Yet if my book names an ending date of 2007, it begs the question of how violence has been represented in the years since then. Are we in a definitely new age and does literary fiction reveal the nature of the transformation? The easy but honest answer—note the rare conjunction—is that it is far too soon to tell. Certainly the political situation in the decade since 9/11 has evolved. Although there were surely voices against the militarization of the U.S. response to the threat of terrorism, the nation's appetite for war is drastically dampened. The conflicts that have been fought in the name of U.S. power have been overt, not covert, but they have continued to provide the American public with new reasons to distrust official accounts. Doctored intelligence, extraordinary renditions, the use of waterboarding, the Abu Ghraib scandal, the Haditha massacre, and as-yet unnamed crimes of soldiers who killed civilians for sport in Afghanistan play like hellish repeats of the scandals over the Gulf of Tonkin resolution and My Lai, only with greater cynicism and a more entrenched sense of powerlessness. Public attention to the loss of *American* life has risen with the number of soldiers killed in action, but rather than seeing footage of combat or coffins in the media, as occurred in Vietnam, we have reports filed from embedded journalists. As occurred after Vietnam, the nation faces a public health crisis in the form of disturbed and sometimes violent veterans; although an entrenched discourse of trauma is available to interpret their distress, medical and therapeutic recourses still lag well behind the need.

On the literary scene, one simply cannot plausibly historicize the past five years. If a gulf opens up on the literary scene that will serve to distinguish the fictions produced in the immediate wake of 9/11 from those produced and honored a few more years later, we will not know it for some time. Novels by Philip Roth continue in their steady drip and with a greater focus on the trials of aged masculinity, but that is hardly a historical indicator. There continues to be a strong countertradition of finely wrought novels of domestic manners and family agon that are recognized in the marketplace of honors and accolades; writers like Jeffrey Eugenides, Marilynne Robinson, Jonathan Franzen, and Michael Chabon all come to mind as standard-bearers of such work.

My suspicion and, I confess, my hope is that the implications of conceiving of violence as both unspeakably real and immaterial is losing its persuasive power as high truth, even if it continues to sound to many like common sense. Junot Diaz's *The Brief Wondrous Life of Oscar Wao* (2007), for example, manages to simultaneously anatomize the role played by the United States in supporting violence abroad, while nonetheless insisting that in real life getting laid and watching movies is just as authentically real as the violence of a repressive state. Edward P. Jones's *The Known World* (2003), although surely not intended as such, reads like a rebuttal of that novel's idea that the horrors of slavery are unspeakable: Jones shows how it was not just speakable, but was lived every day by both slaves and slaveholders. Jones asks us to see that in order for slavery to have worked as efficiently as it did real people had to commit, endure, rationalize, and enable violence every day.

ᴄᴍ

I do not know what fiction of the next forty-five years will bring. But I hope that we can begin to respond to claims for the unspeakable reality of abstract, symbolic, and material violence with a greater curiosity about its sources, meaning, and effects. Ideally, this will not entail a parsimonious hoarding of compassion or empathy, but it will allow us to develop a more nuanced account of the uneven distribution and visibility of violence at home and abroad.

notes

INTRODUCTION. The Prestige of Violence

1. My reading of *Beloved* is indebted to both Walter Benn Michael's seminal essay on the novel and by Amy Hungerford's argument about personification. Michaels' argument that *Beloved* depends upon the ghost of Beloved to function as the technology of the transmission of memory underpins my own argument about the way the novel seeks to disavow its textuality. And Morrison's pun on "pass" is a nicely condensed example of the way that stories become personified and then privileged over the person. My argument runs counter to Hungerford's only to the extent that I see what Hungerford describes as personification as part of a process whereby texts are purged of a contaminating meaningfulness by taking on the attributes of the suffering person. See Michaels, "You Who Never Was There"; Hungerford, *The Holocaust of Texts*.

2. "What is the Best Work of American Fiction of the Last 25 Years?" *New York Times*, May 21, 2006.

3. As I will argue later in this introduction, Cormac McCarthy does not in my view promote the prestige of violence, nor do all the novels singled out by critics. The list includes novels that are largely uninterested in acts of explicit violence, like Marilynne Robinson's *Housekeeping*.

4. Bowie, *Lacan*, 110.

5. Bourdieu, "Cultural Reproduction and Social Reproduction"; Bourdieu, *Distinction*.

6. I am indebted to Yves Winter for his excellent summary of political theories of violence in his unpublished dissertation. Winter, *Beyond Blood and Coercion*.

7. Walzer, *Just and Unjust Wars*.

8. Galtung, "Violence, Peace, and Peace Research," 170.

9. Winter, *Beyond Blood and Coercion*, 4.

10. Bourdieu, *Language and Symbolic Power*.

11. The period from 1962 to 1980 has been called "the Era of the Big Sleep" by the historian Paul Boyer. Boyer, *By the Bomb's Early Light*, 5. Gerald DeGroot has said, "the period after 1962 was characterized by the rapid progression down a road called proliferation." DeGroot, *The Bomb*, ix.

12. Chollet and Goldgeier, *America Between the Wars*.

13. Lutz, *Homefront*; Paglen, *Blank Spots on the Map*.

14. Gaddis, *Strategies of Containment.*

15. For an account of the way governmental and family authorities were implicated in this crisis of confidence, see Zeretsky, *No Direction Home.*

16. For a treatment of what he characterizes as the "contemporary American urban novel of violence" see Giles, *Violence in the Contemporary American Novel.*

17. Harrington, *The Other America*; For an excellent account of the way literature registered this shift see Rotella, *October Cities.*

18. Lukacs, *The Historical Novel*; Watt, *Rise of the Novel*; Bakhtin, *The Dialogic Imagination*; McKeon, *Origins of the English Novel.* See also Lynch, *The Economy of Character.*

19. Hobarek, *The Twilight of the Middle Class*, 25.

20. Bourdieu, "Forms of Capital."

21. McGurl, *The Program Era*, 47.

22. Lowen, *Creating the Cold War University.*

23. Ohmann, "English and the Cold War"; Guillory, *Cultural Capital.*

24. Ohmann, 74.

25. Loren Glass summarizes this aspect of Guillory's argument succinctly: "Guillory sees the moment of theory as a symptomatic reaction to the declining relevance of literary study in American universities and society at large." Glass, "The End of Culture," 194.

26. White, *Metahistory*, x.

27. Hutcheon, *A Poetics of Postmodernism.*

28. Taking up postwar visual art and trying to recuperate for it an avant-garde political value that he believes it has been unjustly denied, Hal Foster understands art in the aftermath of minimalism to be interested in "the Real" in various guises. Foster, *The Return of the Real.*

29. Joseph Tabbi's work on technology as sublime postmodernist object helpfully illuminates how postmodern authors take up Kantean theories of the sublime and make it their own. A greater portion of the work on the postmodern sublime is of a different order entirely. Hayden White, Frank Ankersmit, and Jean Francois-Lyotard have all contributed works that do not so much analyze the connections between the postmodern and the sublime as contribute their own theories of the sublimity of postmodern experience and history. Other critics (such as Amy Elias) split the difference, vacillating between analyzing the draw of theories of the sublime for contemporary literature and endorsing the sublimity of the era. See esp. Tabbi, *Postmodern Sublime*; Elias, *Sublime Desire.*

30. McHale, *Postmodernist Fiction.*

31. For the modernist fascination with violence see Tratner, *Modernism and Mass Politics*; North, *The Political Aesthetic of Yeats, Eliot and Pound*; Hewitt, *Fascist Modernism.*

32. Trilling, *Beyond Culture*, xii.

33. Slotkin, *Gunfighter Nation*, 25. Another model for my analysis is John McClure's brilliant 1994 study of (mostly) postwar novelists. His analysis of the way the romance form is contested and reworked by these authors to articulate their politically ambivalent responses to the project of imperialism is both convincing and illuminating. McClure, *Late Imperial Romance.*

34. Hutcheon, *A Poetics of Postmodernism.*

35. Jameson, *Postmodernism.*

36. Literary critics have been able to quote historians in support of this view. Hayden White, who has had a particularly powerful influence on literary scholarship in the postwar period, explicitly declared the twentieth century "holocaustal" for having generated what he describes as a level of destruction and human suffering "the nature, scope, and implications of which no prior age could have imagined." White, "The Modernist Event," 20.

37. Rothberg, *Traumatic Realism*; Elias, *Sublime Desire*; Felman and Laub, *Testimony*; Caruth, *Unclaimed Experience*; Whitehead, *Trauma Fiction*.

38. For a brilliant look at the way trauma has come to dominate political and humanitarian discourse in Europe, see Fassin and Rechtman, *The Empire of Trauma*.

39. Nearly all of their work on trauma was written in the aftermath of the scandal caused by revelations that de Man had willingly written for a collaborationist Belgian newspaper during World War II. For an excellent analysis of Felman's essay on de Man see Hungerford, "Memorizing Memory."

40. See, for example, Cvetkovich, *An Archive of Feeling*; LaCapra, *Writing History, Writing Trauma*; Gordon, *Ghostly Matters*; Kaplan, *Trauma Culture*; Saltzman and Rosenberg, eds., *Trauma and Visuality in Modernity*.

41. Caruth published the work of the prominent neurobiologist Bessel Van Der Kolk in this same volume. He has since published a widely read work for the general public on trauma, but Caruth's work tends to draw very loose analogical support from his neurobiological studies.

42. Caruth explains that "[t]he Japanese man has, himself, missed the catastrophe at Hiroshima. . . . Through [his missing of the event], his story . . . bears the impact of a trauma." Caruth, *Unclaimed Experience*, 40.

43. Scarry appears to invent a categorical difference where none exists. Is the "object" implied by hunger, thirst, rapture, or excitation really any more concrete than the kind of object implied by pain? The main difference between saying "I'm hungry" and "I'm hurt" is that the latter has much greater affective and ideological resonance. In a sentence that I have omitted for brevity, Scarry makes it clear that her language of objects derives from a philosophic vocabulary rather than a grammatical one. But the point of her analysis ends up collapsing such a philosophical vocabulary into a purely grammatical one. Scarry, *The Body in Pain*.

44. Van der Kolk reports finding that Broca's area, "the part of the left hemisphere [of the brain] responsible for translating personal experiences into communicable language," is not active while PTSD patients are exposed to stresses that lead to the re-experiencing of traumatic events. See Van der Kolk, McFarlane, and Weisacth, *Traumatic Stress*, 293.

CHAPTER ONE. Zembla in the *New York Times*

1. Nabokov, *Lolita*, 312. While I disagree strongly with Brian Boyd's literally fantastic reading of the novel, I think he is right to insist that the antifoundationalist Nabokov promoted by some readings of the novel is not tenable. For more on Boyd, see notes 3 and 6.

2. For the definitive theory of Botkin's authorship see Johnson, *Worlds in Regression*, 1985.

3. The earliest proponent of Shade as the sole author of *Pale Fire* was Andrew Field. Brian Boyd provides one of the later, but now standard, statements of the case. See Field, *Nabokov: His Life in Art*; Boyd, *Vladimir Nabokov: The American Years*, 425–56. Boyd has recently changed his position, offering an elaborate new reading in its stead. His recent book-length study suggests that the correspondences between the poem and commentary are the result of ghostly post-mortem assistance provided first by Hazel Shade and then by John Shade. While I disagree with this argument in too many ways to treat adequately here, his book does provide a useful overview of the history and major players in the criticism of the novel, albeit one heavily slanted toward his former camp's readings. See Boyd, *Nabokov's Pale Fire*, 114–26.

4. The earliest and still one of the only serious proponents of this view is Stegner, *Escape into Aesthetics*.

5. My claim that Nabokov's personal losses are important to the novel is not particularly original. The connection between Shade's assassination and that of Nabokov's father was first explored in depth, albeit to very different ends, in Meyer, *Find What the Sailor Has Hidden*. The loss of language is at the heart of Michael Wood's reading of the novel and of Nabokov's American novels more generally. My argument is indebted to this insight. Like Wood, I assume that while Kinbote is in all likelihood the false alter ego of a man named Botkin, we are left with almost nothing to know about Botkin other than some possible sources of his misery. See Wood, *The Magician's Doubt*.

6. We can see all this play out in Brian Boyd's recent work. Evidence of his argument that Hazel and John Shade's ghosts are responsible for the correspondences between poem and commentary, is available, he claims, to anyone with sufficient curiosity and passion. Yet in Boyd's primer on what "Outside Sources" are and are not essential, Boyd establishes the links between the fictional Zembla and its real world correlates only to dismiss them. Recalling, among other details, the seeds of Nabokov's Zembla in an article the author likely read about the first days of the League of Nations, Boyd says "the exotic details of this and other Zemblan passages . . . often conceal close equivalents in the real world just where they seem strangest, yet identifications like these, while amusing to remember or momentarily exciting to discover, tend to miss the point. If Nabokov wants us to understand something essential, he plants it firmly within the covers of his book, or indicates—if we exercise just a little curiosity, memory and imagination— exactly where we should look for it elsewhere." It is not clear why the use of the word "Dulwich" in Shade's poem is sufficient to initiate Boyd's elaborate spiritualist reading of the novel via Browning's "Pippa Passes," while Zembla, with its less "exotic" "real world" equivalents, should be ignored and its leads dismissed as mere amusements or curiosities. Boyd, *Nabakov's Pale Fire*, 82.

7. Reported in Boyd, *Vladimir Nabakov*, 709.

8. Belletto, "The Zemblan Who Came in From the Cold." Although I am not persuaded by Belletto's argument that Nabakov is critiquing rather than uncritically enacting the conflation of homosexuality with treason that Belletto locates within the logic of cold war containment, he brilliantly demonstrates the centrality of cold war political concerns to the novel as a whole. Belletto is singling out Mary McCarthy's early, ardent, and oddly apolitical review of the novel, which was the first to point out that there was a place on the map that corresponded to Zembla. See McCarthy, "A Bolt From the Blue," 22.

9. Much of the historical background that follows is drawn directly from Paul Boyer's work on the subject, especially *Fallout* but also his study of the early post-nuclear years. See Paul Boyer, *Fallout*, 61–86.

10. Nabokov eventually abandoned plans for the article. Boyd, *Vladimir Nabakov*, 417. Nabokov, *Selected Letters*, 106, 108.

11. See *New York Times*, July 20, 1959; Prescott, "Books of the Times," *New York Times*, July 20, 1959, 23. Also among the items that appear largely unchanged is a quote from Carl Sandburg about the Soviet exhibition at the New York Coliseum and the headline "Iraqi Red Revolt and Army Mutiny Erupt at Kirkuk," *New York Times*, July 20, 1959, 10.

12. "Thirty Children Join Picnic of Nations," *New York Times*, July 20, 1959, 12; "Upset Stomach Troubles Queen; She Cancels Program in Yukon," *New York Times*, July 20, 1959, 10.

13. Wiscari, "Khrushchev Calls Off Plan For a Visit to Scandinavia," *New York Times*, July 21, 1959, A1.

14. Weaver, "State Bar Urges Major Change In Statute on Criminally Insane," *New York Times*, July 21, 1959, A1.

15. Shakespeare, *Timon of Athens, The Arden Shakespeare* (London: Routledge, 1994), IV.iii.439–45.

16. Wood, *Magician's Doubt*, 176.

17. For the most recent and thorough treatment of ghosts in *Pale Fire* see Boyd, *Nabokov's Pale Fire*; Alexandrov, *Nabokov's Otherworld*. An early work on the subject is W. W. Rowe, *Nabokov's Spectral Dimension*.

18. Much of the recent discussion of homophobia and homosexuality in Nabokov's work was initiated by an excellent piece by Lev Grossman. See Grossman, *The Gay Nabokov*. For the debate that ensued among Nabokov scholars, many but not all of whom vehemently defended Nabokov from the perceived slander, see the Nabokov-L archives for May 2000.

19. Grossman, *Gay Nabokov*.

CHAPTER TWO. Monks and "the Mind of Watts"

1. Pynchon, "A Journey Into The Mind of Watts."

2. Frank Palmeri makes a similar point in service of a different argument when he says that "Tristero might not be a historical plot, but its legacy of disinheritance is nevertheless a historical truth." Palmeri, "Neither Literally nor as Metaphor," 993.

3. N. Katherine Hayles has argued that "The . . . ambiguity of the novel rests between a postmodern view that renders irrelevant the distinctions between life and art, and a realism that reaches beyond construction toward a reality that exists whether or not we apprehend it" (97). My own argument differs mainly in my core assumption that the belief in something beyond our constructions does not so much depart from postmodernism as underlie its practice. Hayles, "A Metaphor of God Knew How Many Parts."

4. The theme of the disinherited is treated most explicitly toward the end of the novel during a section explaining the history of the Tristero (132).

5. For a very different reading of the "crying" at the novel's end, see Castillo, "Borges and Pynchon: The Tenuous Symmetries of Art."

6. Mattesich, *Lines of Flight*, 57.

7. See Eddins, *The Gnostic Pynchon*.

8. O'Donnell, *New Essays*, 1.

9. There is also a brief reference to Vietnam made by John Nefastis, who hopes to have sex with Oedipa on the couch while catching some television news on the subject (86).

10. Quoted from Pynchon's letters in Gussow, "Pynchon's letters nudge his mask."

11. Markusen, et al., *The Rise of the Gunbelt*, 82.

12. The technology produced in Southern California allowed soldiers to be distant from those they killed. The ethical implications of the "air war" are a common theme in the firsthand literature on the war produced by veterans and journalists.

13. Karnow, *Vietnam*.

14. Oedipa's trip to Berkeley seems to occur at least a few months after the Sproul Hall steps were declared, following lengthy protests by the Free Speech Movement, an open area for political activity. That decision was made in early January 1965 by the newly appointed acting Chancellor, Martin Meyerson. But the Vietnam Day Committee was not formed until the massive sit-in of May 21–22, 1965, known as Vietnam Day. Pynchon paints himself in much the same light as Oedipa, and echoes many of the same themes as are found in the passage above, in his introduction to *Slow Learner*. Pynchon, *Slow Learner*, 6–7.

15. McCann and Szalay, "Do You Believe in Magic?"

16. That said, the YAF, with its internal conflicts between libertarian antistatists and traditional anticommunists, is certainly relevant to the political questions the novel raises about the proper role of the state. Andrew, *The Other Side of the Sixties*.

17. Quang Duc is important to my reading of *The Armies of the Night* (chapter 4). While I do not discuss *American Pastoral* in my chapter on Philip Roth, the self-immolation by Buddhist monks is an important motif in that novel as well.

18. Hayles, "*A Metaphor of God Knew How Many Parts*"; Palmeri, "Neither Literally nor as Metaphor." See also Cooper, "Metaphor, Model Building, and Paranoia," in *Signs and Symptoms*; Quilligan, "Thomas Pynchon and the Language of Allegory."

CHAPTER THREE. Americanizing Vietnam in Mailer's *The Armies of the Night*

1. See http://www.amazon.com/Armies-Night-History-Novel/dp/sitb-next/0452272793/ref=sbx_con#concordance.

2. McCann, "The Imperiled Republic"; McCann and Szalay, "Do You Believe in Magic?"; Hobarek, "Liberal Anti-Liberalism."

3. Although Arendt deplores the use of violence, she does credit the increasingly militant student left with an awareness, lacking in their elders, of the unpredictable violence to which technology has made us subject. After discussing nuclear and other military technologies, Arendt writes: "To the oft-heard question, Who are they, this new generation? One is tempted to answer, Those who hear the ticking." Arendt, *On Violence*, 18.

4. Mailer reports saying to Lowell that if they are arrested "the papers can't claim that hippies and hoodlums were the only ones guilty" (84).

5. See Manso, *Mailer*.

6. Singer, "Tough Guy," 30.

7. Trachtenberg, "Mailer on the Steps of the Pentagon," 701–02.

8. Kazin, "The Trouble He's Seen."

9. Varon, *Bringing the War Home*.

10. For the centrality of authenticity in the period see Rossinow, *The Politics of Authenticity*; Cheever, *Real Phonies*.

11. Schell, *The Real War*.

12. Herr, *Dispatches*, 20.

13. See Young, *The Vietnam Wars*; Divine, "Historiography: Vietnam Reconsidered"; Levy, *The Debate Over Vietnam*.

14. Mailer, who was persuaded by his publisher to use the euphemism "fug" in place of fuck in *The Naked and the Dead*, found this form of hypocrisy especially galling. Mailer recounts Tallulah Bankhead remarking upon meeting him: "You're the young man that doesn't know how to spell." Lennon, *Conversations with Norman Mailer*, 117.

15. Manso, *Norman Mailer*, 458–59.

16. Mailer again and again equivocates about whether or not there are female demonstrators. He postulates at one point that most demonstrators had never taken part in civil disobedience "if one counted the women," as if one might not (112). He later invents a collective monologue in which the presumptively male demonstrators generously proclaim to the MPs, "We have pot, we have food we share, we have girls. Come over to us and share our girls" (270). And then he imagines that the women beaten during the march are not themselves demonstrators, but merely the property of the demonstrators.

CHAPTER FOUR. Veterans of Sex

1. Scott, "PTSD in DSM-III"; Young, *The Harmony of Illusions*.

2. Young, *The Harmony of Illusions*, 145–263.

3. Sarah Haley, new to the VA after having just finished her MA in social work, treated a veteran who reported witnessing a massacre of women and children at My Lai at a time when the story had only just been broken by the AP and was not yet widely known. Unaware of the story, she nonetheless took his account at face value but met with resistance from her superiors, who all insisted that the man was delusional. See Nicosia, *Home to War*, 184–88; Haley, "When the Patient Reports Atrocities."

4. Young, *The Harmony of Illusions*, 95–117.

5. Scott, "PTSD in DSM-III," 304.

6. Leys, *Trauma*, 2.

7. Looking ahead just five years after the publication of DSM-III, we can see how the *therapeutic* discourse surrounding PTSD and that of feminist clinicians was committed to a model of the essential *speakability* of violence. An oft-cited issue of *Women and Therapy* from 1986, republished the same year under the title *Another Silenced Trauma*, features a Navy nurse whose physical and mental health was seriously mishandled by the VA in the years after her stint in the United States handling casualties from the Tet Offensive and then in South Vietnam at the primary facility for Navy and Marine casualties. Nearly all the therapists who study and comment on her case see her initial silence as a product of noxious social repression, one that a properly feminist therapy seeks to ameliorate. The nurse indeed reports that she was counseled by one of her therapists at the VA to try to forget about what she witnessed. Rosenblum and Cole, *Another Silenced Trauma*.

8. Judith Herman describes feminists as equal partners in the coalition that sought medical recognition of trauma. I have found little evidence that feminists played an important role *qua feminists* in the initial stages of advocacy. Herman, *Trauma and Recovery*.

9. Feminists spearheaded the movement to change the definition of PTSD in the DSM-IV (2000), which no longer stated that the traumatogenic event need be "outside the range of normal human experience." The major statistical work on rape in the period was by Menachim Amir. Although his analysis was contested, nearly all the works published on rape in the period use his data. See Amir, *Patterns in Forcible Rape*. Often credited as the first significant essay on rape as a political problem is Susan Griffin's "Rape: The All-American Crime." Griffin is in turn hailed in a number of other sources that are roughly contemporaneous with Susan Brownmiller's book. See Medea and Thompson's *Against Rape*; Russell, *The Politics of Rape*. Throughout the second half of the decade the literature on rape as a social and political problem explodes; nearly all of it is predicated on the novel dictum that rape is an act of violence and a mechanism of social control rather than a socially unacceptable expression of male sexual desire. See Chappell, Geis, and Geis, eds., *Forcible Rape*. For a sociological history of the feminist antirape movement, see Matthews, *Confronting Rape*.

10. Brownmiller's index has no entry for trauma, while the chapter on "Rape and Psychotherapy" in the New York Radical Feminist's Sourcebook focuses on the rape of women by their analysts. New York Radical Feminists, *Rape*, 76–81.

11. The New York Radical Feminists were at the center of the antirape movement. As Lynn Shapiro summarizes in a recent overview of the group's activities: "Consciousness-raising about the sexual abuse of women and children . . . started with the January 24, 1971, Rape Speakout. This was soon followed by the April 17, 1971, Rape Conference." See http://www.archive.org/details/RadicalFeminismNewYorkRadicalFeministsRevisedHistoryOverview.

12. Fassin and Rechtman make this point effectively in their account of the problem of traumatized war criminals in the Vietnam War: "The issue in the decision of whether or not the psychological sequelae of Vietnam veterans belonged in the category of PTSD, was to decide also whether perpetrators and the victims of atrocities could be combined in a single category." Fassin and Rechtman, *Empire of Trauma*, 91–92.

13. Chappell, Geis, and Geis, eds., *Forcible Rape*, 66.

14. I am indebted to Claire Potter for her insights into the way the controversies over Susan Saxe and Jane Alpert impacted theoretical discussion by radical feminists about leftist violence committed by women. See, for instance, Jane Alpert, "Mother Right"; Susan Saxe, "Letter to the Movement."

15. Kapuscinksi offers an excellent examination of the way Atwood interrogates, in *Surfacing* and other works, the narrative of Canadian peacefulness through brutal women. Kapuscinski, "Negotiating the Nation."

16. During the time of the novel's composition Atwood was active in the Toronto antidraft movement. Adams, "Going to Canada."

17. I am grateful to Bill Stowe for his challenging and resonant suggestion that the husband and living child are psychological phantasms, stand-ins for the not-yet-

remembered child the heroine aborted. I am skeptical, however, that adequate textual evidence can be amassed to confidently dematerialize these characters.

18. Farland, "Total System, Total Solution, Total Apocalypse."

19. Dworkin, *Intercourse.*

20. Young, *The Harmony of Illusions,* 126.

21. Ibid., 142.

22. In an astute early essay on this and other feminist novels, Judith Kegan Gardiner criticizes the entirety of Piercy's utopian vision on similar grounds: "The good alternative world is portrayed as a private female fantasy; the public realm has disappeared into it. . . . Her vision of a wonderful, different public world can also be seen as a private, escapist daydream." Gardiner, "Evil, Apocalypse, and Feminist Fiction," 75.

23. Silbergleid, "Women, Utopia, and Narrative."

24. Solay and Philmus, "Towards an Open-Ended Utopia"; Booker, "Woman on the Edge of a Genre."

CHAPTER FIVE. "Words generally only spoil things"

1. Sedaris, "Possession."

2. While I analyze Roth's embrace of traumatic history as it relates to the Holocaust, a similar story could be limned in relationship to American politics moving from *Our Gang* to *American Pastoral* and *The Human Stain*. For an account of Roth's political engagement as a novelist and essayist, see Lee, *Philip Roth,* 45–61. For a discussion of the concept of cultural trauma, see my introduction.

3. My analysis takes for granted that, although Zuckerman is not reducible to Roth, his views about literature and Jewish life are derived from and consistent with Roth's own. For the relationship between Roth and Zuckerman see Lee, *Philip Roth,* 17, 33, 69–74; Goodheart, "Counterlives," *Novel Practices.*

4. Greenspan cites Raul Hilberg and Edward Linenthal in support of his argument. Greenspan, "Imagining Survivors," in *The Americanization of the Holocaust*; Novick, *The Holocaust In American Life.*

5. For an early defense of Roth see Solataroff, "Philip Roth and the Jewish Moralists." Two important later attacks on Roth, in essays by Norman Podhoretz and Irving Howe, were published in the same issue of Commentary 1972.

6. Zuckerman explains that the story was inspired by a family quarrel over money. Like many of Roth's Jewish critics, Zuckerman's father fears that such a story will reinforce negative stereotypes of Jewish avarice. For an excellent and nuanced account of Roth's attitudes about Zionism, diasporic Judaism, anti-Semitism, and the polemic context in which Roth's work has been received, see Omer-Sherman, *Diaspora and Zionism in Jewish-American Literature.*

7. See Hungerford, *The Holocaust of Texts.*

8. Michael Rothberg's nuanced response to Walter Benn Michael's reading of Roth's *The Plot Against America* cites these same lines as evidence of the novelist's resistance to "the sentimentalization and instrumentalization of the Holocaust in American culture" (305). But Rothberg misses what I will describe as an important transformation in Roth's thinking on this matter. He argues that *Operation Shylock* is consistent with *The Ghost*

Writer in its assessment of the importance of the Holocaust to Americans. Rothberg, "Against Zero-Sum Logic," 303–11.

9. Focusing on this last feature, Amy Hungerford has argued that "what Nathan identifies with in *The Ghost Writer* is not the Jewish community, his family, and the history they both hold out as the reason why he should identify with them, but with his nascent art and the individual 'madness of art' revered by James, Lonoff, and Nathan himself." My only amendment to this helpful formulation is that the madness of art throughout Roth's and Zuckerman's career is understood to derive *from* the Jewish community, a community whose *true* character is masked by the pious history being held out by Wapter and his ilk. Zuckerman's mad lust for Amy, like Amy and Lonoff's mad lust for each other, is not offered to us as wild invention but as the very realistic substance of Jewish life. That strangeness and madness are what the author must try to match. Hungerford, *The Holocaust of Texts*, 139.

10. This focus on the failing body returns as a major theme of Roth's fiction especially in the period after *The Plot Against America*. In the final Zuckerman books Roth returns, as it were, to the core focus of his earlier books. But in *American Pastoral* for instance, where Zuckerman's prostate cancer and the Swede's own death is narrated, we are asked to either forget the suffering of the author's body or read it as a symptom of an entirely symbolic violence done to the patriarchal body politic undone by feminism and the erosion of America's manufacturing base.

11. For an excellent essay on the issues of self and subjectivity in the novel, one informed by attention to Roth's draft manuscripts, see Shostak, "The Diaspora Jew."

12. Wanda's surname connects her to the theme of erotic possession that was central to *The Ghost Writer*.

13. The diaries turn out to have been forged by the Mossad for the purposes of recruiting Roth, but the lesson he draws from them is validated not by the diary itself but by Klinghoffer's fate and the larger historical backdrop of the novel.

14. While much of his analysis is compelling, I take issue with Andrew Furman's characterization of Ziad as delivering "a fundamentalist diatribe." Although he is one of the many unhinged characters in the novel, he is also ardently secular. Furman commends Roth for what he sees as a less-demonizing portrayal of "the Arab other" in Jewish American fiction about Israel, but dismisses too quickly and without adequate textual support Ziad's critique of the use of the Holocaust to justify occupation. The ambiguous status of this critique is central to the power of the novel; its eventual and hard-won rejection is the text's organizing project. See Furman, "A New 'Other' Emerges in American Jewish Literature."

15. Although the novel is endlessly destabilizing, within the reality of the novel created by Philip Roth about Philip Roth, the character Roth has in fact undertaken the mission.

16. Felman and Laub, *Testimony*, 5.

17. Felman draws from the work of J. L. Austin for her model of the speech act. Walter Benn Michaels offers a particularly trenchant critique of the work that her model of the speech act performs. My own interest here lies in her less technical and theoretically specific conception of how testimony is at once both linguistic and supralinguistic. Michaels, " 'You Who Never Was There.' "

18. Michael Wood offers the most eloquent summary of such readings: "Two current plots against America spring immediately to mind. There is the global plot of al-Qaida against the evils of capitalism, substantively and symbolically centred in the U.S. . . . And there is, settling down now as a major fear of many Americans, the plot of the Bush administration to abolish many civil liberties and concentrate autocratic powers in the hands of the president." Wood, "Just Folks."

19. Roth, "The Story Behind *The Plot Against America*."

20. Michaels, "Plots Against America."

21. There is a bizarre moment late in the novel when the narrator likens Jews to the colonists who usurped the land properly belonging to the Delaware and Algonquin tribes (357).

22. The statistic on civilian casualties in both wars is contested and varies enormously. Reports on civilian casualties in the Iraq War have been compiled by the U.S. military, the United Nations, Iraq Body Count, and the Brookings Institution. A comparison of the numbers gathered by these and other groups is available at http://www.npr.org/news/specials/tollofwar/tollofwarmain.html. For numbers on civilian casualties in the Afghan War see http://www.guardian.co.uk/news/datablog/2009/nov/19/afghanistan-civilian-casualties-statistics-data.

23. He says, "Some readers are going to want to take this book as a roman á clef to the present moment in America. That would be a mistake." Roth, "The Story Behind *The Plot Against America*."

CHAPTER SIX. "The hammers striking the page"

1. Don DeLillo, "An Interview with Don DeLillo."

2. Amy Hungerford details the connections between Tap's name, the tapping of DeLillo's own typewriter keys, and the hammers the cultists use to kill their victims and inscribe initials into their flesh. Hungerford, "Don DeLillo's Latin Mass."

3. Amy Hungerford makes a similar argument (and one to which I am much indebted) in her recent essay on Don DeLillo. Her essay seeks to demonstrate through textual and biographical evidence that DeLillo's denarrativized and desemanticized language derives from the mystical and incarnational logic of the pre-Vatican II Latin mass. She shows how DeLillo recuperates Catholic *structures* of belief even as he seeks an alternative to the apocalyptic violence that she argues he associates with the twin specters of "fundamentalism" and "cults." The murderous cult in *The Names*, for instance, is in Hungerford's reading an instructively "dangerous limit case" that DeLillo rejects along with the conspiratorial violence of *Libra*, the nuclear weaponry of *Underworld*, and the terrorism of *Mao II*. Contrary to Hungerford, I will suggest that DeLillo cannot give up such an investment in violence because, whatever his humanistic horror of it, he never abandons his commitment to death and violence as the ultimate source of the real.

4. DeLillo has said: "Eventually it becomes clear (or almost clear) that the book is being 'written' in the year 1999. The narrator-protagonist is living on a small island where he contemplates his celluloid adventures as a young man. He uses as source material not only his mental recollections of that period but the movie he began making while traveling west and finished during a period of time merely alluded to in the

book. The time frame narrows and widens from 1999 to the 1960s, from island to continent, from movie-being-made to the events which inspired the movie." DeLillo, "Notes Toward a Definitive Meditation (by Someone Else) on the Novel *Americana*," 328.

5. In the same short piece in *Epoch*, DeLillo spoke of his efforts this way: "The author evidently constructed two planes of incest in 'Americana.' One is based on relations (or near-relations) between the protagonist and his mother. The second might be called political incest—the notion that baseless patriotism is an elaborately psychotic manifestation of love for mother country." DeLillo, "Notes Toward a Definitive Meditation (by Someone Else) on the Novel *Americana*," 328.

6. Wood, "Americans on the Prowl," 27.

7. The fabrication of a patsy, and its convergence with Oswald's self-fabrication, has been noted by many of *Libra*'s critics. For an analysis of how this fabrication undermines humanist conceptions of the individual, see Carmichael, "Lee Harvey Oswald and the Postmodern Subject"; Lentricchia, "*Libra* as Postmodern Critique."

8. It is not easy to say who speaks this phrase. The narrative voice in Libra often makes oracular utterances that are not attached to any particular character. Frank Lentricchia offers a similar analysis of *Libra*'s narrator, although he identifies that voice as a "DeLillo" character that is subject to "virtuoso changes of point of view." See Lentricchia, "*Libra* as Postmodern Critique," 210.

9. This phrase has also been associated with the novel's critique of the paranoid culture of secret-keeping. See Osteen, *American Magic and Dread*.

10. Shawn James Rosenheim's historicization of the hermeneutics of suspicion is very useful in this regard. He demonstrated how cold war intelligence practices, and their cryptographic correlates in literature, gave rise to a heightened awareness of textuality as both a form of encoded information, and as a material order in itself. Rosenheim, *The Cryptographic Imagination*, 3.

11. DeLillo, "American Blood," 22.

12. See Keesey, *Don DeLillo*, 175.

13. Junod, "The Falling Man."

14. DeLillo has both Martin and Hammad articulate connections between American hegemony and terrorism, but the novel does not endorse them. Instead, they appear as distastefully inadequate.

works cited

Adams, Rachel. "Going to Canada: The Politics and Poetics of Northern Exodus." *Yale Journal of Criticism* 18.2 (2005): 409–33.

Alexandrov, Vladimir E. *Nabokov's Otherworld*. Princeton, N.J.: Princeton University Press, 1991.

Alpert, Jane. *Mother Right: A New Feminist Theory*. 1974. Available at http://scripto rium.lib.duke.edu/wlm/mother/.

Amir, Menachim. *Patterns in Forcible Rape*. Chicago: University of Chicago Press, 1971.

Andrew, John A. *The Other Side of the Sixties: Young Americans for Freedom and the Rise of Conservative Politics*. New Brunswick, N.J.: Rutgers University Press, 1997.

Ankersmit, Frank. *Sublime Historical Experience*. Palo Alto, Calif.: Stanford University Press, 2005.

Arendt, Hannah. *On Violence*. New York: Harvest Books, 1970.

Atwood, Margaret. *Surfacing*, 1972. New York: Random House, 1973.

Bakhtin, Mikhail. *The Dialogic Imagination: Four Essays*. Austin: University of Texas Press, 1981.

Belletto, Steven. "The Zemblan Who Came in from the Cold, or Nabokov's *Pale Fire*, Chance, and the Cold War." *English Literary History* 73.3 (Fall 2006): 775–80.

Booker, M. Keith. "Woman on the Edge of a Genre: The Feminist Dystopias of Marge Piercy." *Science Fiction Studies* 21.3 (November 1994): 337–50.

Bourdieu, Pierre. "Cultural Reproduction and Social Reproduction." In *Knowledge, Education and Social Change*, edited by R. Brown, 71–84. London: Taylor & Francis, 1974.

———. *Distinction: A Social Critique of the Judgment of Taste*. Cambridge, Mass.: Harvard University Press, 1984.

———. "The Forms of Capital." In *Handbook of Theory and Research for the Sociology of Education*, edited by John G. Richardson, 241–58. New York: Greenwood, 1986.

———. *Language and Symbolic Power*. Edited by John B. Thompson. Cambridge, Mass.: Harvard University Press, 1991.

Bowie, Malcolm. *Lacan*. Cambridge, Mass.: Harvard University Press, 1991.

Boyd, Brian. *Nabokov's Pale Fire: The Magic of Artistic Discovery*. Princeton, N.J.: Princeton University Press, 1999.

————. *Vladimir Nabokov: The American Years*. Princeton, N.J.: Princeton University Press, 1991.

Boyer, Paul. *By the Bomb's Early Light: American Thought and Culture at the Dawn of the Atomic Age*. New York: Pantheon, 1985.

————. *Fallout*. Columbus: Ohio State University, 1998.

Brownmiller, Susan. *Against Our Will: Men, Women and Rape*. New York: Simon and Schuster, 1975.

Carmichael, Thomas. "Lee Harvey Oswald and the Postmodern Subject: History and Intertextuality in Don DeLillo's *Libra*, *The Names*, and *Mao II*." *Contemporary Literature* 34.2 (1993): 204–18.

Caruth, Cathy, ed. *Trauma: Explorations in Memory*. Baltimore, Md.: Johns Hopkins University Press, 1995.

————. *Unclaimed Experience: Trauma, Narrative, and History*. Baltimore, Md.: Johns Hopkins University Press, 1996.

Castillo, Debra A. "Borges and Pynchon: The Tenuous Symmetries of Art." In *New Essays on The Crying of Lot 49*, edited by Patrick O'Donnell, 21–46. Cambridge: Cambridge University Press, 1991.

Chappell, Duncan, Robley Geis, and Gilbert Geis, eds. *Forcible Rape: The Crime, the Victim and the Offender*. New York: Columbia University Press, 1977.

Cheever, Abigail. *Real Phonies: Cultures of Authenticity in Post–World War II America*. Athens: University of Georgia Press, 2010.

Chollet, Derek, and James Goldgeier. *America Between the Wars*. New York: Public Affairs, 2008.

Connell, Noreen, and Cassandra Wilson. *Rape: The First Sourcebook for Women by New York Radical Feminists*. New York: New American Library, 1974.

Cooper, Peter L. *Signs and Symptoms: Thomas Pynchon and the Contemporary World*. Berkeley: University of California Press, 1983.

Cvetkovich, Ann. *An Archive of Feeling: Trauma, Sexuality and Lesbian Public Cultures*. Durham: Duke University Press, 2003.

DeGroot, Gerald J. *The Bomb: A Life*. Cambridge, Mass.: Harvard University Press, 2004.

DeLillo, Don. American Blood. *Rolling Stone*, December 8, 1983, 22.

————. *Americana*. Boston: Houghton Mifflin, 1971.

————. *End Zone*. Boston: Houghton Mifflin, 1972.

————. *Falling Man*. New York: Scribner, 2007.

————. *Great Jones Street*. Boston: Houghton Mifflin, 1973.

————. "An Interview with Don DeLillo." Edited by Maria Nadotti and translated by Peggy Boyars. *Salmagundi* Fall (1993): 96.

————. *Libra*. New York: Viking Penguin, 1988.

————. *Mao II*. New York: Viking Penguin, 1991.

————. *The Names*. New York: Random House, 1982.

————. "Notes Toward a Definitive Meditation (by Someone Else) on the Novel *Americana*." *Epoch* 21.3 (1972): 327–29.

Didion, Joan. *The Book of Common Prayer*. New York: Random House, 1977.

————. *Play It As It Lays*. New York: Farrar, Straus and Giroux, 1970.

————. *Salvador*. New York: Washington Square Press, 1983.

————. *Slouching Towards Bethlehem.* New York: Farrar, Straus and Giroux, 1968.

————. *The White Album.* New York: Farrar, Straus and Giroux, 1979.

Divine, Robert A. "Historiography: Vietnam Reconsidered." In *The Vietnam Reader,* edited by Walter H. Capps, 100–15. New York: Routledge, 1991.

Dworkin, Andrea. *Intercourse.* New York: The Free Press, 1987.

Eddins, Dwight. *The Gnostic Pynchon.* Bloomington: University of Indiana Press, 1990.

Elias, Amy. *Sublime Desire: History and Post-1960s Fiction.* Baltimore, Md.: Johns Hopkins University Press, 2001.

Farland, Maria. "Total System, Total Solution, Total Apocalypse: Sex Oppression, Systems of Property, and 1970s Women's Liberation Fiction." *Yale Journal of Criticism* 18.2 (2005): 381–407.

Fassin, Didier, and Richard Rechtman. *The Empire of Trauma: An Inquiry into the Condition of Victimhood.* Princeton, N.J.: Princeton University Press, 2009.

Felman, Shoshanna, and Dori Laub. *Testimony: Crises of Witnessing in Literature, Psychoanalysis, and History.* New York: Routledge, 1992.

Field, Andrew. *Nabokov: His Life in Art.* Boston: Little Brown, 1967.

Foster, Hal. *The Return of the Real: The Avant-Garde at the End of the Century.* Cambridge, Mass.: MIT Press, 1996.

Furman, Andrew. "A New 'Other' Emerges in American Jewish Literature: Philip Roth's Israel Fiction." *Contemporary Literature* 36.4 (Winter 1995): 633–53.

Gaddis, John Lewis. *Strategies of Containment: A Critical Appraisal of American National Security Policy During the Cold War.* New York: Oxford, 1982, 2005.

Galtung, Johan. "Violence, Peace, and Peace Research." *Journal of Peace Research* 6.3 (1969): 167–91.

Gardiner, Judith Kegan. "Evil, Apocalypse and Feminist Fiction." *Frontiers: A Journal of Women Studies* 7.2 (1983): 74–80.

Giles, James R. *Violence in the Contemporary American Novel: An End to Innocence.* Columbia: University of South Carolina Press, 2000.

Glass, Loren. "The End of Culture." In *Historicizing Theory,* edited by Peter C. Herman, 191–208. Albany: State University of New York Press, 2004.

Goodheart, Eugene. *Novel Practices.* New Brunswick: Transaction Press, 2004.

Gordon, Avery. *Ghostly Matters: Haunting and the Sociological Imagination.* Minneapolis: University of Minnesota Press, 1997.

Greenspan, Henry. "Imagining Survivors: Testimony and the Rise of Holocaust Consciousness." In *The Americanization of the Holocaust,* edited by Hilene Flanzbaum, 45–67. Baltimore, Md.: Johns Hopkins University Press, 1999.

Griffin, Susan. "Rape: The All American Crime." *Ramparts* 10 (1971): 26–35.

Grossman, Lev. The Gay Nabokov. *Salon,* May 17, 2000.

Guillory, John. *Cultural Capital: The Problem of Literary Canon Formation.* Chicago: University of Chicago Press, 1993.

Gussow, Mel. "Pynchon's letters nudge his mask." *New York Times,* March 4, 1998.

Haley, Sarah. "When the Patient Reports Atrocities: Specific Treatment Considerations of the Vietnam Veteran." *Archives of General Psychiatry* 30.2 (1974): 191–96.

Harrington, Michael. *The Other America: Poverty in the United States.* New York: Simon and Schuster, 1962.

Hayles, Katherine. " 'A Metaphor of God Knew How Many Parts': The Engine that Drives *The Crying of Lot 49*." In *New Essays on The Crying of Lot 49*, edited by Patrick O'Donnell, 97–125. Cambridge: Cambridge University Press, 1991.

Herman, Judith. *Trauma and Recovery*. New York: Basic Books, 1992.

Herr, Michael. *Dispatches*. New York: Vintage International, 1977.

Hewitt, Andrew. *Fascist Modernism: Aesthetics, Politics and the Avant-Garde*. Palo Alto, Calif.: Stanford University Press, 1993.

Hirsch, Marianne. *Family Frames: Photography, Narrative and Postmemory*. Cambridge, Mass.: Harvard University Press, 1997.

Hobarek, Andrew. "Liberal Anti-Liberalism: Mailer, O'Connor, and the Gender Politics of Middle-Class *Ressentiment*." *Women's Studies Quarterly* 33:3 and 4 (Fall/Winter 2005): 22–47.

———. *The Twilight of the Middle Class: Post World War II American Fiction and White Collar Work*. Princeton, N.J.: Princeton University Press, 2005.

Howe, Irving. "Philip Roth Reconsidered." *Commentary* December 1972: 69–77.

Hungerford, Amy. "Don DeLillo's Latin Mass." *Contemporary Literature* XLVII, 3 (2006): 343–80.

———. *The Holocaust of Texts: Genocide, Literature, and Personification*. Chicago: University of Chicago Press, 2003.

———. "Memorizing Memory." *Yale Journal of Criticism* 14.1 (2001): 67–92.

Hutcheon, Linda. *A Poetics of Postmodernism: History, Theory, Fiction*. New York: Routledge, 1988.

Jameson, Fredric. *Postmodernism, or, the Cultural Logic of Late Capitalism*. Durham, N.C.: Duke University Press, 1991.

Johnson, D. Barton. *Worlds in Regression*. Ann Arbor: Ardis, 1985.

Junod, Tom. "The Falling Man." *Esquire*, September 2003.

Kal, Tali. *Worlds of Hurt*. Cambridge: Cambridge University Press, 1996.

Kaplan, E. Ann. *Trauma Culture: The Politics of Terror and Loss in Media and Literature*. New Brunswick, N.J.: Rutgers University Press, 2005.

Kapuscinski, Kiley. "Negotiating the Nation: The Reproduction and Reconstruction of the National Imaginary in Margaret Atwood's *Surfacing*." *English Studies in Canada* 33.3 (2007): 95–123.

Karnow, Stanley. *Vietnam: A History*. New York: Penguin, 1983.

Kazin, Alfred. "The Trouble He's Seen." *New York Times*, May 5, 1968. Available at http://www.nytimes.com/books/97/05/04/reviews/mailer-armies.html.

Keesey, Douglas. *Don DeLillo*. Twayne's United States Authors Series, New York: Twayne, 1993.

LaCapra, Dominick. *Writing History, Writing Trauma*. Baltimore, Md.: Johns Hopkins University Press, 2000.

Lee, Hermione. *Philip Roth*. London: Methuen, 1982.

Lennon, J. Michael. *Conversations with Norman Mailer*. Jackson: University Press of Mississippi, 1988.

Lentricchia, Frank. "*Libra* as Postmodern Critique." In *Introducing Don DeLillo*, edited by Frank Lentricchia, 193–215. Durham, N.C.: Duke University Press, 1991.

Levy, David W. *The Debate Over Vietnam*. Baltimore, Md.: Johns Hopkins University Press, 1991.

Leys, Ruth. *Trauma: A Genealogy*. Chicago: University of Chicago Press, 2000.

Lowen, Rebecca C. *Creating the Cold War University: The Transformation of Stanford*. Berkeley: University of California Press, 1997.

Lukacs, Georg. *The Historical Novel*. Lincoln: University of Nebraska Press, 1962.

Lutz, Catherine. *Homefront: A Military City and the American Twentieth Century*. Boston: Beacon Press, 2001.

Lynch, Diedre. *The Economy of Character: Novels, Market Culture, and the Business of Inner Meaning*. Chicago: University of Chicago Press, 1998.

Lyotard, Jean-Francois. *Lessons on the Analytic of the Sublime*. Translated by Elizabeth Rottenberg. Palo Alto, Calif.: Stanford University Press, 1994.

Mailer, Norman. *The Armies of the Night: History as a Novel, the Novel as History*. New York: Plume, 1968.

———. *Why Are We in Vietnam?* New York: Putnam, 1967.

Mandel, Naomi. *Against the Unspeakable: Complicity, the Holocaust, and Slavery in America*. Charlottesville: University of Virginia Press, 2006.

Manso, Peter. *Mailer: His Life and Times*. New York: Simon and Schuster, 1985.

Markusen, Ann, Peter Hall, Scott Campbell, and Scott Deitrick. *The Rise of the Gunbelt: The Military Remapping of Industrial America*. New York: Oxford, 1991.

Mattesich, Stefan. *Lines of Flight: Discursive Time and Countercultural Desire in the Work of Thomas Pynchon*. Durham, N.C.: Duke University Press, 2002.

Matthews, Nancy A. *Confronting Rape: The Feminist Anti-Rape Movement and the State*. New York: Routledge, 1994.

McCann, Sean. "The Imperiled Republic: Norman Mailer and the Poetics of Anti-Liberalism]." *English Literary History* 67.1 (2000): 293–336.

McCann, Sean, and Michael Szalay. "Do You Believe in Magic?: Literary Thinking After the New Left." *The Yale Journal of Criticism* 18.2 (2005): 435–68.

McCarthy, Mary. "A Bolt From the Blue." *New Republic* 4 (June 1962): 22.

McClure, John. *Late Imperial Romance*. New York: Verso, 1994.

McGurl, Mark. *The Program Era: Postwar Fiction and the Rise of Creative Writing*. Cambridge, Mass.: Harvard University Press, 2009.

McHale, Brian. *Postmodernist Fiction*. New York: Routledge, 1987.

McKeon, Michael. *The Origins of the English Novel: 1600–1740*. Baltimore, Md.: Johns Hopkins University Press, 1987.

Medea, Andrea, and Kathleen Thompson. *Against Rape*. New York: Farrar, Straus and Giroux, 1974.

Meyer, Priscilla. *Find What the Sailor has Hidden: Vladimir Nabokov's Pale Fire*. Middletown, Conn.: Wesleyan University Press, 1988.

Michaels, Walter Benn. "Plots Against America: Neoliberalism and Antiracism." *American Literary History* 18.2 (2006): 288–302.

———. "'You Who Never was There': Slavery and the New Historicism, the Holocaust and Deconstruction." *Narrative* 4.1 (January 1996): 1–16.

Millard, Bill. "The Fable of the Ants: Myopic Interaction in DeLillo's *Libra*." *Postmodern Culture* 4.2 (January 1994).

Millett, Kate. *Sexual Politics*. New York: Doubleday, 1970.

Morrison, Toni. *Beloved*. New York: Plume, 1987.

Nabokov, Vladimir. *Lolita*. New York: Vintage, 1955.

———. *Pale Fire*. New York: Random House, 1962.

———. *Selected Letters: 1940–1977*. Edited by Dmitri Nabokov and Matthew J. Bruccoli. San Diego: Harcourt Brace Jovanovich, 1989.

———. *Speak, Memory*. New York: Vintage International, 1967.

New York Radical Feminists. *Rape : the first sourcebook for women*. Edited by Noreen Connell and Cassandra Wilson. New York: Plume, 1974.

Nicosia, Gerald. *Home to War: A History of the Vietnam Veterans Movement*. New York: Crown, 2001.

North, Michael. *The Political Aesthetic of Yeats, Eliot and Pound*. Cambridge: Cambridge University Press, 1991.

Novick, Peter. *The Holocaust in American Life*. New York: Houghton Mifflin, 1999.

O'Donnell, Patrick. "Introduction." In *New Essays on The Crying of Lot 49*, edited by Patrick O'Donnell, 1–20. Cambridge: Cambridge University Press, 1991.

Ohmann, Richard. "English and the Cold War." In *The Cold War and the University: Toward an Intellectual History of the Postwar Years*, edited by Noam Chomsky, 73–106. New York: The New Press, 1997.

Omer-Sherman, Ranen. *Diaspora and Zionism in Jewish-American Literature*. Hanover: University of Brandeis Press, 2002.

Osteen, Mark. *American Magic and Dread: Don DeLillo's Dialogue with Culture*. Philadelphia: University of Pennsylvania Press, 2000.

Paglen, Trevor. *Blank Spots on the Map: The Dark Geography of the Pentagon's Secret World*. New York: Dutton, 2009.

Palmeri, Frank. "Neither Literally nor as Metaphor: Pynchon's *The Crying of Lot 49* and the Structure of Scientific Revolution." *English Literary History* 54.4 (Winter 1987): 979–99.

Podhoretz, Norman. "Laureate of the New Class." *Commentary* December 1972: 4, 7.

Pynchon, Thomas. *The Crying of Lot 49*. New York: Harper Collins, 1966.

———. "A Journey Into The Mind of Watts," *New York Times*, June 12, 1966, 34–35, 78, 80–82, 84.

———. *Slow Learner: Early Stories*, New York: Little, Brown and Company, 1984.

Quilligan, Maureen. "Thomas Pynchon and the Language of Allegory." In *Critical Essays on Thomas Pynchon*, edited by Richard Pearce, 187–212. Boston: G.K. Hall, 1981.

Rosenblum, Esther D., and Ellen Cole, eds. *Another Silenced Trauma: Twelve Feminist Therapists and Activists Respond to One Woman's Recovery from War*. New York: Harrington Press, 1986.

Rosenheim, Shawn James. *The Cryptographic Imagination: Secret Writing from Edgar Poe to the Internet*. Baltimore, Md.: Johns Hopkins University Press, 1997.

Rossinow, Doug. *The Politics of Authenticity: Liberalism, Christianity and the New Left*. New York: Columbia University Press, 1998.

Rotella, Carlo. *October Cities: The Redevelopment of American Literature*. Berkeley: University of California Press, 1998.

Roth, Philip. *American Pastoral*. New York: Random House, 1997.

———. *The Anatomy Lesson*. New York: Random House, 1983.

———. *The Counterlife*. New York: Random House, 1986.

———. *The Ghost Writer*. New York: Random House, 1979.

———. *Goodbye, Columbus*. Cambridge: The Riverside Press, 1959.

———. *Operation Shylock: A Confession*. New York: Random House, 1993.

———. *The Plot Against America*. New York: Random House, 2004.

———. *Portnoy's Complaint*. New York: Random House, 1967.

———. "The Story Behind *The Plot Against America*." *New York Times*, September 19, 2004.

———. *Zuckerman Unbound*. New York: Farrar, Straus and Giroux, 1981.

Rothberg, Michael. "Against Zero-Sum Logic: A Response to Walter Benn Michaels." *American Literary History* 18.2 (2006): 303–11.

———. *Traumatic Realism: The Demands of Holocaust Representation*. Minneapolis: University of Minnesota Press, 2000.

Rowe, W. W. *Nabokov's Spectral Dimension*. Ann Arbor: Ardis, 1981.

Russell, Diana E. H. *The Politics of Rape*. New York: Stein and Day, 1974.

Saltzman, Lisa, and Eric Rosenberg, eds. *Trauma and Visuality in Modernity*. Hanover, N.H.: Dartmouth College Press, 2006

Saxe, Susan. "Letter to the Movement." *Liberation*, December 1975.

Scarry, Elaine. *The Body in Pain: The Making and Unmaking of the World*. New York: Oxford University Press, 1985.

Schell, Jonathan. *The Real War*. New York: Pantheon, 1987.

Scott, Wilbur J. "PTSD in DSM-III: A Case in the Politics of Diagnosis and Disease." *Social Problems* 37.3 (1990): 294–310.

Sedaris, David. "Possession." *New Yorker*, April 19, 2004.

Shakespeare, William. *Timon of Athens*. The Arden Shakespeare, London: Routledge, 1994.

Shostak, Debra. "The Diaspora Jew and the 'Instinct for Impersonation': Philip Roth's *Operation Shylock*." *Contemporary Literature* 38.4 (Winter 1997): 726–54.

Silbergleid, Robin. "Women, Utopia and Narrative: Towards a Postmodern Citizenship." *Hypatia* 12. 4 (Autumn 1997): 156–77.

Singer, Mark. "Tough Guy." *The New Yorker*, May 27, 2007.

Slotkin, Richard. *The Fatal Environment: The Myth of the Frontier in the Age of Industrialization, 1800–1890*. Norman: University of Oklahoma Press, 1985.

———. *Gunfighter Nation: The Myth of the Frontier in Twentieth-Century America*. Norman: University of Oklahoma Press, 1998.

———. *Regeneration Through Violence: The Mythology of the American Frontier, 1600–1860*. Norman: University of Oklahoma Press, 1973.

Solataroff, Theodore. "Philip Roth and the Jewish Moralists." *Chicago Review* 8.4 (Winter 1959): 87–99.

Solay, Bulent, and Robert M. Philmus. "Towards an Open-Ended Utopia." *Science Fiction Studies* 11.1 (March 1984): 25–38.

Stegner, Page. *Escape into Aesthetics: The Art of Vladimir Nabokov*. New York: Dial, 1966.

Tabbi, Joseph. *Postmodern Sublime: Technology and American Writing from Mailer to Cyberpunk*. Ithaca: Cornell University Press, 1995.

Trachtenberg, Alan. "Mailer on the Steps of the Pentagon." *The Nation* 206.22 (May 27, 1968): 701–02.

Tratner, Michael. *Modernism and Mass Politics: Joyce, Woolf, Eliot, Yeats*. Stanford: Stanford University Press, 1995.

Trilling, Lionel. *Beyond Culture: Essays on Literature and Learning*. New York: Viking, 1965.

Van der Kolk, Bessel A., Alexander C. McFarlane, and Lars Weisaeth. *Traumatic Stress: The Effects of Overwhelming Experience on Mind, Body, and Society*. New York: Guilford Press, 1996.

Varon, Jeremy. *Bringing the War Home: The Weather Underground, the Red Army Faction, and Revolutionary Violence in the Sixties and Seventies*. Berkeley: University of California Press, 2004.

Walzer, Michael. *Just and Unjust Wars: A Moral Argument with Historical Illustrations*, 2nd ed. New York: Basic Books, 1992.

Watt, Ian. *The Rise of the Novel*. Berkeley: University of California Press, 1957.

Weaver, Warren, Jr. "State Bar Urges Major Change In Statute on Criminally Insane." *New York Times*, July 21, 1959, A1.

Weissman, Gary. *Fantasies of Witnessing: Postwar Efforts to Experience the Holocuast*. Ithaca: Cornell University Press, 2004.

White, Hayden. *The Content of the Form: Narrative Discourse and Historical Representation*. Baltimore, Md.: Johns Hopkins University Press, 1987.

———. *Metahistory: The Historical Imagination in Nineteenth Century Europe*. Baltimore, Md.: Johns Hopkins University Press, 1973.

———. "The Modernist Event." In *The Persistence of History: Cinema Television and the Modern Event*, edited by Vivian Sobchack, 18–24. New York: Routledge, 1995.

Whitehead, Anne. *Trauma Fiction*. Edinburgh: Edinburgh University Press, 2004.

Winter, Yves. *Beyond Blood and Coercion: A Study of Violence in Machiavelli and Marx*. Unpublished Dissertation.

Wiscari, Werner. "Khrushchev Calls Off Plan For a Visit to Scandinavia." *New York Times*, July 21, 1959, A1.

Wood, Michael. "Americans on the Prowl." *New York Times Book Review*, October 10, 1982.

———. "Just Folks." *London Review of Books* 26.21, November 4, 2004.

———. *The Magician's Doubt: Nabokov and the Risks of Fiction*. Princeton, N.J.: Princeton University Press, 1994.

Woolf, Virginia. *Mrs. Dalloway*. New York: Harvest Books, 1925.

Young, Allan. *The Harmony of Illusions: Inventing Post-Traumatic Stress Disorder*. Princeton, N.J.: Princeton University Press, 1995.

Young, Marilyn B. *The Vietnam Wars: 1945–1990*. New York: Harper Collins, 1991.

Zeretsky, Natasha. *No Direction Home: The American Family and the Fear of National Decline, 1968–1980*. Chapel Hill: University of North Carolina Press, 2007.

index

Middle Passage, 1
Millett, Kate, 92
M'Naghten, Daniel, 38
Modernism, antirealism in, 17–18
Moral economy, 142–143
Morrison, Toni, 1, 5, 23, 24. *See also*
	Beloved
Mrs. Dalloway, 18
My Lai, massacre at, 90, 143, 151n3
My Life as a Man, 107
Mystery, politics of, 75

Nabokov, Vladimir, 9, 25, 30
	brother's death, 45
	critique of rape, 91
	father's death, 38–39, 45, 47
	loss of homeland, 34–35
	See also specific texts
The Naked and Dead, 80–81, 84, 151n14
The Names, 123, 124, 128–131, 137, 138, 141
National Book Award, 80
Native Son, 12
Nazification of America, 119
NBC, 108
Nefastis, John, 150n9
The New Republic, 81
New York Radical Feminists, 152n11
	Manifesto, 91–92
New York Review of Books, 80
New York State Bar Association, 38
New York Times, 2, 36, 37, 80, 81, 119, 120
New York Times Book Review, 128
New York Times Sunday Magazine, 48
New Yorker, 35, 106
Newark, riots in, 11
Nixon, Richard:
	resignation of, 11
	Vietnam and, 81–82
No Place to Hide, 35
Nonexperience, 21
Novaya Zemlya, 34–36
Nuclear fallout:
	metaphorical usage of the, 37
	in *Pale Fire,* 34–38
	threat of, 10–11

Nuclear testing:
	in America, 37
	in Soviet Union, 35

O'Donnell, Patrick, 60
Ohmann, Richard, 15
Old Testament, 23
On Violence, 8, 73
Operation Shylock, 111–117, 119, 121
Oswald, Lee Harvey, 123, 132
The Other America, 12
"Other America," 25
Our Gang, 153n2

Paglen, Trevor, 10
Pale Fire, 9, 25, 148n3
	"accidental" victims, 38–41
	cold war commentary, 34–38
	The Crying of Lot 49 and, 50
	historical violence and, 43–45
	influence on subsequent texts, 33
	multilayered meanings in title, 41–43
	nuclear fallout, 34–38
	overview, 30–34
	the real of literary art, 46–47
Palestine Liberation Organization (PLO),
	111, 116
Palmeri, Frank, 149n2
Parody, tone and, 59
Pastiche, aesthetic of, 77
Peel, Sir Robert, 38
Pentagon Papers, 11
"Philip Roth and the Jewish Moralists,"
	153n5
Physical pain, 23–24
Piercy, Marge, 26, 88, 99–105. *See also*
	specific texts
Play It as It Lays, 88
The Plot Against America, 27, 107, 117–122,
	124, 154n10
Poets, language, 17
Political violence, in *Pale Fire,* 39–40, 46
Pornography, 91
Portnoy's Complaint, 107, 118, 119
"Possession," 106–107

CPSIA information can be obtained at www.ICGtesting.com
Printed in the USA
242566LV00003B/16/P

9 780820 339108